WORLD BANK LATIN AMERICAN
AND CARIBBEAN STUDIES

Viewpoints

THE LONG MARCH:
A REFORM AGENDA FOR
LATIN AMERICA AND
THE CARIBBEAN IN
THE NEXT DECADE

by Shahid Javed Burki
and Guillermo E. Perry

THE WORLD BANK
WASHINGTON, D.C.

Copyright © 1997
The International Bank for Reconstruction
and Development/THE WORLD BANK
1818 H Street, N.W.
Washington, D.C. 20433, U.S.A.

This publication is part of the World Bank Latin American and Caribbean Studies series. Although these publications do not represent World Bank policy, they are intended to be thought-provoking and worthy of discussion, and they are designed to open a dialogue to explore creative solutions to pressing problems. Comments on this paper are welcome and will be published on the LAC Home Page, which is part of the World Bank's site on the World Wide Web. Please send comments via e-mail to laffairs@worldbank.org or via post to LAC External Affairs, The World Bank, 1818 H Street, N.W., Washington, D.C. 20433, U.S.A.

Cover illustration by Nip Rogers.

Shahid Javed Burki is regional vice president and Guillermo E. Perry is chief economist in the Latin America and the Caribbean Regional Office of the World Bank.

Library of Congress Cataloging-in-Publication Data

Burki, Shahid Javed.
    The long march : a reform agenda for Latin America and the
Caribbean in the next decade / by Shahid Javed Burki and Guillermo
E. Perry.
        p. cm.
    Includes bibliographical references.
    ISBN 0-8213-3985-0
    1. Latin America—Economic policy. 2. Caribbean Area—Economic
policy.   3. Economic stabilization—Latin America. 4. Economic
stabilization—Caribbean Area 5. Poverty—Government policy—Latin
America   6. Poverty—Government policy—Caribbean Area I. Perry,
Guillermo.   II. Title.
HC125.B769   1997
338.9729—dc21   97-13357
                                                           CIP

Contents

Acknowledgments viii

Prologue ix

Chapter I: Consolidating Stabilization Gains...1

    A.   Fiscal Policy 4

        1. Unfunded Social Security Systems and Other Contingent Fiscal Liabilities.............4

        2. Quasi-Fiscal Losses 5

        3. Intergovernmental Fiscal Relations...6

        4. Procyclical Fiscal Policy in Commodity Booms 7

        5. Efficiency of Tax Collections 8

        6. Expenditure Efficiency and Budgetary Institutions 8

    B.   The Financial Sector 9

        1. Macroeconomic Factors...9

        2. Microeconomic Factors 10

        3. Recent Experiences in the Region...11

    C.   The External Sector 13

        1. Balance of Payments Crises 13

        2. Exchange Rate Policy 13

        3. Dealing with Volatile Capital Flows 14

    Notes to Chapter I..17

    Appendix to Chapter I..19

Chapter II: Structural Reform and Economic Progress 27

    A.   International Trade Openness 28

        1. Policy Indicators of Trade Liberalization 28

        2. Outcome Indicators of Trade Liberalization 30

    B.   Financial Development 33

        1. Banking Sector Development 34

        2. Stock-Market Development 36

    C.   Labor Market Liberalization 37

    D.   Proper Use on Public Resources and Efficiency of Revenue Generation 44

        1. Indicators on the Proper Use of Public Resources 44

        2. Indicators on the Efficiency of Revenue Generation 48

    E.   Governance 53

    F.   Concluding Remarks 57

    Notes to Chapter II 57

Chapter III: Strategic Priorities for Accelerating Growth 61

    A.   LAC's Growth in the 1990s 61

    B.   Strategic Priorities for Accelerating Growth in LAC...63

    C.   Quality Investment in Human Development 67

        1. Education 67

        2. Health 69

            a. Fiscal Implications of Rising Costs in Health Services 69

            b. Improving the Quality and Efficiency of Health Services 70

    D.   Developing Efficient Financial Markets 71

        1. Competition and Efficiency in the Banking Sector 71

            a. Privatizing State-Owned Banks 71

            b. Liberalizing Foreign Competition in Banking Services 72

            c. Competition with Non-banking Entities 72

2. Developing Efficient Bond and Equity Markets 73

    a.   Equity and Bond Markets 73

    b.   Asset-Backed Securities 74

    c.   Government Bonds 74

    d.   Municipal Finance 74

    e.   Pension Funds 74

    f.   Mutual Funds 74

    g.   Insurance 75

3. Financial Market Infrastructure 75

E.   Improving the Legal and Regulatory Environment 76

    1.   Transaction Costs and Asymmetric Information 76

    2.   Property Rights and Security of Contracts 76

    3.   Reducing the Burden of Unnecessary Regulations 77

    4.   Deregulating Labor Markets 77

    5.   Competition Laws and Enforcement 78

    6.   Regulatory Regimes for Private Investment in Infrastructure and Social Services 79

F.   Public Administration and Governance 79

    1.   Reforming the Civil Service 80

    2.   Decentralization and Service Delivery 81

    3.   Judicial Reform 82

    4.   Governance 83

        a. Accountability, Transparency, and Corruption 83

        b. Crime and Violence 83

Notes to Chapter III 84

Chapter IV: The Challenge of Poverty Reduction 87

A.   The Incidence of Poverty 87

    1.   The Poverty Profile in the Region 87

    2.   Trends in Poverty 88

B.   Growth and Poverty 88

C.   The Pattern and Quality of Growth 90

    1.   Labor Markets 91

        a. Understanding the Diversity of the Informal Sector 92

        b. Educating and Training Workers 92

      c. Focusing on Women in the Labor Force 92

    2. Credit Markets 93

    3. Land Markets and Rural Poverty 95

D.   Human Capital Development 97

    1. Education 97

    2. Health 100

E.   Poverty and Targeted Programs 102

    1. Transfer Programs...103

    2. Employment Schemes...104

    3. Social Investment Funds...104

    4. Social Security Reform 106

    Notes to Chapter IV 107

References

References 109

Tables

Table 1.1   Selected Economic Indicators 2

Table 1.2   Net Private Capital Flows to LAC...15

Table 1.3   Real GDP Growth Rate 19

Table 1.4   Inflation Rate 20

Table 1.5   Non-Financial Public Sector Balance...21

Table 1.6   Current Account Balance 22

Table 1.7   Gross Domestic Investment 23

Table 1.8   Gross National Savings 24

Table 1.9   Rate of Unemployment..25

Table 2.1   Indicators of Trade Openness 28

Table 2.2   Trade Regime 30

Table 2.3   Percentage Change in the Ratio of the Volume of Trade Relative to GDP 31

Table 2.4   Black Market Premium on Foreign Exchange 31

Table 2.5   Indicators of Labor-Market Reforms 40

Table 2.6   Proceeds from Privatization..46

Table 2.7   VAT Indicators for Selected Countries...52

Table 3.1   The Impact of Economic Reforms on LAC's Growth Rates 62

Table 3.2   Growth of Gross Domestic Investment in LAC, 1980-1995 62

Table 3.3   World Merchandise Trade, 1981-1995 63

Table 3.4   Investment and Savings Rates in LAC, 1985-1995 63

Table 3.5   Investment and Savings Rates in East Asia, 1985-1995 64

Table 3.6   Output-Capital Ratios in LAC and East Asia, 1985-1990..64

Table 3.7   Homicides per 100,000 Population..66

Table 4.1   Income Shares of Lowest and Highest Quintiles, 1960's-1990's 89

Table 4.2   School Enrollment, Primary 98

Table 4.3   Mortality Rate, Infant 100

Figures

Figure 2.1   Trade Liberalization Index...29

Figure 2.2   Weighted Tariffs and Para-Tariff and Weighted Incidence of Non-Tariff Measures
               for LAC and Asian NICs 29

Figure 2.3   Structure-Adjusted Trade Intensity 32

Figure 2.4   Comparison By Regions 33

Figure 2.5   Banking Development Index..35

Figure 2.6   Stock Market Development Index I...36

Figure 2.7   Stock Market Development Index II...37

Figure 2.8   Banking Development Indicators 38

Figure 2.9   Stock Market Development Indicators 39

Figure 2.10   Labor-Market Liberalization Index I 43

Figure 2.11   Labor-Market Liberalization Index II...43

Figure 2.12   Wages and Salaries as a Percentage of Primary Expeditures..45

Figure 2.13   Private Investment as a Percentage of Gross Domestic Investment 47

Figure 2.14   Total Tax Revenue as a Percentage of GDP 49

Figure 2.15   Trade Taxes as a Percentage of Total Tax Revenue 50

Figure 2.16   Added VAT Revenue Productivity Ratio...51

Figure 2.17   Government Indices 54

Figure 2.18   ICRG Governance Indicators 56

Figure 3.1   Per Capita Growth Rates by Region 62

Figure 3.2   Banking Operating Costs 66

Figure 3.3   Educational Achievement and Expeditures 67

Figure 3.4   Enrollment and Educational Attainment...67

Figure 4.1   International Comparisons of Land Inequality...89

Figure 4.2   Growth and Poverty in LAC, 1979-1994 90

Acknowledgments

THIS REPORT IS THE PRODUCT OF EXTENSIVE DISCUSSIONS AMONG STAFF OF THE LATIN AMER-ican and Caribbean (LAC) regional office of the World Bank. Initial background papers were prepared by the Lead Economists of the various country departments and by the Lead Specialists in the Human and Social Development Group (LASHD). Economists and other specialists working in LAC participated in a two-day retreat in November, 1996, to discuss issues raised by this background work. From that meeting elements of a consensus emerged regarding the policy challenges facing the countries of Latin America and the Caribbean in the years to come, together with the implications for the World Bank's future activities in the region. That consensus is reflected in this report. We extend our appreciation and gratitude to all who participated in that instructive and fruitful meeting.

The research and writing of this report were conducted by a team in the Office of the Chief Economist for LAC (LACCE), under the overall direction of Guillermo E. Perry. Team members were Saul Lizondo (Chapter 1); Norman Loayza and Luisa Palacios (Chapter 2); Daniel Lederman (Chapter 3); and Robert Ayres (Chapter 4). Valuable inputs to specific sections of the report were provided by Xavier Coll, Fernando Reimers, Donald Winkler and Myriam Waiser of the Human and Social Development Group; Sri-Ram Aiyer, Luis Guasch, Malcolm Rowat, and Hemant Shah of the LAC Technical Department; William Dillinger, Paul Levy, and David Rosenblatt of LAC Country Department 1; and John Heath of LAC Country Department 3. The LAC Lead Economists—Ian Bannon, Norman Hicks, Homi Kharas, Zia Qureshi, and John Underwood—commented on drafts of Chapters 1, 2, and 3. Phil Keefer, Ross Levine, Lant Pritchett, and Martin Rama of the World Bank's Policy Research Department, and Carmen Pages of the Inter-American Development Bank, also provided very helpful advice and comments on Chapter 2. We are grateful to Juan Jose Echavarria of the Trade Unit at the Organization of American States, Ricardo Infante of the International Labor Office for Latin America and the Caribbean, and Eduardo Lora of the Inter-American Development Bank for providing data used in Chapter 2. The team also received many useful comments and suggestions from other LAC staff members, too numerous to mention here, who read preliminary drafts of Chapter 3.

Essential research assistance was provided by Beatriz Alonso, Charles Chang, Conrado Garcia-Corado, Jorge Forgues, and Shayma Saiyid.

Prologue

THREE YEARS AGO, THE PREVAILING MOOD AMONG POLICYMAKERS IN LATIN AMERICA AND the Caribbean (LAC), international investors, and other interested observers was one of euphoria. Authorities in most countries had taken decisive actions that were expected to lead to high growth rates. These actions included fiscal adjustment, trade liberalization, financial deregulation, the welcoming of foreign investment, and the privatizing of a substantial number of public enterprises. Macroeconomic stabilization and structural reforms contributed to growth rates that were indeed higher in the early 1990s than they had been in the "lost decade" of the 1980s. Projections of growth rates over 6 percent per year for the second half of the 1990s were commonplace. The region was flooded with private capital, which grew from a net inflow of US$12.5 billion in 1990 to $54.1 billion in 1993, in inflation-adjusted dollars. Moreover, Mexico was invited to become a member of clubs traditionally reserved for industrialized countries, such as the North American Free Trade Agreement (NAFTA) and the Organization for Economic Cooperation and Development (OECD). Doubters and skeptics were a small minority and their voices were drowned out by the crescendo of the alleluia.

The Mexican peso crisis of December 1994 changed the mood dramatically. Gloom, anxiety, and uncertainty replaced euphoria. Many predicted that capital flows to the region would dry up for many years to come, as had happened after the Mexican crisis of the early 1980s. Some feared generalized contagion effects and net capital outflows. Such fears were reinforced by the initial drop in most stock-market indexes in the region. They were kept alive for several months in 1995 as the Argentine authorities fought a difficult battle against instability, which they finally won.

The toll was high for Mexico and Argentina. In 1995, per capita income in Mexico declined by approximately US$770, and in Argentina by about US$130. Largely as a consequence of developments in Mexico and Argentina, the LAC region's economic growth rate plunged from 5.4 percent in 1994 to 0.9 percent in 1995. However, contrary to expectations, the crisis was largely confined to those two countries, and the rest of the region grew at a healthy 4.3 percent in 1995.

A stronger than expected recovery in the Mexican and Argentine economies pushed the region's growth rate to 3.5 percent in 1996. In contrast to most predictions, net private capital inflows surged from US$46.5 billion in 1995 to US$62 billion in 1996, far exceeding the peak of 1993. Most analysts believe that this level of private capital inflows will continue for at least a few years. Authorities in the LAC region are trying hard to keep these international capital surges from financing new consumption and lending booms and from excessively appreciating their countries' currencies, in order to prevent the economic vulnerabilities that spawned the crises of late 1994 and 1995. It is to be hoped that managers of international funds have also learned from these crises and will do their homework better in the future to avoid both the risky excesses during the booms and the exaggerated reactions during the downturns.

The mood today is more serene and optimistic than that of the first half of 1995. There are valid reasons for such optimism. Recent studies conducted at the World Bank and the Inter-American Development Bank (IDB) estimate that stabilization and economic reforms have raised the average annual growth rate of the region's per capita income by about two percentage points.[1] At the same time, the mood is more sober than it was before the Mexican crisis of late 1994. Projections of future annual growth rates range between 4 percent and 5 percent over the next few years for most LAC countries. Such growth rates will not be high enough, however, to reduce substantially the poverty that still afflicts a large percentage of the region's population. The large inequalities in both income and asset distribution that characterize most LAC countries mean that higher growth rates are needed to reduce poverty. At the same time, these large inequalities hinder the region's growth prospects. The economic reforms undertaken in the region to date have had little impact on inequality, and because growth has been moderate in recent years, these reforms have not reduced poverty significantly.

As a result, there is now a general awareness among policymakers that additional reforms need to be undertaken if LAC economies are to grow more than 6 percent a year, which is the growth rate that is widely believed necessary to lower the number of people living in poverty in the region. Policymakers also believe that many of the reforms vaguely referred to as "second generation" reforms are different from, and more problematic than, the "first generation" reforms. Few attempts have been made, however, to develop and organize the remaining reform agenda. This report offers a proposal for discussion.

• • •

The agenda proposed in this volume is based on recent theoretical and empirical work on the sources of economic growth and poverty reduction; on empirical measures of the LAC region's progress in terms of policies and economic factors that affect economic growth, and on comparisons between the LAC region and rapidly growing regions, such as the East Asian countries, and more developed economies, such as the OECD countries. The report identifies items in the reform agenda required to *consolidate macroeconomic stability* in the region (see Chapter 1), a nec-

essary condition for sustaining high rates of growth. It also specifies the additional structural reforms needed to *accelerate growth* in the medium and long term (see Chapters 2 and 3) and the policies required to broaden the reach of economic growth in order to confront the *challenge of poverty reduction* in the LAC region (see Chapter 4).

This three-pronged analysis has yielded a reform agenda for LAC in the next decade. This agenda comprises the following five broad policy areas, which are all interconnected.

A. Quality Investment in Human Capital

Despite substantial progress in expanding the coverage of education and health services in LAC, the quality of these services remains dismal in comparison to that of other regions, such as East Asia, Central Europe, and the industrialized OECD countries. Moreover, inequality of opportunities in health and education is one of the main determinants of current income distribution and poverty. Improving the quality of educational and health services is essential both to foster medium- and long-term competitiveness and productivity growth, and to enhance the poverty-reducing effect of economic growth.

The reform agenda in this area focuses on institutional, incentive-based reforms of the educational and health systems. The main objectives are to improve the quality and efficiency of *basic* education and health services, and to remove present-day biases against the poor. The agenda for education reform is particularly important to accelerate growth and reduce poverty. It includes fostering school autonomy under parental and community control, promoting competition among public and private providers, extending time in school (by lengthening both the school day and the school year), remunerating teachers on the basis of their performance, reforming teacher-training institutions, and increasing the provision and educational content of public and private daycare services, especially for the poor.

B. Efficient Financial Markets

Weak financial sectors are a threat to macroeconomic stability. At the same time, recent research on the determinants of growth has shown empirically that the development of both banking and capital markets increases investment and makes it more efficient. Indexes of financial development in the LAC region still lag well behind those of East Asian and OECD countries. Financial deepening is low, intermediation margins are high, and bond and equity markets are small, illiquid, and highly concentrated. Concentrated access to financial markets also contributes to the highly concentrated pattern of growth that characterizes most of LAC. Poor access to credit by microenterprises, small rural producers, and the poor prevents economic growth from having the full impact that it might in creating jobs and reducing poverty.

Needed reforms in this area include the following: improving regulation and supervision of financial markets, fostering domestic and foreign competition, privatizing inefficient publicly owned banks, intervening to develop deep and liquid bond and equity markets, and integrating the segmented financial markets for microenterprise, rural, and housing finance.

C. Enhanced Legal and Regulatory Environment

Recent theoretical and empirical work has established that property rights and adequate legal and regulatory systems are critically important for growth because they promote higher investment and more efficient investment. Available evidence indicates that both foreign and domestic investors perceive that in the protection of property rights, in the enforcement of contracts, and in the credibility of the legal and regulatory framework, the LAC region lags substantially behind other regions, especially the East Asian and OECD countries.

Weak property rights are a major hindrance to the advancement of the poor. Excessive regulation, especially of labor markets, fosters informality and stimulates labor-saving patterns of growth, both of which limit the poverty-reducing effects of economic growth. Despite advances in some LAC countries, private investment in infrastructure remains a costly and risky proposition because it leads either to low investment levels or to excessive government guarantees that hinder efficiency and may threaten fiscal prudence and macroeconomic stability. This is especially important since the LAC region needs a substantial increase both in investment and in the efficiency of infrastructure to sustain high growth rates. Achieving the required level of investment and degree of efficiency is not possible through public investment alone, because of the need to increase (or at least maintain) public investment in human capital and at the same time, to maintain fiscal discipline.

The reform agenda in this area includes enhancing the protections provided by property rights, expanding titling programs, developing efficient competition laws, and eliminating unnecessary or inefficient regulation of economic activity. Two main priorities emerge in this area, labor market reform, and regulatory frameworks, for private investment in infrastructure and the social services.

1. Labor market reform

Reforming labor markets includes enhancing flexibility in contracting, deploying, and collective bargaining; reforming severance payment systems; and reducing taxation on labor use, provided that the fiscal situation permits this. The aim is to improve the efficiency of labor markets and to reduce anti-employment biases, which are the result of inadequate regulation that imposes excessive costs and risks on employers. These reforms may significantly enhance the employment-creation effects of growth, and thus contribute in an important way to the reduction of poverty. Indeed, improving the functioning of labor markets is an important complement to improving the quality of investments in human capital.

2. Regulatory frameworks for private investment in infrastructure and the social services

These reforms include improving regulatory frameworks, establishing autonomous regulatory agencies staffed by highly skilled officials, and improving the allocation and management of risks that are associated with private investment in infrastructure projects. Regarding the latter, it is particularly important that fiscal contingencies embodied in the government-provided guarantees offered to private investors are adequately valued and budgeted.

D. Quality Public Sector and Governance

For these reforms to be designed and executed properly, the governments of the LAC region must be credible, efficient, and accountable. After all, the best legal and regulatory framework is of little use if the laws and regulations are not obeyed and enforced.

The recently published *World Development Report, 1997: The State in a Changing World* establishes clearly that the quality of government matters for development.[2] Available evidence indicates that investors in LAC perceive that the LAC region is lagging others in terms of the quality of public bureaucracies, the credibility of government, the reliability of the judiciary, and personal security. These perceptions are also closely associated with investment and economic growth. Furthermore, studies of individual countries in LAC suggest that the exceptionally high levels of crime and violence in parts of the region exact a high economic toll.

Therefore, the proposed reform agenda aims to achieve result-oriented, accountable, and transparent governments, and to strengthen the rule of law in LAC. More specifically, the desired improvements include *efficient decentralization of government, civil service reform, and reform of the judiciaries.*

Decentralization is proceeding swiftly in many LAC countries. Responsibilities for the delivery of services and public expenditures are being shifted increasingly to subnational governments. Since the popular election of mayors in many cities in the region, a number of improvements in the performance of local governments have emerged in the LAC region. Despite anecdotal evidence, however, improvements in governance are still not widespread and we lack enough evidence to conclude that these reforms will produce the desired effects. The quality of social services delivered by local governments depends both on the quality of local institutions and on the effectiveness of local governance. Efficient local taxation and revenue sharing are essential to make the decentralization process more efficient and to maintain overall fiscal balance. When decentralization depends excessively on the transfer to local governments of revenues collected by central governments and not on local tax efforts, local officials have few incentives either to use resources efficiently or to submit to local community control.

E. Fiscal Strengthening

Last but not least, fiscal strengthening is a precondition for the success of the rest of the agenda. In today's world of extensive financial integration and volatile capital flows, fiscal prudence and flexibility are the cornerstones of macroeconomic stability, which is itself necessary to sustain high growth rates. Fiscal prudence and flexibility also help to keep national savings rates high and to maintain adequate levels of investment in human capital and infrastructure.

Although most LAC countries have successfully made fiscal adjustments in recent years, a "second generation" of fiscal reforms is required to guarantee long-term fiscal sustainability, to enhance efficiency, and to promote equality. Most prominent among them are: *social security reform,* to ensure that social security systems are financially viable and

to cover present unfunded liabilities, and *subnational government fiscal reform,* to guarantee that fiscal adjustments at the national level are not undermined either by inadequate fiscal management at the subnational level or by poorly designed revenue-sharing mechanisms. In addition, social security reforms already initiated in seven countries in the region have shown important synergies with both labor market and health reforms. Also, fiscal reform of subnational governments is closely linked to achieving efficient decentralization, as was mentioned earlier. Other fiscal reforms include the adequate budgeting and funding of other contingent liabilities (such as the quasi-fiscal operations of central and publicly owned banks, and guarantees to exporters and to private investors in infrastructure), improved tax enforcement, and better budgetary institutions.

• • •

We recognize that this is an ambitious and complex agenda. It is technically, administratively, and politically demanding. Hence the title of this report: *The Long March,* which implies that achieving high sustained growth and reducing poverty significantly both require a well-planned and demanding itinerary of reforms, the results of which will take some time and effort to realize. There are no easy answers. Successful countries, such as the newly industrialized countries (NICs) in East Asia and Chile in the LAC region, have patiently implemented reforms and improved policies for more than a decade. Thus, policymakers in the LAC region are well advised to continue marching ahead with their reform and stabilization efforts without hesitation and without succumbing to despair.

We are convinced that the systematic application of the reform agenda proposed in these pages will take the LAC economies to higher sustained-growth plateaus than they now enjoy and will achieve the moral imperative of reducing poverty significantly. After all, Chile has proven both that a country in the Western Hemisphere can grow 7 percent annually over an extensive period of time and that it can at the same time reduce the number of people living in poverty by almost half, from approximately 40 percent of its population in 1987 to 23 percent in 1994.[3] It should come as no surprise that Chile is the only country in the region to show substantial progress (approaching East Asian standards) in the five areas of reform proposed in this report.

It remains unclear whether there exists the political commitment and conditions necessary for these reforms to be promoted and successfully implemented. There is much talk about a possible backlash against reform in the region. We do not share the pessimistic view in this regard. After all, both Mexico and Argentina rapidly came out of the 1995 crisis and deepened their commitment to reform. The only country in the region to experience a backlash was Venezuela, but it adopted the reform path again in 1995 with very promising results. We have to remember that 15 years ago, most analysts were convinced that the prevailing political interests in the region, which benefited from protectionism and other policies, would effectively impede progress in the reform of trade and investment policies. The same is said today with respect to entrenched interests in public-sector bureaucracies, and specifically in the educational and health sectors. We are skeptical of those who doubt that the region is capable of implementing the next stage of reforms. We believe in the power of ideas and in the strength of the movement—worldwide and in the LAC region—towards modernization and equity. Thus, although we are fully aware of the obstacles to progress, we remain moderately optimistic about the LAC region's prospects for achieving sustained growth and reducing poverty.

Notes To The Prologue

1. See Easterly, Loayza, and Montiel (1997), Lora and Barrera (1997), and Fernández-Arias and Montiel (1997).

2. See World Bank (1997i).

3. These "headcount" indices are based on a "poverty line" of 30,100 Chilean pesos per month at 1994 prices. Similar results are obtained when the poverty line is defined as 15,050 real pesos (the index having been reduced from 12.7 percent in 1987 to 5.1 percent in 1994), and when it is defined as 34,164 real pesos (the index having been reduced from 47.3 percent in 1987 to 29 percent in 1994).

I
Consolidating
Stabilization Gains

I T IS NOW CLEAR THAT AN UNSTABLE MACROECONOMIC ENVIRONMENT ADVERSELY AFFECTS economic growth. This conclusion follows from numerous studies that have used a variety of indicators to represent macroeconomic instability. The evidence from a large number of countries reveals a negative relationship between economic growth and inflation, particularly for high rates of inflation.[1] Also, large public-sector deficits and large differences between parallel and official exchange rates, which usually result from exchange controls and unsustainable macroeconomic policies, are associated with low rates of economic growth.[2] In addition, evidence suggests that the Latin America and Caribbean region in particular has been harmed by a turbulent macroeconomic environment, especially by volatile terms of trade, and by volatile real exchange rates which have resulted, in part, from unstable fiscal and monetary policies and from the adoption of unsustainable exchange rate regimes.[3]

Macroeconomic instability leads to lower economic growth because it reduces both the level of investment and the rate of productivity growth in the economy. An unstable macroeconomic environment is usually characterized by high and variable rates of inflation, by sudden changes in economic policies that cause sharp changes in relative prices, and by the imposition of controls that distort economic activities. The resulting uncertainty and misallocation of resources reduce the efficiency of the price mechanism and shorten the planning horizon of investors, leading to lower levels of investment and to a suboptimal allocation of this investment. A stable macroeconomic environment is thus crucial for sustained economic growth.

The LAC countries made significant progress towards macroeconomic stability during the early 1990s. Following the implementation of stabilization programs and the introduction of structural reforms in a number of these countries, economic growth picked up while inflation fell for the region overall. Large capital inflows during this period were accompanied by a rapid growth of domestic investment and a significant accumulation of international reserves. Progress during the 1990s, however, was not steady. In particular, the Mexican peso crisis of December 1994 resulted in a large output fall in Mexico, and also had adverse consequences for Argentina and Uruguay. The region has recovered substantially from this crisis: capital inflows resumed after a relatively short interruption, economic growth picked up, and inflation continued its declining trend.

Real gross domestic product (GDP) for the region grew at an average annual rate of 3.2 percent during 1991–96, compared to 1.9 percent during 1980–90.[4] (See Tables 1.1 and 1.3.) The experience of individual countries, of course, has not been uniform; the GDPs of about two-thirds of LAC countries grew, on average, at higher rates during 1991–96 than during the 1980s. In addition to this increase in the level of the growth rate, there was a decline in the volatility of the growth rate; both reflect the more stable macroeconomic environment of the 1990s.[5]

TABLE 1.1

Selected Economic Indicators

Real GDP Growth Rate
(In percent)

| | AVERAGE | | | | | | | | | |
	1980–85	1986–90	1991–96	1991	1992	1993	1994	1995	1996	1997
Mean	1.8	3.4	3.2	3.2	3.8	2.9	3.3	2.7	3.4	4.0
GDP-Weighted Mean	1.8	1.9	3.2	3.3	2.4	3.7	5.4	0.9	3.5	4.4
GDP-Weighted Mean w/o Arg. and Mex.	2.0	2.3	3.3	2.0	0.9	4.3	5.2	4.3	2.9	4.0
Median	2.0	3.6	3.6	3.1	4.4	3.4	4.2	3.5	3.1	4.0

Inflation Rate
(In percent)

| | AVERAGE | | | | | | | | | |
	1980–85	1986–90	1991–96	1991	1992	1993	1994	1995	1996	1997
Mean	107.1	321.9	73.0	149.9	52.3	87.6	111.2	23.2	14.0	11.7
GDP-Weighted Mean	137.3	716.9	457.9	236.1	427.4	898.0	1114.4	49.3	22.4	12.2
GDP-Weighted Mean w/o Brazil	134.4	450.2	31.3	85.2	23.8	16.5	14.0	22.5	25.6	15.0
Median	13.6	15.7	13.6	24.3	15.1	10.6	10.6	11.0	9.8	9.3

Non-Financial Public Sector Balance
(As percentage of GDP)

| | AVERAGE | | | | | | | | | |
	1980–85	1986–90	1991–96	1991	1992	1993	1994	1995	1996	
Mean	−8.6	−7.0	−2.6	−3.2	−2.7	−2.4	−2.7	−2.3	−2.4	
GDP-Weighted Mean	−7.5	−5.6	−1.2	−0.1	−1.0	−0.1	−0.9	−3.0	−2.2	
Median	−6.3	−5.1	−1.8	−1.8	−2.2	−1.1	−2.1	−1.7	−2.1	

Current Account Balance
(As percentage of GDP)

| | AVERAGE | | | | | | | | | |
	1980–85	1986–90	1991–96	1991	1992	1993	1994	1995	1996	1997
Mean	−5.8	−3.7	−5.4	−5.0	−6.5	−6.3	−5.4	−4.7	−4.5	−4.6
GDP-Weighted Mean	−2.9	−1.1	−2.2	−1.6	−2.3	−2.7	−2.6	−2.1	−2.2	−2.8
GDP-Weighted Mean w/o Arg. and Mex.	−3.3	−1.0	−1.4	−0.3	−0.2	−1.5	−0.9	−2.6	−2.8	−3.3
Median	−5.1	−2.9	−3.8	−3.5	−4.1	−4.6	−3.8	−3.8	−2.8	−3.3

Gross Domestic Investment
(As percentage of GDP)

| | AVERAGE | | | | | | | | | |
	1980–85	1986–90	1991–96	1991	1992	1993	1994	1995	1996	
Mean	21.9	21.5	21.7	22.0	21.8	22.3	21.3	21.4	21.2	
GDP-Weighted Mean	21.1	20.7	20.3	19.7	20.5	20.3	20.8	20.7	20.1	
Median	21.6	20.6	20.5	19.6	21.1	21.0	21.3	20.0	20.1	

Gross National Savings
(As percentage of GDP)

| | AVERAGE | | | | | | | | | |
	1980–85	1986–90	1991–96	1991	1992	1993	1994	1995	1996	
Mean	15.2	15.6	15.9	16.1	15.1	15.2	15.9	16.5	16.4	
GDP-Weighted Mean	18.2	19.6	18.2	18.2	18.2	17.7	18.2	18.8	17.9	
Median	15.8	15.6	16.3	16.0	15.1	15.5	16.6	17.4	17.1	

Rate of Unemployment
(In percent)

| | AVERAGE | | | | | | | | | |
	1980–85	1986–90	1991–96	1991	1992	1993	1994	1995	1996	
Mean	10.5	10.2	9.4	9.4	9.8	10.0	9.1	8.7	9.6	
Population-Weighted Mean	7.4	6.0	6.7	5.9	6.4	6.4	6.4	7.2	7.8	
Population-Weighted Mean w/o Arg.	7.7	6.0	6.2	5.8	6.3	6.1	6.0	6.3	6.9	
Median	9.5	9.7	7.9	8.1	8.0	8.2	7.8	7.1	8.1	

Sources: See Tables 1.3–1.9

Inflation in the region fell sharply in the 1990s. (See Tables 1.1 and 1.4.) Excluding Brazil, which plays a dominant role due to its size and the high inflation it experienced during these years, the average annual rate of inflation in LAC countries dropped from about 300 percent in 1980–90 to 31 percent in 1991–96. Inflation in Brazil fell more recently. Following the introduction of a successful stabilization program in mid-1994, it dropped from about 2700 percent in 1994 to 18 percent in 1996. Including all the countries, in 1996 the average rate of inflation in the region was 22.4 percent, and more than half of the countries had rates of inflation below 10 percent.

As a crucial component of their recent stabilization efforts, LAC countries strengthened significantly their public finances. (See Tables 1.1 and 1.5.) The average public-sector deficit in the region declined from 6.5 percent of GDP during 1980–90 to 1.2 percent of GDP during 1991–96.[6] This improvement reflected stronger public finances throughout the region. Out of the 26 LAC countries for which data are available, 23 countries attained a more favorable fiscal outcome during 1991–96 than during 1980–90. In 1996, however, 10 countries still had fiscal deficits above 3 percent of GDP.

During the 1990s, capital inflows to the region increased significantly, reflecting both external factors and improved domestic prospects in LAC economies; these inflows were only temporarily interrupted by developments associated with the 1994 Mexican peso crisis. The renewed access to external financing allowed LAC countries to make greater use of foreign savings. The external current-account deficit for the region, which had declined from an average of 5 percent of GDP in 1980–82 to 1 percent of GDP in 1983–90 as a result of the debt crisis of the 1980s, increased to 2.2 percent of GDP in 1991–96. (See Tables 1.1 and 1.6.) This primarily reflected higher average current-account deficits in Mexico, and to a lesser extent, in Argentina, Colombia, and a few other countries. The average deficit for the region remained relatively stable during 1991–96. While the deficit decreased in Mexico and Argentina after 1994, this decline was offset by an increase in the deficit in Brazil.

Countries in the LAC region are expected to experience higher output growth and lower inflation in 1997. The average rate of growth of real GDP is expected to increase from 3.5 percent in 1996 to about 4.4 percent in 1997, reflecting higher growth in most of the largest countries in the region, including Argentina, Brazil, Colombia, Peru, and Venezuela. Similarly, the average rate of inflation is expected to continue to decline, mainly reflecting lower inflation in Brazil, Mexico, and Venezuela.

Despite these favorable developments, several aspects of the macroeconomic situation in LAC countries remain far from satisfactory. First, economies in the region remain vulnerable to domestic and external factors that may threaten the stability achieved in recent years. Second, real GDP growth has improved since the 1980s, but it still remains below the levels needed to reduce poverty significantly and help ensure social stability. Third, and related to the previous point, gross domestic investment (GDI) continues at the low level of approximately 20 percent of GDP, and gross national savings declined from about 19 percent of GDP in 1980–90 to about 18 percent of GDP in 1990–96. (See Tables 1.1, 1.7 and 1.8.) Countries in the region will need to increase markedly their levels of savings and investment if they are to attain significantly higher rates of output growth on a sustained basis. Fourth, higher economic growth in the 1990s has not resulted in lower unemployment. In fact, in recent years the average rate of unemployment in the region has risen above the average level registered during the 1980s, mainly reflecting substantially higher unemployment in Argentina, and to a lesser extent also in Mexico and Venezuela (See Tables 1.1 and 1.9). This chapter addresses the first issue mentioned above; the other three issues are addressed elsewhere in this document.

This chapter discusses the policies needed to reduce macroeconomic vulnerability and to help consolidate the stabilization gains achieved by LAC countries in recent years. It examines various features of the region's public finances that contribute to large fiscal deficits and to volatile fiscal policies. These features include the following: unfunded social security systems and other contingent fiscal liabilities, quasi-fiscal losses, inappropriate intergovernmental fiscal relations, mismanagement of commodity booms, deficiencies in tax collection, and inefficiencies in public expenditure. The chapter then describes the macroeconomic and microeconomic factors that have led to problems in the financial sector, and examines the proper policies for handling those problems. Finally, it discusses issues associated with external vulnerability, including the factors that lead to balance-of-payments crises, the role of exchange rate policy, and the best way to deal with volatile capital flows.

A. Fiscal Policy

Fiscal policy has important implications for macroeconomic stability, and thus, for economic growth.[7] The two aspects of fiscal policy most relevant in this regard are the volatility of fiscal policy and the magnitude of fiscal deficits.

The relationship between fiscal volatility and economic growth is particularly clear in the case of tax policy. A volatile tax regime increases uncertainty about the future net returns on private-sector investment, leading to lower levels of investment, and thus to lower economic growth. Sharp changes in public-sector expenditure and fiscal deficits also increase uncertainty and reduce investment and growth because both generally lead to large changes in relative prices, which affect investment profits. In fact, evidence shows that uncertainty about tax revenue, public-sector consumption expenditure, and public-sector deficits all can negatively affect economic growth.[8]

The magnitude of fiscal deficits also affects economic growth. Large fiscal deficits lead sooner or later to high rates of inflation, with the negative consequences for growth that were mentioned previously. Fiscal discipline is also important because of its direct contribution to national savings.[9] Increasing the rate of national savings reduces macroeconomic vulnerability by lessening the need to rely on potentially volatile capital inflows to finance a given level of domestic investment. Evidence shows that countries with strong and flexible fiscal policies are in a better position to deal with the consequences of volatile capital flows.[10]

As mentioned above, LAC countries have significantly strengthened their public finances in recent years. However, their tasks in the area of fiscal policy are far from complete. Fiscal deficits remain above 3 percent of GDP in several countries in the region (including, for instance, Brazil and Costa Rica) and they are rising once again in others (such as Ecuador and Jamaica). Also, several countries have underinvested in human capital and in infrastructure for a long period, and they may need not only to reallocate but also to increase public expenditure in the future if they want to achieve sustained higher rates of economic growth.

In addition, LAC countries must address other structural pressures and problems if they are to ensure long-term fiscal sustainability and thus macroeconomic stability. Those pressures and problems can be classified as arising from

1. unfunded social security systems and other contingent fiscal liabilities,

2. quasi-fiscal losses,

3. inappropriate intergovernmental fiscal relations,

4. mismanagement of commodity booms,

5. deficiencies in tax collections, and

6. inefficiencies in public expenditure,

All of these problems are not present in every country, and the particular form and relevance of each of them varies significantly from country to country. So the detailed reform agenda is highly country-specific. Still, it is useful to discuss the general blueprint.

1. Unfunded social security systems and other contingent fiscal liabilities

The most prominent area of unfunded fiscal liabilities in LAC, as elsewhere, is the social security system. Virtually all LAC countries at one time had financially unsound social security systems in which the present value of expected benefits far exceeded the present value of reserves and expected contributions. The basic imbalance between benefits and contributions was compounded by low enforcement of contribution payments and mismanagement of reserves. Most countries essentially operated pay-as-you-go systems in which the contributions of active workers were used to pay the current benefits of the old, retired, sick, and incapacitated workers. These systems were able to run for many years without cash deficits because initial ratios of contributors to beneficiaries were high; these countries had relatively young populations, and social security systems in their early stages have few beneficiaries. Eventually, however, cash deficits emerged, first in Argentina, Brazil, and Uruguay, and subsequently in other countries as well.

Following the pioneering example of Chile in the early 1980s, a handful of LAC countries (Argentina, Bolivia, Colombia, Mexico, Peru, and Uruguay) have recently undertaken reforms to develop fully funded social security systems. Although these reforms are likely to be reflected in higher cash deficits than otherwise during the transition from the old to the new systems, they have undoubtedly strengthened the public finances when assessed from an appropriate long-term perspective.

In some cases, however, the new systems provide only partial coverage, and they still have some serious design problems. For example, public employees are often excluded, and in most reformed systems the regulations imposed on pension fund managers have created segmented financial markets, high commercialization costs, and insufficient choices for the beneficiaries.[11] In some countries, competition between the old and the new systems is neither transparent nor efficient.[12] Reform is thus high on the agenda for countries that have not yet reformed their social security systems, and substantial improvement is still to be made in countries that have undertaken reforms.

A number of other contingent fiscal liabilities are not explicitly budgeted in LAC countries, including, for instance, export guarantees and guarantees to private investors in infrastructure. As private investment in infrastructure grows, countries that offer generous payment and minimum traffic guarantees, for instance, or minimum energy purchase agreements, may find themselves committed to high unbudgeted expenditures in the future. For example, debt-restructuring deals for private investors in toll roads in Mexico amounted to a significant portion of the quasi-fiscal costs that were incurred after the Mexican peso crisis of December 1994. A recent conference sponsored by the World Bank was devoted to examining the proper way to reduce and allocate the risks of private investment in infrastructure, as well as to price and budget government guarantees to investors in these projects.[13]

2. Quasi-fiscal losses

The losses of public financial institutions have represented a significant fiscal burden in a number of LAC countries. Those losses generally result from quasi-fiscal operations, in which the central bank and other public financial institutions provide explicit or implicit subsidies for certain economic activities.[14] In the case of central banks, quasi-fiscal operations include the provision of subsidized credit, subsidized foreign exchange, exchange rate guarantees, and subsidized exchange-rate risk insurance. The sterilization of capital inflows, although not a quasi-fiscal operation, also has adversely affected the financial position of those central banks in the region that acquired low-yield foreign assets by issuing high-yield liabilities. The most important source of quasi-fiscal losses in several LAC countries in recent years, however, has been the bailout of banks in distress.[15] This has been the case, for instance, in Brazil, Jamaica, Mexico, and Venezuela. Quasi-fiscal losses originating from public financial institutions other than the central bank, such as federal and state-owned banks, primarily reflect the provision of credit at subsidized interest rates and of credit to insolvent borrowers without adequate collateral.

Losses arising from quasi-fiscal operations are a source of concern because they may have a substantial impact on the public finances and they may go undetected for a long time. The reasons for this are two-fold. First, the operational results of public financial institutions are normally not reflected in the budget. Second, because of the nature of some of the operations, losses arising from contingent liabilities, such as exchange rate guarantees or implicit commitments to bail out banks, will not materialize until some time after the obligation has been incurred. Thus, the central bank and other public financial institutions may be accumulating economic losses that are not captured by the traditional measures of fiscal stance. Only when those financial institutions need to be recapitalized will those losses be clearly reflected in the fiscal accounts.

Two steps must be taken to deal with the problem of losses from quasi-fiscal operations. First, the fiscal character of these operations must be brought into the open by presenting information on the profits and losses of public financial institutions together with the budget figures. Also, the contingent liabilities of these institutions must be estimated and provisioned.

Second, the underlying sources of the losses must be addressed. At the level of the central bank, this would involve, for instance, eliminating credit subsidies. While it may be impossible for the central bank to avoid completely the costs that arise from occasional difficulties in the banking system, by strengthening bank regulation and supervision the likelihood of such difficulties emerging in the future will be reduced. Also, losses to the central bank can be reduced to some extent by requiring that deposit insurance schemes be financed by participating financial institutions rather than by the central bank.

The basic problem of the public financial institutions other than the central bank is that they are not run on a commercial basis, mainly because their owners (national and subnational governments) tend to use them for political purposes and for avoiding hard budget constraints. In this context, privatization or liquidation of these institutions is highly desirable.

3. Intergovernmental fiscal relations

For a number of years now, there has been a trend toward fiscal decentralization in a number of LAC countries, including Argentina, Brazil, Bolivia, Colombia, Guatemala, and Venezuela, among others. The rationale for fiscal decentralization is based primarily on microeconomic considerations; decentralization is expected to lead to a more efficient provision of public goods for a number of reasons, which are explained in Chapter 3.

In addition to its effect on allocation efficiency, however, fiscal decentralization has important implications for the design and implementation of macroeconomic policy.[16] Subnational governments have frequently contributed to the creation of large fiscal deficits, and thus to macroeconomic instability, in part because they see macroeconomic stabilization as a responsibility of the national government. Also, subnational governments often lack strong incentives for fiscal discipline since, on many occasions, they have been bailed out by the national government. A number of factors in intergovernmental fiscal relations usually contribute to macroeconomic instability.

An important problem in some LAC countries has been the implementation of revenue-sharing schemes, through which an important fraction of revenues collected by the national government is automatically transferred to subnational governments. This has been the case, for instance, in Argentina, Brazil, and Colombia. Under these circumstances, national governments find it difficult to reduce overall fiscal deficits by increasing taxes because subnational governments are usually inclined to spend their share of additional revenue. Also, as subnational governments finance a large part of their expenditures using these transfers, they are disinclined to exploit their own tax base. That increases in unrestricted revenue sharing have discouraged subnational governments from generating their own revenue has been confirmed in studies of Brazil, Colombia, Ecuador, Guatemala, and Mexico, among other countries.[17]

National governments have sometimes avoided this problem by increasing selected taxes that generate revenues not shared with lower-level governments. However, in many cases this has produced highly distorted tax structures. To avoid these problems, an effort should be made to provide subnational governments with adequate revenue sources over which they have control but the burden of which they cannot shift to taxpayers outside the locality. Admittedly, in some countries, administrative factors may limit how much revenue can be collected at the local level.

The use of discretionary and negotiated grants to transfer resources to subnational governments also has been a problem in some LAC countries. This practice has often resulted in funds being allocated according to considerations other than sound economic principles. To the extent possible, these types of grants should be avoided, and any necessary transfer of funds should be governed by clear and automatic rules. Also, the ambiguous assignment of expenditure responsibilities among the various levels of government is likely to result in higher deficits, because subnational governments then have incentives to evade those responsibilities and to shift the burden to the national government. On occasion, this has been a problem, for instance, in Brazil and Mexico.[18]

To control overall public-sector deficits, subnational governments need to have effective limits placed on their borrowing.[19] In some countries, such as Argentina and Brazil, borrowing by subnational government was facilitated by the access to financing that state (or provincial) governments had from their own banks. It would be unrealistic to rely exclusively on market discipline to contain the deficits of subnational governments. For market discipline to work, these governments should have no captive source of funds, there should be abundant and accurate information on their finances, and there should be no expectation of a bailout by the national government. Although the recent move to privatize state banks has limited somewhat this source of captive funds, the other conditions for effective market discipline are not present. Thus, explicit limits on borrowing by subnational governments are needed. As in the case of grants, these limits should be set according to rules rather than left to discretion.[20]

Recently, some states and provinces, plagued by financial crisis, have been undertaking fiscal adjustment programs supported by their federal governments and by multilateral institutions. Such programs typically include downsizing, revenue enhancement, debt restructuring, and privatization (or at least restructuring) of state and provincial banks and other subnational public enterprises. To date, 12 Brazilian states have signed adjustment agreements with the federal government, and 11 provincial banks in Argentina have been privatized.

4. Procyclical fiscal policy in commodity booms

Another significant source of macroeconomic instability in the LAC region has been the mismanagement of commodity booms in countries with a large concentration of exports of a particular commodity.[21] The LAC experience in this regard has been, with a few exceptions, highly traumatic. Increases in commodity prices are typically accompanied by overspending booms that are fueled not only by higher incomes, but also by the increased indebtedness that results from the country's improved access to foreign financing. Inflationary pressures and marked appreciation of the currency ensue, and often the external current account balance deteriorates significantly even before the boom is over. When this occurs, access to foreign credit is sharply reduced and traumatic adjustments are required.

Fiscal policy has often been highly procyclical during commodity booms, and thus it has played an important role in the developments mentioned above. As commodity booms generate important additional fiscal revenues—which is especially true when the commodities are produced by state enterprises or yield large royalty and tax revenues (as in the case of oil and other minerals)—governments find themselves with increased capacity to spend and with access to foreign and domestic credit. Even if the governments initially decide to exercise some control, very soon, under political pressures and for reasons of convenience, they relax their restraint. This leads to higher (and often improvised and inefficient) current and capital expenditures, to tax reductions, and to increased indebtedness. When the boom ends, adjustment is deferred as long as possible because firing employees, reducing wages, and suspending the execution of public investment are difficult, costly, and politically inconvenient measures. Eventually, the adjustment comes, and it is usually traumatic. It is not uncommon for countries to end up worse off than before the boom started. A prominent example of this was the mismanagement by most LAC oil-exporting countries (notably Venezuela, Mexico, Ecuador, and Peru) of the oil boom that took place between 1973 and 1980; when the boom ended, these countries were among the ones hardest hit by the debt crises.

In order to avoid the procyclical aspect of fiscal policy associated with commodity booms, public-sector expenditures must be planned and carried out on the basis of long-term revenues.[22] This requires both an appropriate forecast of those revenues, and rules to ensure that expenditure commitments are consistent with the forecast. The uncertainty about fiscal revenues could be reduced by using market-based hedging instruments (such as futures, options, and swaps).[23] The use of such instruments would reduce uncertainty about export revenues and profitability, and thus would permit a better forecasting of fiscal revenues. Market-based hedging instruments have been used to reduce price uncertainty by a number of public enterprises in the LAC region, including copper companies in Chile and Mexico, and oil companies in Brazil, Ecuador, and Mexico. For most commodities, however, market-based hedging instruments are available only for short-term maturities, and thus are not very helpful in dealing with longer-term price uncertainty. Also, the use of hedging instruments entails costs (such as payment of premiums, deposit of margins, establishment of appropriate accounting and monitoring systems, and training of traders) that could end up making it an unattractive alternative for some firms.

Independent of the accuracy achieved in forecasting fiscal revenues, in order to prevent the problems of a highly procyclical fiscal policy driven by commodity booms and busts, it is crucial to smooth the path of public expenditure. In general terms, this is achieved by saving the additional fiscal revenues accrued during periods of high commodity prices, and using those savings to finance expenditure during the periods of low commodity prices. Because political pressures usually make it difficult to save resources in affluent times, institutions need to be created to make it easier to resist those pressures.[24] A useful tool for formalizing such institutions has been commodity stabilization funds.

Typically, the structure of commodity stabilization funds includes a reference price which responds, in part, to the evolution of international market prices. Revenues based on the reference price are allocated to the general budget. Excess revenues that arise when market prices are above the reference price are deposited in the fund, and any deficiency in revenues that arises when the market price is below the reference price is financed by withdrawing from the fund. The optimal rules for determining the reference price and other aspects of how the stabilization fund functions will depend, among other things, on the particular stochastic process that the price of the commodity follows.[25]

Successful examples in the LAC region include the Copper-Stabilization Fund instituted by Chile in 1985, which facilitated the management of the copper price boom in the late 1980s. In 1994 Colombia instituted an elaborate Oil Stabilization Fund to mitigate the effect of variations in spending capacity that arise both from increased production (resulting from new discoveries) and from price variations. It is too early to evaluate the usefulness of this fund, as it became operative only last year and the largest revenue increases are still to be felt. However, public expenditure expanded after the new oil discoveries, perhaps in anticipation of future revenue, and this may limit the fund's usefulness. Other oil-exporting countries, such as Ecuador and Venezuela, have been considering the possibility of adopting a similar mechanism.

For stabilization funds to be effective in smoothing public expenditure, pressures to spend the resources of the fund in excess of the amount established by the rules must be resisted. This is why such rules need to be included in a law. Furthermore, stabilization funds are just institutional mechanisms aimed at smoothing public expenditure; they will have a chance of being effective only if their intent is not violated in some other way. For example, it would be useless to deposit the revenues from a commodity price boom in a stabilization fund if, at the same time, the public sector finances increases in expenditure through additional borrowing.

5. Efficiency of tax collections

Most LAC countries have reformed considerably their tax systems in the last decade, driven both by the requirements of trade and financial opening, and by the need for fiscal adjustment. As a result of trade reforms, export taxes have been eliminated almost everywhere and revenue from import taxes has declined sharply. At the same time, the competition for foreign direct investment (FDI) and other capital flows has led LAC countries to reduce the marginal rates for both corporate and personal income taxes and to eliminate double taxation of dividend income. Some minor distortionary taxes also have been eliminated because, in the more competitive environment, they were a hindrance to domestic production. Revenue losses from such reforms, however, needed to be more than offset by other revenue measures because of the need for fiscal adjustment. This has been achieved mainly through value-added taxes (VAT)—either by introducing them, by increasing their rates, or by broadening their bases—which have become the major individual source of tax revenue in the region. To a lesser extent, revenue increases have also been obtained by broadening the bases of income taxes, by using presumptive taxation mechanisms such as the "assets tax," and by improving tax administration.[27]

However, relative to tax rates, tax yields remain low in most countries because of widespread evasion and exemptions. Thus, there is still ample scope to strengthen the public finances through an increase in tax collection, which

can be achieved by improving tax administration, by removing exceptions, and by closing loopholes. This is the unfinished agenda in tax reform. Although this is well understood, most LAC countries do not possess the political will to change the current state of affairs, mainly because the necessary reform lacks glamour and its benefits are not appreciated directly while its direct costs fall on the very vocal high- and middle-income groups.

6. Expenditure efficiency and budgetary institutions

In a number of LAC countries, the reduction or elimination of inefficient expenditure could make a significant contribution to strengthening the public finances and to improving efficiency. Public administrations, both at the national and subnational levels, continue to be unduly large. In some countries, like Brazil, the necessary downsizing has been precluded by constitutional or legal norms that make employee layoffs exceedingly difficult and costly. Other countries, such as Ecuador, still have expensive and highly inefficient and regressive energy subsidies. Military expenditures continue to be excessively high in some cases, although the region as whole does not seem to spend an exorbitant share of its GDP for military purposes.

Expenditures in many countries are still not well focused on the areas that should have priority, such as basic education, health, and infrastructure. As discussed in Chapters 3 and 4, many countries are already spending high fractions of their national incomes in social sectors, but allocation is strongly biased towards higher levels of education and sophisticated health services. Inefficiencies tend to be larger in social expenditures than in other areas.

To a large extent, the misallocation of scarce public funds is an outcome of political systems strongly shaped by patron-client relationships. Such systems benefit from unstructured and underdeveloped budgetary processes and institutions. It has been documented that public funds are less likely to be badly allocated when budgetary institutions are stronger; when budgetary allocations require sound technical supporting analysis, such as feasibility studies for investment projects and cost-effectiveness estimates for current expenditure allocations; and when the executive, and in particular, the central economic ministries, such as finance and planning, have more control of the budgetary process. Budgetary institutions tend to be weaker in subnational governments, where basic problems of accounting and reporting remain to be solved.[28] Inefficiencies in government spending, especially in the social sectors, are, however, systemic in nature. Present institutions do not provide adequate incentives for quality and efficiency. Public-sector reform appears essential to achieve substantial advances in this area. (See Chapters 3 and 4.)

B. The Financial Sector

A sound financial system is crucial for maintaining macroeconomic stability. Problems in the financial system, and particularly in the banking system, can spread rapidly through the rest of the economy with serious consequences for economic activity and, more generally, for overall economic performance.[29]

Banking problems may lead to macroeconomic difficulties in a variety of ways.[30] A weak banking system generates an inefficient allocation of credit; banks that have lost an important share of their capital are subject to moral hazard and so may tend to lend for excessively risky projects. Also, a weak banking system constrains economic policy; the authorities may be reluctant to tighten credit, even if it is needed to contain inflation or defend the currency, because doing so would have an adverse impact on the financial health of banks. In addition, a generalized loss of confidence in the banking system may induce a large portfolio shift towards foreign assets, putting pressure on the domestic currency and provoking a balance-of-payment crisis.[31] Finally, banking problems, and particularly banking crises, usually entail high fiscal costs. For instance, these costs have been estimated at 13 percent of GDP for Argentina in 1982, 20 percent of GDP for Chile in 1985, 6 percent of GDP for Colombia in 1985, and 13 percent of GDP for Venezuela in 1994.[32] Similarly, fiscal costs arising from recent banking problems in Mexico have been estimated at 10 to 12 percent of GDP; although estimates of the fiscal costs for Brazil and Jamaica are not readily available, they surely amount to several percentage points of GDP. In view of the serious consequences that banking problems may have on the economy, it is crucial to understand the sources of those problems and to design policies to help prevent them.

1. Macroeconomic factors

The emergence of credit booms, sometimes associated with financial liberalization and with the success of stabilization programs, has contributed to banking problems in a number of developing countries.[33] These problems have been particularly serious when financial liberalization was undertaken in the presence of weak bank regulation and supervision. Typically, either the relaxation or elimination of controls over international and domestic financial transactions, or the optimism brought about by a sharp reduction of domestic inflation, has induced large capital inflows that are intermediated by the banking system. Initially, there is a consumption boom, an expansion of economic activity, and a rapid increase in stock and real estate prices. Since many borrowers remain liquid during this phase of the cycle, assessing loan risk becomes more difficult, and banks may be unable to detect a deterioration in the underlying quality of their loan portfolio. However, when the expansion of economic activity slows down or stops, the true quality of loans becomes evident, and stock and real estate prices fall sharply, reducing the value of collateral and imposing large losses on banks.

This schematic description of the consequences of domestic and external financial liberalization without proper regulation—capital inflows, followed by a credit boom, large increases in asset prices, a consumption boom, and eventually, a financial crisis—fits very well the developments in the Mexican economy prior to its recent crisis. More generally, countries that have undertaken financial liberalization without first ensuring a proper regulatory framework have invariable invited financial crises. Thus, financial liberalization should be implemented gradually, particularly after a long period of financial repression and when bank regulation and supervision are not sufficiently strong. Also, sterilization operations and increases in reserve requirements can help to contain credit booms. In addition, a tightening of fiscal policy can reduce pressures on interest rates and thus reduce capital inflows, while at the same time limiting the expansion of domestic demand. The introduction of restrictions on capital inflows seems to have helped contain these inflows in some countries, although this effect appears to have been temporary in most cases.

In addition to credit booms, other policy-induced macroeconomic developments may generate banking problems. For instance, an unbalanced policy mix that is based on lax fiscal policy and tight credit can result in excessively high interest rates, thus leading to a deterioration in the quality of bank portfolios. Similarly, bank portfolios may worsen as a result of large changes in the real exchange rate resulting from the collapse of unsustainable exchange rate regimes. In addition, the health of the banking system is directly affected when state-owned banks are not run on a commercial basis and are used for quasi-fiscal activities. The most direct way of dealing with these problems is to reverse the policies that created the difficulties. Measures that could be taken to deal with the problems mentioned here include tightening fiscal policy, ensuring consistency between monetary and fiscal policies and the exchange rate regime, and liquidating or privatizing state-owned banks.

Macroeconomic developments affecting the banking system may also have an external origin. For instance, volatility in the terms of trade, over which countries have little or no control, may lead to a serious deterioration in the quality of bank portfolios, particularly in economies with a high concentration of exports. Similarly, volatile capital flows may lead to sudden changes in the availability of funding for banks. To help deal with these problems, economic agents need to have access to financial instruments (such as swaps, options, and future contracts) to reduce their exposure. Also, banks must be sufficiently capitalized, and the central bank must hold an adequate level of international reserves. The experience of Argentina also has shown that changing bank liquidity requirements can be an useful tool for dealing with capital outflows in the context of a currency board regime.

2. Microeconomic factors

Poor bank management, usually the result of poor prudential regulations and weak bank supervision, has been responsible for bank problems in a number of cases. Typical features of badly managed banks include overextension, poor loan evaluation, excessive loan concentration, connected lending, term and currency mismatch, poor loan recovery, and weak internal controls. [34]

Dealing with these problems requires putting in place stringent rules for access to banking to ensure sufficient capital and fit managers, strict exit policies, adequate minimum capital requirements (which in LAC should be higher than the 8 percent of risk-adjusted assets recommended by the Bank for International Settlements [BIS], as is the case in Argentina), a good accounting system, proper asset classification and provisioning rules, limits on loan concentration and connected lending, proper information disclosure, a legal system that ensures the enforcement of financial contracts, loan recovery and realization of collateral, and an obligatory deposit insurance scheme financed by the banks and covering

only small deposits. Supervision activities should include frequent on-site inspections; supervisors should have access to all relevant information, have enforcement powers, and be independent from political pressures. Also, these activities should be complemented by mandatory external audits.

There is ample room for improving regulation and supervision in the LAC region. These activities are particularly demanding in today's world of high financial integration and volatile capital flows. Regulation of conglomerates (through the consolidation of balance sheets and disclosure requirements) and the supervision of offshore banking are especially weak in most LAC countries. Also, regulators and supervisors in many of the region's countries are not technically prepared to deal with the risks posed by sophisticated derivative markets, securitization, and other changes associated with rapid financial innovation. Also, enforcement of sanctions in the event of noncompliance is uncommon. In addition, the need to promote international cooperation in the regulation of financial systems is clear, although little progress has been achieved by LAC in this area.

Measures that enhance the effectiveness of market discipline also can help improve the performance of banks. Bank creditors can provide banks with incentives to behave prudently by requiring higher interest rates and, if necessary, by withdrawing their funds from institutions that follow unsound practices. When it is effective, market discipline increases the likelihood that poorly managed banks are driven out of the market before they create systemic problems, thus contributing to a healthier banking system. To be effective, however, it requires participants who are well informed and whose funds are not fully protected (so that they have incentives to monitor the performance of banks and to respond accordingly). Market discipline can be enhanced by removing deposit insurance schemes that provide excessive protection, and by ensuring that the market receives prompt and accurate information about the situation of the banks. Chile and New Zealand, for instance, have adopted some market-based regulations. (See Box 1.) Even in industrial countries, however, the ability of the market to assess the real situation of banks has been limited. Thus, market discipline should be considered a complement to, rather than a substitute for, proper regulation and supervision.

The liberalization of FDI regimes for financial services can also contribute to financial stability. Lack of competition in the domestic financial market often breeds inefficiencies, and thus raises the cost of capital in domestic markets. Also,

BOX 1

Two Examples of Market-Based Regulations

Chile

1. Loans are classified in four groups based not on past due payments but on current assessment of the repayment capacity, past record, and collateral of borrowers.
2. Auditors review banks 3 times per year and summary ratings (such as CAMEL—Capital, Assets, Management, Earnings, Liquidity) are published in newspapers.
3. Private rating agencies review instruments issued by banks and publish the ratings.
4. Loans must be disclosed to members/affiliates in the group.
5. Banks' net worth is adjusted several times per year. When any bank's net worth falls below 40 percent of the value on January 1, it must recapitalize.
6. The law forbids superintendency from delaying loss recognition.
7. Each bank must maintain a reserve that is 2.5 times its capital to prevent/reduce runs on deposits.
8. Government guarantees liquid liabilities of small depositors (below US$2,000).

New Zealand

1. Reserve Bank licenses banks, monitors published reports, and enforces capital standards.
2. Banks disclose credit quality on a quarterly basis and are audited semi-annually. Credit quality is posted at each branch.
3. Any bank must stop lending when its capital falls below 6 percent of risk-weighted assets; management is replaced when capital falls to 3 percent.
4. Reserve Bank retains the right to seek additional information as lender of last resort.
5. There is no explicit deposit insurance.

greater internationalization is a way of importing good regulation and supervision, which are embodied in the business practices of foreign financial affiliates operating in developing countries. In addition, these affiliates may have better access to external financing than do domestic banks when domestic financial markets become turbulent.

3. Recent experiences in the region

Several countries in the region experienced banking and financial crises during 1994–1996, including Argentina, Brazil, Jamaica, Mexico, and Venezuela. Banking sectors in LAC remain fragile, and many require restructuring and/or recapitalization. The following several examples highlight some of the problems and policy responses in each of the countries just mentioned.

Argentina had already begun to strengthen bank regulation and supervision when the 1995 banking crisis occurred. This crisis was triggered by the sharp outflow of deposits from the nation's banks following the devaluation of the peso in Mexico, and it exposed significant weaknesses in many of the publicly owned and private banks. The risks for the financial system were exacerbated by the restrictions placed on the central bank's ability to provide emergency credit to illiquid banks by Argentina's Convertibility Law. A rapid response from the authorities and the visible support of international financial institutions, including the World Bank, were important in restoring confidence. Several weak private banks were closed or merged, and many of the provincial banks were privatized. Also, in response to the crisis, the authorities created a limited deposit insurance program to protect small depositors, raised significant external credit in order to provide emergency liquidity if needed, and further increased the requirement for capital adequacy. They also reduced reserve requirements at the height of the crisis in order to provide some liquidity to the banks.

In Brazil, several banks were seriously affected by a number of factors: the sharp reduction of inflation that began in mid-1994, and which deprived them of their share of the inflation tax; the very high real interest rates that followed; and a slowdown in economic activity in mid-1995, which worsened their loan portfolio. To address these problems, the central bank initially took control of 29 private banks and 6 state-owned banks. Some small private banks were closed, while a few others were merged with other banks and returned to the private sector. The authorities also introduced a deposit insurance scheme and a program of financial assistance to facilitate the restructuring of private banks, increased the central bank's power to deal with problem banks, enhanced the role of external auditors, increased capital requirements, and tightened controls over offshore operations. They are also making progress in improving bank supervision. In addition, the authorities introduced a mechanism to facilitate the liquidation, privatization, or restructuring of state-owned banks as part of the program to reschedule state debts, and they recapitalized the largest Brazilian bank, which is under majority ownership of the federal government.

In Mexico, the financial crisis of December 1994 had a severe impact on the banking system, which was already weak as a result of a previous rapid expansion of credit in the presence of poor regulation and supervision. To strengthen the banking system, the authorities introduced a numbers of programs, some of which were designed to support debtors and others to provide direct assistance to banks in difficulties. They also reinforced bank supervision and prudential regulation. The reform agenda for Mexico includes (1) expeditiously resolving the difficulties of problem banks and bank assets to restore the system's financial strength while limiting fiscal costs, which are currently estimated at 10 to 12 percent of GDP, but may go higher; (2) improving the incentives regime to reduce moral hazard, and focusing particularly on the comprehensive bank liability insurance currently in place; and (3) strengthening the regulatory and institutional framework, which includes improving accounting standards, establishing disclosure requirements, and reforming the legal and regulatory framework for bank transactions and contracts in general, including bankruptcy.

In Venezuela, unprecedented political and social unrest in 1992–93 led to macroeconomic turbulence that exposed systemic deficiencies in the banking sector. The collapse in February 1994 of Banco Latino, the country's second largest bank in terms of deposits, unveiled a serious financial crisis that affected numerous institutions. By the end of 1995, 19 financial institutions, accounting for about 70 percent of the financial system's deposits, had been intervened and/or nationalized. Official funds used to recapitalize and support institutions in difficulty amounted to about 13 percent of GDP in 1994 and 4 percent of GDP in 1995. Since the emergence of the crisis, the authorities have made progress in improving prudential regulation (including, for example, tighter limits on loans to insiders and higher capital requirements), and in strengthening supervision. They also facilitated the access by regulatory agencies and by the general public to information on financial institutions, introduced new accounting standards, and approved the rules for universal banking. The conversion of an important number of specialized institutions

into universal banks in the near future is expected to improve efficiency in the banking sector. Also, owing to the wider scope of their activities, universal banks should be better able than specialized institutions to diversify risk and to adjust to changes in the economic environment. In addition, the opening of the financial sector to foreign participation has resulted in the presence of new international financial groups in the domestic market, which should help strengthen the health of the financial sector.

The roots of the recent problems in the Jamaican financial sector lie in the poor management of financial firms, the lack of regulatory controls over the structure of the financial institutions, inadequate regulations, and weak supervision of the sector. Different reserve requirements among the various types of financial institutions encouraged disintermediation from commercial banks to merchant banks in the early 1990s, and more recently, from merchant banks to building societies. Consequently, both the number and the assets of the unregulated building societies grew quite rapidly. Further difficulties resulted from the formal associations between insurance companies, which were largely unsupervised, and other types of deposit-taking institutions. In several cases, the insurance companies drew upon the resources of the deposit-taking institutions to fund the holding of illiquid real estate assets. The collapse and subsequent interventions at three institutions has given rise to the debate about the need for more orderly and rational oversight.

C. The External Sector

The evolution of the external accounts is closely related to virtually all important aspects of macroeconomic policy, some of which have already been mentioned in this chapter. This section focuses on three issues of macroeconomic stability associated with developments in the external sector. First, it summarizes briefly the empirical findings about leading indicators of currency crises. Second, it discusses the role of exchange rate policy in maintaining macroeconomic stability. Finally, it examines the experience of developing countries with the surge in capital inflows that took place in the 1990s in order to derive lessons for dealing with volatile capital flows.

1. Balance of payments crises

The extensive literature that examines the theoretical and empirical aspects of balance-of-payments crises suggests many variables as leading indicators of crises. [35] Early theoretical models emphasized that these crises were caused by expansionary monetary and fiscal policies, which led to a persistent loss of international reserves that ultimately forced the authorities to abandon the parity. [36] According to these models, the period preceding the crisis is accompanied by a real appreciation of the domestic currency and a deterioration of the trade balance. More recent models have pointed out that the authorities may decide to abandon the parity for reasons other than that international reserves have been depleted. For instance, they may be concerned that the policies needed to defend the parity, such as an increase in interest rates, will adversely effect other key economic variables, such as the level of employment, the cost of servicing the public debt, or the health of the banking system. According to these models, therefore, high unemployment, large public debt, or a weak financial system will increase the likelihood of a crisis.

Empirical studies support various leading indicators of currency crises that have been identified in the theoretical literature. The most consistent result across studies has been the presence of an increasing real appreciation of the currency in the period leading to a crisis. Although it is well known that the "equilibrium" real exchange rate is not constant, and thus, that every real appreciation cannot be taken as a sign of misalignment, it is clear that a large real appreciation with respect to the recent historical mean should be seen as a signal of potential problems that calls for close scrutiny of the situation. Obviously, a careful assessment must take into consideration other variables, as well as the particular circumstances in the country in question. Other leading indicators of currency crises include declining international reserves, a weakening of export growth, and a deterioration of the trade balance. Also, empirical studies show that expansionary monetary and fiscal policies increase the probability of crises, as traditional models have suggested. In addition, evidence suggests that a slowdown in real GDP growth and a decline in stock prices (usually at the end of credit booms) play a role in determining the likelihood of a crisis. A number of other variables (foreign, institutional, and political) also seem to be relevant, but drawing firm conclusions about their effects is difficult because they have been used only in a few studies.

The policy implications that can be derived from these studies are familiar. To reduce the probability of a balance-of-payments crisis, it is necessary to follow disciplined monetary and fiscal policies, avoid an excessive real appreciation of the currency, contain credit booms, and strengthen the banking system.

2. Exchange rate policy

In addition to these policy implications, there is the issue of the role that exchange rate policy could play in reducing the likelihood of an exchange rate crisis. In particular, the strong evidence about the dangers of excessive real appreciations raises the question of whether exchange rate policy should be geared toward avoiding such appreciations. This question, of course, cannot be answered definitively. The benefits of using the exchange rate to maintain international competitiveness must be compared with possible benefits of keeping a fixed exchange rate, and the result of this comparison is likely to be country-specific.

It is now generally agreed that there is no one exchange rate system that would be the best under every conceivable set of circumstances. Recent discussions about the relative merits of alternative exchange rate systems have focused on the roles that the exchange rate may play as an anchor for prices and as a tool for facilitating necessary adjustments in relative prices. [37] To be sustainable, a fixed exchange rate imposes restrictions on fiscal and credit policies. Those in favor of fixed exchange rates argue that, because of the costs of reneging on a commitment to fixed exchange rates, countries with this system will instead implement prudent macroeconomic policies to help ensure a low rate of inflation. Proponents of more flexible regimes, on the other hand, argue that a fixed exchange rate makes the adjustment to adverse exogenous shocks, such as a deterioration of the terms of trade, too costly because of downward rigidity of wages and prices. Furthermore, they argue that a fixed exchange rate by itself does not impose discipline. In the absence of discipline, the fixed exchange rate just postpones the problem, transforming what would have been a gradual adjustment under a flexible regime into a traumatic one.

The empirical evidence about long-term macroeconomic performance under alternative exchange rate systems does not favor conclusively one system over another. [38] In general, countries with fixed exchange rates have experienced significantly lower and more stable rates of inflation than have countries under other regimes. There are also indications that this relationship between fixed exchange rates and low inflation is a causal one, and not one of reverse causality, in which countries that prefer low inflation tend to choose fixed exchange rates. Of course, the countries that operated under fixed exchange rates but adjusted the parity frequently experienced higher rates of inflation than did those that adjusted the parity only sporadically. While the evidence regarding inflation seems to favor fixed exchange rates over flexible regimes, the evidence regarding other variables of interest seems to favor flexible regimes. Countries with fixed exchange rates have experienced slightly lower and more volatile rates of output growth, and more volatile levels of employment, than have countries with flexible regimes.

Countries in the LAC region are presently implementing a variety of exchange rate systems. Argentina, Belize, Panama, and a group of Caribbean countries have their currencies pegged to the U.S. dollar, whereas the rest of LAC countries operate some form of flexible exchange rate arrangement. These include countries that are implementing exchange rate bands (such as Brazil, Chile, and Colombia), countries in which the currency floats relatively freely (such as in Mexico and Peru), and countries that have other types of managed regimes. Even within the countries using exchange rate bands, there are significant differences. Brazil has a fixed (although adjustable) band and intervenes to keep the exchange rate within a narrow "internal" band, whereas Chile and Colombia implement crawling bands and allow for larger variations in the exchange rate than does Brazil

As mentioned above, there is no optimal solution that can be applied uniformly, because each country may be facing a different tradeoff between the discipline imposed by a fixed exchange rate and the flexibility offered by other regimes. For example, the use of crawling exchange rate bands has been credited as an important component of the package of policies that accounts for Chile's sustained good economic performance. It is also seen as having helped Colombia prevent an excessive real appreciation of its currency and avoid serious repercussions from both the Mexican peso crisis of 1994 and its own domestic political difficulties in 1995.[39] At the same time, however, the use of a fixed exchange rate clearly has been a crucial component in the policy package that brought price stability to Argentina, which has had a long history of high inflation, and that facilitated the introduction of a number of important structural reforms there. Of course, a crucial task now in Argentina is to enhance the flexibility in the labor market to reduce unemployment.

Also worth mentioning again is that overall economic performance depends not only on the exchange rate

regime, but also fundamentally on the other underlying macroeconomic policies. For instance, while Chile and Colombia have had a favorable experience with exchange rate bands, Mexico's experience with this exchange rate system ended in a crisis. Although there may still be some disagreement about the relative contribution of political, external, and policy factors in generating this crisis, it is clear that several developments, which could have been prevented or corrected by proper policy actions, played a crucial role. These developments included the growing real appreciation of the currency, the widening current account deficit, the expansive credit policy of 1994, and the use of short-term financing.

3. Dealing with volatile capital flows

The LAC region is becoming increasingly integrated with the world's financial markets. This brings a number of benefits: the possibility of higher levels of investment financed by foreign savings, the knowledge-spillover effects of foreign direct investment, a better smoothing of consumption in the presence of fluctuations in income, and the possibility of better portfolio diversification by domestic investors. However, the process of integration also increases the risks that face these economies as they become more vulnerable both to external factors, such as fluctuations in international interest rates and disturbances in any of the major markets, and to changes in foreign investors' perceptions of the prospects of the economy.

The recent experience with capital flows in a number of developing countries in the LAC region and in other parts of the world can be used to derive lessons about the proper way of dealing with volatile capital flows. Capital inflows to developing countries increased sharply in the 1990s, after having declined in the 1980s partly in response to the debt crisis initiated in 1982. Private capital inflows (measured in constant 1990 U.S. dollars) to all developing countries, after declining from an annual average of US$82 billion in 1980–82 to US$40 billion in 1983–90, increased to US$131 billion in 1991–96. Private capital inflows to LAC countries followed a similar pattern, although the recovery during the 1990s was less pronounced. They declined from an annual average of US$47 billion in 1980–82 to US$10 billion in 1983–90, and then increased to US$43 billion in 1991–96. (See Table 1.2.) During 1991–96, these inflows increased, interrupted temporarily by the consequences of the Mexican peso crisis of 1994. Whereas private capital inflows to LAC

TABLE 1.2

Net Private Capital Flows to LAC

(In billions of 1990 U.S.$)

	1980	1981	1982	1983	1984	1985	1986	1987	1988	1989	1990	1991	1992	1993	1994	1995	1996
Total Private Flows	39.0	59.3	42.6	19.4	13.6	8.9	3.7	8.7	9.6	2.9	12.5	22.0	26.7	54.1	47.2	46.5	62.0
Debt Flows	29.2	47.6	34.0	14.6	9.5	3.6	−0.5	1.9	0.6	−6.1	3.3	4.0	7.2	16.8	14.3	20.7	26.7
Commercial banks	16.7	21.7	20.2	15.6	12.5	5.8	1.3	4.9	4.5	−6.6	2.8	1.3	3.8	−0.7	5.0	10.6	13.3
Bonds	1.3	2.0	5.4	−1.1	−1.3	−1.0	−1.6	−2.3	−1.5	−1.3	0.1	4.0	4.4	18.9	11.4	11.2	23.7
Others	11.3	23.9	8.5	0.0	−1.7	−1.3	−0.2	−0.7	−2.4	1.7	0.4	−1.3	−1.1	−1.5	−2.1	−1.2	−10.4
Net Foreign direct investment	9.7	11.5	8.6	4.7	4.1	5.3	4.2	6.7	8.8	8.6	8.1	12.0	11.9	12.7	21.4	19.6	21.6
Portfolio equity flows	0.0	0.2	0.0	0.0	0.0	0.0	0.0	0.1	0.2	0.5	1.1	6.0	7.7	24.6	11.6	6.2	13.7

Source: World Development Indicators database.
Note: 1996 Commercial banks data is a LAC staff estimate.

countries totaled US$12 billion in 1990, they reached US$62 billion in 1996.

Both external and domestic factors account for this sharp increase in capital inflows to developing countries, including those in LAC. On the external side, in the early 1990s economic activity in industrial countries slowed, international interest rates declined, and a growing trend towards international diversification by institutional investors developed and became increasingly important. On the domestic side, economic prospects improved as a number of countries implemented successful stabilization programs, undertook important structural reforms (including trade liberalization, the relaxation of restrictions to international capital flows, privatization, and tax reforms), and in some cases, reestablished orderly relationships with foreign creditors. In some countries, however, the high domestic interest rates resulting from stabilization programs that relied heavily on tight credit policy to contain inflation were responsible for attracting capital inflows.[40]

These large capital inflows allowed many developing countries to accumulate international reserves and to finance higher rates of investment. However, their economies also showed signs of overheating, as reserve accumulation was accompanied by rapid expansion of both monetary aggregates and bank credit, by consumption booms, and by inflationary pressures. Also, these developments sometimes contributed to bubbles in the stock market and in real estate prices, weakening the health of the financial sector.

Developing countries implemented a variety of policies to deal with these adverse consequences of capital inflows.[41] Some of these policies aimed to contain the accumulation of international reserves by

1. reducing gross capital inflows (for example, by imposing minimum maturity conditions, taxes, or unremunerated reserve requirements on foreign borrowing, as was done by Colombia and Chile);
2. increasing gross capital outflows (for instance, by allowing domestic residents to make portfolio investments abroad and by easing restrictions on profits and capital repatriation by foreign firms);
3. allowing the exchange rate to appreciate; and
4. liberalizing imports.

Other policies were aimed at (1) limiting the impact of reserve accumulation on the monetary base (mainly, by using open market operations to sterilize capital inflows); (2) containing the impact of the increase of the monetary base on monetary aggregates and bank credit (for example, by increasing reserve requirements and imposing limits on certain type of credit operations); and (3) offsetting the effect of monetary and credit expansion on domestic demand (through fiscal tightening).

These policies have not been equally effective in dealing with the adverse consequences of capital inflows, and many of them have entailed some costs. Restrictions on gross capital inflows seem to have been somewhat effective in altering the magnitude and the composition of capital inflows, at least in the short run.[42] However, they become less effective with time as economic agents find ways to evade them, and thus they need to be reinforced and broadened repeatedly.[43] Also, controls on capital flows may have some efficiency costs.[44] The policy of lifting of restrictions on capital outflows seems to have contributed to some gross outflows, but has been largely ineffective in reducing net inflows. Presumably, the market may interpret this policy as signaling a friendlier environment for foreign investment, which may increase expected returns and thus lead to additional gross inflows.[45]

Allowing the currency to appreciate helps to limit the impact of capital inflows on inflation and also reduces the incentive for inflows because the greater variability of the exchange rate increases uncertainty about net returns. However, a large real appreciation may have serious adverse effects on the current account, and the higher variability of the real exchange rate may have a negative impact on growth.

A number of countries have successfully used open market operations to sterilize capital inflows. However, these operations prevent an equilibrating reduction in domestic interest rates, and so they lead to higher than usual capital inflows. Also, sterilization entails fiscal costs because the central bank acquires international reserves in exchange for liabilities that carry higher rates of return. The alternative of increasing bank reserve requirements (remunerated at lower-than-market rates) shifts at least part of the costs of sterilization to the banking system. While this reduces the fiscal cost, it also may lead to disintermediation and a weakening of the banking system.

Tightening fiscal policy has been an effective means of containing domestic demand and reducing the inflationary pressures arising from capital inflows. However, at times it has been difficult to obtain political support for fiscal tightening when fiscal policy is already tight. In addition, fiscal policy needs to be based not just on short-term fluctuations in capital flows but also on long-term considerations.

The experiences of countries that received large capital inflows during the 1990s suggest a number of conclusions regarding the proper response to such inflows. The most successful countries relied on a set of instruments, including sterilization, fiscal tightening, some exchange rate appreciation, and on certain direct measures, such as taxes or controls, to reduce the magnitude of the inflows. While most countries initially intervened with sterilization, they eventually also adopted other policies. A tightening of fiscal policy seems to be the most effective way to contain the real appreciation of the currency and the widening of the current-account deficit in the medium term. Using the exchange rate as a nominal anchor while relying mainly on credit tightening to contain demand has usually resulted in a credit boom, a sharp real appreciation of the currency, and a large deterioration of the current account.

Net capital inflows to developing countries are likely to continue as the integration of the world's capital market

proceeds.[46] In the absence of large disturbances in the major markets, flows may be expected to be relatively stable at an aggregate level but not necessarily at the individual-country level. As integration deepens and investors are increasingly able to discriminate among countries, the distribution of aggregate flows will become more sensitive to domestic conditions and to the quality of the economic policies of individual countries. Prudent economic policies will be rewarded by the markets, and unsound policies will be punished faster than before.

The experience reviewed above, and the issues discussed earlier in this chapter, suggest the following recommendations for LAC countries in an environment of increased financial integration.

Maintaining a strong long-term fiscal position that precludes the emergence of doubts about fiscal solvency that might seriously weaken investor confidence is very important. Also, to the extent possible, fiscal policy needs to be flexible enough to play a short-run stabilizing role.

Direct measures to control capital inflows have proven effective at least in the short run and may be useful in preventing excessive capital inflows. However, the effectiveness of this type of measure is likely to decline as markets become more integrated and sophisticated. Obviously, introducing controls to contain capital outflows will seriously weaken confidence and is likely to result in larger capital outflows than otherwise.

As capital flows are playing an increasingly important role in total external transactions, it is clear that assessing the adequacy of international reserves should take into account the magnitude of possible shocks to the capital account rather than be based primarily on the level of imports. What is not yet clear, however, is the specific yardstick that should be used to estimate possible shocks to the capital account. Experience indicates that the outstanding stock of short-term public debt should play a role in such a calculation. In this regard, it is also important to avoid the clustering of public-debt maturities that might lead to refinancing difficulties during periods of market turbulence.

Finally, as mentioned previously, ensuring a healthy banking system is important. This will prevent banking problems from becoming a source of macroeconomic disturbances and from introducing additional constraints on macroeconomic policy.

Notes To Chapter I

1. See Fischer (1993), Barro (1995, 1996), Bruno and Easterly (1995), and de Gregorio (1996).

2. See Fischer (1993), Easterly and Schmidt-Hebbel (1994), Barro (1995), and Bruno and Easterly (1995).

3. See Inter-American Development Bank (1995).

4. Unless otherwise indicated, the figures for the LAC region mentioned in this chapter were calculated as the average of individual countries' figures, weighted by GDP, measured in 1990 U.S. dollars. The country-coverage of regional averages differs across variables depending on the availability of data.

5. Gavin (1997) examines the decline in macroeconomic volatility in the 1990s.

6. The coverage of the fiscal accounts is not entirely uniform across countries, but this should not affect the trend in the fiscal outcomes. Also, in obtaining these figures, the concept of "operational" deficit (which excludes the inflation component of interest payments on domestic debt) was used for Brazil. If the more comprehensive concept of public-sector borrowing requirement (PSBR) were used for Brazil, the fiscal trends for the region would be similar to those for inflation (when including Brazil), showing high deficits through 1994 and a sharp drop in the deficits afterwards.

7. Tanzi and Zee (1996) contains a comprehensive discussion of the effects of fiscal policy on long-run economic growth, including the effects that work through macroeconomic stability (emphasized here), as well as those that work through resource allocation and income distribution.

8. See Aizenman and Marion (1993) and Easterly and Rebelo (1993).

9. Although increases in public savings are partially offset by reductions in private savings, they still make a significant contribution to national savings. The "offset" coefficient has been estimated at 50 percent for Latin America; see Edwards (1997).

10. See World Bank (1997f).

11. In Mexico, all public employees are excluded. In other countries, the military, teachers, and oil state enterprise employees are excluded. For a discussion of the design problems, see Shah (1997).

12. This is notably the case in Colombia.

13. This conference, "Managing Government Exposure In Private Infrastructure Development," was held in Cartagena in May 1997.

14. See Mackenzie and Stella (1996).

15. Whether the loss from the bailout of financial institutions appears as a quasi-fiscal loss or directly as a fiscal cost depends on whether the bailout is undertaken by the central bank or by the treasury.

16. See Tanzi (1996).

17. See Peterson (1997).

18. See Peterson (1997).

19. See Ter-Minassian (1996) for a discussion of alternative approaches to control borrowing by subnational governments.

20. For a discussion of the case of Colombia, see Perry and Huerta (1997).

21. A basic description of the problems associated with commodity booms and busts is presented in Varangis, Akiyama, and Mitchell (1995).

22. The need to identify the transitory components of fiscal revenues applies not only to revenue windfalls arising from commodity booms, but also to transitory revenues from other sources. For example, the initial stages of exchange-rate-based stabilization programs are usually accompanied by consumption booms that generate significant additional tax revenues. These additional revenues, however, are only transitory. In these circumstances, assessing the fiscal situation by looking at total revenues leads to an overestimation of the strength of fiscal policy. See Talvi (1996).

23. In addition to reducing price uncertainty, these instruments may be useful in providing some price stability, but this is usually possible only for relatively short periods (less than a year). For a discussion of the use of commodity derivative instruments to manage price uncertainty, see Varangis and Larson (1996).

24. This reflects the view that, to a large extent, procyclical fiscal policy in the presence of transitory revenue windfalls is not the result of policy mistakes but an equilibrium determined by the pressures of different interest groups. See, for example, Lane and Tornell (1996) and Talvi and Vegh (1996).

25. See, for instance, Arrau and Claessens (1992). This paper derives optimal rules for the functioning of the Chilean Copper Stabilization Fund and for the use of the windfall gains that oil exporters received as a result of the Persian Gulf crisis; it takes into account the process followed by copper and oil prices, and uses a model of precautionary savings with liquidity constraints.

27. For an overview of recent trends in tax reform in the region, see Perry and Herrera (1994) and Shome (1992).

28. In Colombia, for example, most municipalities had neither uniform, complete, and acceptable accounting practices, nor budgetary classifications until 1994.

29. Financial crises are usually accompanied by deep recessions. For example, the depth of the recession experienced by Argentina during 1995 can be partly explained by the credit squeeze that was associated with the capital outflows. See Calvo (1997).

30. See Lindgren, Garcia, and Saal (1996).

31. See Kaminsky and Reinhart (1996) for empirical evidence of the relationship between banking and balance-of-payments crises.

32. See Rojas-Suarez and Weisbrod (1996). These estimates primarily reflect central bank lending to banks as a consequence of the crises, and assume no recovery from future sale of assets. Alternative definitions and estimates of the fiscal costs can be found in Rodriguez (1994) for Argentina, Marshall and Schmidt-Hebbel (1994) for Chile, and Caprio and Klingebiel (1996) and Lindgren et al. (1996) for various countries. In all cases, estimated costs amount to a significant fraction of GDP.

33. See, for example, Gavin and Hausmann (1996) and Goldstein and Turner (1996).

34. See, for instance, de Juan (1996).

35. See Kaminsky, Lizondo, and Reinhart (1997) for a brief review of the theoretical and empirical literature on currency crises.

36. Although the argument is presented for a fixed exchange rate, a similar argument also applies to other types of exchange rate regimes in

which there is an official commitment to defend the currency under certain rules, such as a crawling peg, an exchange rate band, etc.

37. Early comparisons among alternative exchange rate systems were based on optimality criteria that included the variability of employment, of output, of consumption, or of the price level, around their long-run equilibrium level. Typically, the results of those comparisons depended on the specific objective function, the type of shocks affecting the economy (demand or supply, domestic or external, nominal or real), and the structure of the economy (degree of indexation, openness, international capital mobility, and labor mobility). See, for example, Argy (1990). This particular way of looking at the problem, focusing on the volatility of macroeconomic variables around long-term levels, did not address the main problems in developing countries, which continue to be relatively high rates of inflation and balance-of-payments difficulties.

38. See Gosh et al. (1995).

39. See Williamson (1996).

40. While it is clear that both external and domestic factors played a role in attracting capital inflows, their relative importance is still unclear. Schadler et al. (1993) maintain that external factors were not very important, while Calvo, Leiderman, and Reinhart (1996) argue that they account for a large share of the inflows, particularly in Latin American countries. Fernandez-Arias (1996) finds that external factors played a dominant role in the countries in his sample (except for Mexico, Argentina, and Korea). Fernandez-Arias and Montiel (1996), however, caution that some of the results against domestic factors may arise because of difficulties in measurement and because some papers focus on portfolio flows, thus excluding foreign direct investment which may be more sensitive to domestic factors.

41. The organization of the discussion below is based on Montiel (1996).

42. See Montiel (1996) and World Bank (1997f).

43. Dooley (1996) presents evidence that these types of restrictions are largely ineffective when potential arbitrage profits are large.

44. For a discussion of the conditions under which there would be efficiency costs, see Montiel (1996), and Fernandez-Arias and Montiel (1996).

45. Lifting restrictions on capital outflows eliminates a source of irreversibility in foreign investment (Laban and Larrain [1993]) and could also be interpreted as signaling a more favorable tax environment in the future (Bartolini and Drazen [1996]).

46. See World Bank (1997f).

Appendix to Chapter I

TABLE 1.3

Real GDP Growth Rate

(In percent)

COUNTRY NAME	AVERAGE			1991	1992	1993	1994	1995	1996	1997
	1980–85	1986–90	1991–96							
Antiqua and Barbuda	5.3	7.4	1.8	5.1	0.2	3.4	4.2	−4.2		
Argentina	−1.1	0.4	5.1	8.9	8.6	6.0	7.4	−4.6	4.4	6.0
The Bahamas	4.4	2.1	−0.6	−2.7	−2.0	1.9	0.3	−0.3		
Barbados	0.1	3.7	−0.2	−2.7	−4.9	1.2	4.7	0.4		
Belize	2.9	9.7	3.7	3.1	9.3	3.3	1.8	3.3	1.5	2.4
Bolivia	−1.4	2.3	3.9	4.6	2.8	4.1	4.2	3.7	4.0	4.5
Brazil	2.5	2.0	2.8	0.5	−1.2	4.5	5.8	4.1	2.9	4.0
Chile	2.3	6.5	7.4	7.3	11.0	6.3	4.2	8.5	7.2	7.0
Colombia	2.6	4.6	4.1	2.0	4.0	5.4	5.8	5.4	2.1	3.5
Costa Rica	0.5	4.6	3.9	2.2	7.7	6.3	4.5	2.5	0.0	2.0
Dominica	7.9	5.6	2.3	2.2	2.7	1.9	2.1	1.8	3.2	3.1
Dominican Republic	2.4	3.8	4.2	0.9	7.8	2.9	4.0	2.5	7.0	5.0
Ecuador	2.7	2.1	3.2	5.0	3.6	2.0	4.3	2.3	2.0	2.6
El Salvador	−4.0	2.0	5.6	3.6	7.5	7.4	6.0	6.3	2.5	4.5
Grenada	4.1	5.5	2.2	3.6	1.2	0.9	2.5	3.0		
Guatemala	−0.3	2.9	4.1	3.7	4.8	3.9	4.0	4.9	3.1	4.2
Guyana	−3.2	−2.4	7.2	6.4	8.4	8.3	9.0	4.5	6.7	5.0
Haiti	0.4	0.2	−3.7	−3.0	−14.8	−2.6	−10.6	4.5	4.5	4.5
Honduras	1.6	3.1	3.4	3.1	5.7	6.5	−1.5	3.6	3.0	4.0
Jamaica	−0.8	4.9	2.1	0.7	6.7	3.8	1.1	0.5	0.0	1.0
Mexico	3.1	1.5	1.8	3.6	2.9	0.7	4.5	−6.2	5.1	4.4
Nicaragua	1.2	−3.1	2.2	−0.2	0.4	−0.2	3.3	4.2	5.5	5.5
Panama	4.9	−1.1	5.6	9.5	8.5	5.4	4.7	3.5	2.0	3.5
Paraguay	4.0	3.9	2.9	2.5	1.8	4.1	3.1	4.7	1.3	2.4
Peru	0.6	−0.8	5.1	2.9	−1.8	6.4	13.1	7.0	2.8	4.0
St. Kitts and Nevis	5.3	7.1	4.1	1.9	3.0	5.0	5.5	3.7	5.8	5.9
St. Lucia	n/a	9.3	3.5	2.2	7.0	2.0	2.1	4.1	3.8	
St. Vincent	6.6	6.9	3.3	3.1	4.9	2.1	−0.4	6.7		
Suriname	4.9	8.6	2.4	7.4	13.7	−12.3	−2.3	4.0	4.0	
Trinidad and Tobago	0.1	−2.2	1.6	2.7	−1.7	−1.7	4.2	3.3	2.9	3.2
Uruguay	−1.9	3.7	3.9	3.2	7.9	3.0	6.8	−2.4	4.9	4.5
Venezuela	−1.5	2.8	2.5	9.7	6.1	0.3	−2.8	2.2	−0.5	3.5
Mean	1.8	3.4	3.2	3.2	3.8	2.9	3.3	2.7	3.4	4.0
GDP-Weighted Mean	1.8	1.9	3.2	3.3	2.4	3.7	5.4	0.9	3.5	4.4
GDP-Weighted Mean w/o Arg. and Mex.	2.0	2.3	3.3	2.0	0.9	4.3	5.2	4.3	2.9	4.0
Median	2.0	3.6	3.6	3.1	4.4	3.4	4.2	3.5	3.1	4.0

Source: World Development Indicators database and World Bank staff estimates.

TABLE 1.4

Inflation Rate

(In percent)

COUNTRY NAME	AVERAGE			1991	1992	1993	1994	1995	1996	1997
	1980–85	1986–90	1991–96							
Argentina	335.6	1192.7	35.8	172.0	24.6	10.6	4.3	3.3	0.2	2.5
The Bahamas	7.0	5.1	3.4	7.0	5.6	2.7	1.7	2.1	1.4	
Barbados	8.8	3.8	3.0	6.0	6.6	0.9	0.0	1.9	2.8	
Belize	6.1	2.2	3.0	3.0	2.9	1.0	2.8	2.9	6.4	3.0
Bolivia	2,249.9	68.0	11.7	21.0	12.4	8.8	7.4	10.2	10.2	6.5
Brazil	141.9	1,056.9	1,061.0	441.0	1,009.1	2,150.0	2,663.0	84.5	18.2	8.5
Chile	23.8	19.4	12.8	21.8	15.4	12.7	11.4	8.2	7.4	7.0
Colombia	23.1	25.0	24.0	30.0	27.0	22.4	22.8	20.9	20.8	20.0
Costa Rica	34.1	17.0	19.1	29.0	21.7	9.6	13.4	23.2	17.5	12.5
Dominica	5.5	3.8	−2.0	−5.5	−5.5	−1.6	0.0	−1.3	1.7	1.8
Dominican Republic	16.9	35.0	15.1	54.0	4.5	5.0	8.3	12.6	6.0	10.0
Ecuador	25.5	47.0	37.1	48.7	54.6	44.8	27.3	22.9	24.4	31.0
El Salvador	15.2	23.7	12.4	14.0	11.4	18.5	10.6	10.1	9.8	8.0
Grenada	10.4	2.4	2.9	2.6	3.8	2.7	2.6	3.0		
Guatemala	8.2	22.5	14.4	33.0	10.5	11.6	11.6	8.5	11.1	9.0
Guyana	18.7	16.8	29.2	101.5	28.2	11.7	13.6	12.3	7.7	
Haiti	10.6	4.8	23.8	15.0	20.0	22.5	42.6	25.5	17.1	14.9
Honduras	8.8	8.9	21.4	34.0	9.0	10.3	21.7	29.5	23.8	18.0
Jamaica	18.6	13.2	36.9	51.0	77.5	22.0	35.2	19.9	15.8	12.0
Mexico	56.4	75.7	21.6	23.0	15.5	9.8	7.1	34.9	39.0	21.0
Nicaragua	61.6	4,809.1	504.0	2,950.0	23.6	20.2	7.9	11.0	11.6	9.5
Panama	5.0	0.4	1.2	1.0	2.0	1.0	1.0	1.0	1.3	1.3
Paraguay	17.1	28.1	16.9	24.3	15.1	18.2	20.7	13.5	9.8	10.0
Peru	97.4	2,341.4	96.3	409.5	73.5	48.6	23.7	11.1	11.6	7.1
St. Kitts and Nevis	7.0	2.1	2.5	4.0	2.9	1.8	1.4	3.0	2.0	4.0
St. Lucia	7.2	3.8	3.9	6.0	4.7	0.8	2.7	5.9	3.2	
St. Vincent and the Grenadines	7.9	3.0	3.4	5.9	3.8	4.3	0.4	1.7	4.4	
Suriname	8.2	20.4	136.7	26.0	43.7	143.6	368.0	235.9	3.0	
Trinidad and Tobago	13.3	9.7	7.1	4.0	6.7	9.9	9.0	5.2	7.7	7.7
Uruguay	48.8	79.0	49.5	81.5	58.9	52.9	44.1	35.4	24.3	15.0
Venezuela	12.7	38.9	54.1	34.0	31.3	38.6	60.7	59.9	99.9	40.0
Mean	107.1	321.9	73.0	149.9	52.3	87.6	111.2	23.2	14.0	11.7
GDP-Weighted Mean	137.3	716.9	457.9	236.1	427.4	898.0	1,114.4	49.3	22.4	12.2
GDP-Weighted Mean w/o Brazil	134.4	450.2	31.3	85.2	23.8	16.5	14.0	22.5	25.6	15.0
Median	13.6	15.7	13.6	24.3	15.1	10.6	10.6	11.0	9.8	9.3

Source: IMF, International Financial Statistics database, and World Bank staff estimates.

TABLE 1.5

Non-Financial Public Sector Balance

(As percentage of GDP)

COUNTRY	AVERAGE			1991	1992	1993	1994	1995	1996
	1980–85	1986–90	1991–96						
Antigua	−5.6	−17.8	−5.1	−5.2	−3.1	−3.8	−4.9	−8.3	−5.1
Argentina	−14.5	−6.4	−1.8	−2.4	−0.4	−0.2	−1.8	−3.2	−2.9
Belize	−6.4	1.3	−5.8	−4.1	−7.6	−6.5	−5.1	−5.1	−6.5
Bolivia	−10.3	−6.3	−3.8	−4.5	−4.7	−6.5	−3.2	−2.0	−1.9
Brazil	−4.3	−3.9	−1.5	1.5	−2.2	0.2	0.5	−4.8	−3.9
Chile	−1.2	1.9	2.2	2.1	2.8	1.8	2.2	3.4	0.7
Colombia	−5.7	−1.1	−1.0	−0.3	−0.6	−0.8	−0.5	−1.2	−2.6
Costa Rica	−6.9	−1.6	−3.3	−0.5	−0.8	−0.9	−8.0	−3.8	−5.5
Dominican Republic	−5.1	−5.7	−0.4	0.1	1.3	−0.3	−0.3	−0.1	−0.3
Ecuador	−2.6	−4.6	−1.5	−1.9	−2.2	−0.4	−0.4	−1.3	−3.0
El Salvador	−5.5	−1.8	−2.1	−3.2	−4.6	−1.6	−0.6	−0.1	−2.3
Guatemala	n/a	−4.7	−1.4	−1.8	0.0	−2.2	−2.6	−0.9	−0.7
Guyana	−41.7	−39.3	−12.5	−23.5	−16.4	−14.0	−6.8	−8.5	−5.6
Haiti	−6.2	−2.7	−5.2	−5.0	−2.1	−2.9	−3.0	−8.2	−10.0
Honduras	−10.7	−6.7	−5.7	−3.6	−4.4	−10.2	−7.6	−3.5	−5.1
Jamaica	−15.3	−6.5	1.3	−0.4	2.2	1.6	1.6	1.6	−8.0
Mexico	−11.3	−10.6	0.1	−0.6	1.5	0.3	−0.2	0.0	−0.7
Nicaragua	−16.7	−16.5	−10.3	−7.7	−8.4	−8.8	−12.4	−11.1	−13.4
Panama	−5.7	−5.1	−0.1	−1.3	1.5	−1.3	0.3	0.2	
Paraguay	−5.4	−0.4	1.6	2.8	0.0	1.1	1.5	2.5	1.8
Peru	−8.0	−7.7	−2.2	−2.0	−2.6	−2.4	−2.3	−2.7	−1.2
St. Lucia	−2.9	0.7	−0.2	−1.6	−1.4	1.5	−0.9	1.3	0.2
Suriname	−10.9	−18.4	−5.9	−17.4	−11.4	−9.4	−2.3	2.5	2.5
Trinidad and Tobago	−7.9	−5.3	1.3	0.1	−2.2	1.3	3.7	3.3	1.3
Uruguay	−4.0	−5.2	−0.3	−0.3	1.2	2.0	−1.0	−2.5	−1.1
Venezuela	0.0	−3.9	−4.2	−3.3	−6.3	−1.3	−13.9	−8.2	7.6
Mean	−8.6	−7.0	−2.6	−3.2	−2.7	−2.4	−2.7	−2.3	−2.4
Weighted Mean	−7.5	−5.6	−1.2	−0.1	−1.0	−0.1	−0.9	−3.0	−2.2
Median	−6.3	−5.1	−1.8	−1.8	−2.2	−1.1	−2.1	−1.7	−2.1

Source: World Bank

TABLE 1.6

Current Account Balance

(As percentage of GDP)

COUNTRY NAME	AVERAGE			1991	1992	1993	1994	1995	1996	1997
	1980–85	1986–90	1991–96							
Argentina	−3.6	−1.6	−2.5	−1.5	−3.7	−2.9	−3.7	−1.4	−2.0	−2.5
Bahamas	−5.6	−1.9	−4.1	−7.5	−3.5	−2.6	−4.4	−4.3	−2.4	−1.9
Bolivia	−6.6	−7.5	−6.5	−5.3	−10.2	−9.4	−4.0	−3.5	−6.6	−9.9
Brazil	−3.2	−0.4	−0.8	−0.4	1.6	0.0	−0.2	−2.6	−3.2	−3.8
Chile	−9.4	−3.1	−1.8	0.3	−1.6	−4.6	−1.2	0.2	−3.7	−4.0
Colombia	−5.1	0.5	−2.0	5.6	1.8	−4.0	−4.7	−5.4	−5.5	−5.3
Costa Rica	−10.7	−7.3	−3.7	−1.8	−5.5	−8.3	−3.2	−1.5	−1.6	−1.6
Dominican Republic	−5.7	−3.9	−2.7	−1.9	−7.9	−4.6	−0.6	−1.1	−0.2	−0.7
Ecuador	−4.2	−6.8	−3.9	−6.1	−1.7	−4.7	−4.9	−4.1	−1.9	−2.4
El Salvador	−4.0	−3.8	−2.3	−4.0	−3.3	−1.2	−0.2	−2.9	−2.1	−2.4
Guatemala	−3.7	−3.8	−4.7	−2.0	−6.8	−6.6	−5.4	−4.0	−3.2	−3.5
Haiti	−6.8	−1.7	−5.2	−8.3	−2.2	−5.0	0.2	−6.2	−10.0	−8.4
Honduras	−9.7	−6.0	−8.9	−8.4	−10.3	−8.8	−12.2	−7.3	−6.6	−5.4
Jamaica	−11.1	−3.6	−4.2	−6.5	0.8	−4.4	0.4	−5.6	−9.9	−6.8
Mexico	−1.4	−1.0	-4.4	−5.1	−7.3	−5.8	−7.0	−0.6	−0.5	−1.4
Nicaragua	−21.4	−25.9	−46.7	-48.9	−59.3	−48.0	−54.0	−37.5	−32.5	−30.0
Panama	−4.3	6.1	−3.6	−3.9	−4.6	−2.2	−4.4	−4.4	−2.3	−3.0
Paraguay	−6.6	−4.0	−8.5	−5.3	−9.7	−7.6	−9.7	−11.8	−7.0	−9.2
Peru	−3.2	−6.0	−5.2	−3.0	−4.8	−5.1	−5.1	−7.2	−5.8	−5.3
Trinidad and Tobago	−2.5	−1.4	3.0	−0.1	2.6	2.4	4.4	5.5	3.0	2.0
Uruguay	−3.3	0.6	−1.4	0.4	−1.0	−2.5	−2.7	−1.2	−1.5	−1.8
Venezuela	4.2	1.1	1.4	3.2	-6.2	-3.3	4.4	3.0	7.2	5.7
Mean	−5.8	−3.7	−5.4	−5.0	−6.5	−6.3	−5.4	−4.7	−4.5	−4.6
GDP-Weighted Mean	−2.9	−1.1	−2.2	−1.6	−2.3	−2.7	−2.6	−2.1	−2.2	−2.8
GDP-Weighted Mean w/o Arg. and Mex.	−3.3	−1.0	−1.4	−0.3	−0.2	−1.5	−0.9	−2.6	−2.8	−3.3
Median	−5.1	−2.9	−3.8	−3.5	−4.1	−4.6	−3.8	−3.8	−2.8	−3.3

Source: World Development Indicators database and World Bank staff estimates.

TABLE 1.7
Gross Domestic Investment

(As percentage of GDP)

COUNTRY NAME	AVERAGE			1991	1992	1993	1994	1995	1996
	1980–85	1986–90	1991–96						
Argentina	21.4	17.0	17.7	14.6	16.7	18.2	19.9	18.3	18.5
Barbados	21.1	17.5	13.5	17.1	9.5	12.8	13.4	13.8	14.5
Belize	22.7	25.3	25.9	29.7	29.9	32.0	24.4	20.0	19.4
Bolivia	11.4	11.3	14.8	13.9	15.7	15.1	14.7	14.4	15.0
Brazil	19.9	22.1	20.3	19.6	19.6	20.4	20.8	21.9	19.5
Chile	17.2	23.1	27.0	24.5	26.8	28.8	26.8	27.4	27.7
Colombia	19.7	19.7	21.0	17.2	17.2	21.2	23.3	23.5	23.4
Costa Rica	25.5	26.1	26.6	25.2	29.3	29.9	26.8	24.8	23.5
Dominican Republic	21.9	25.0	20.5	17.0	21.1	22.4	20.2	19.7	22.9
Ecuador	21.2	20.6	19.8	22.2	21.2	21.1	19.0	18.7	16.9
El Salvador	12.6	13.5	18.1	15.4	18.5	18.6	18.7	20.6	16.7
Grenada	36.8	37.1	36.6	40.4	34.4	37.4	38.4	32.2	
Guatemala	13.5	13.0	16.0	14.3	18.3	17.4	15.7	15.4	15.0
Guyana	29.0	29.2	35.9	42.2	42.3	33.6	31.6	35.3	30.4
Haiti	16.9	13.7	6.3	11.2	3.7	3.8	1.7	8.6	8.9
Honduras	18.1	18.9	26.6	25.4	26.5	30.7	27.6	24.4	25.0
Jamaica	21.3	21.5	21.2	19.8	19.3	20.3	22.0	17.4	28.2
Mexico	23.1	20.7	21.9	23.4	24.4	21.0	21.9	19.7	20.9
Nicaragua	21.2	21.8	21.6	19.3	20.1	18.0	20.2	25.0	26.9
Paraguay	25.9	24.2	23.3	24.8	22.9	22.9	23.4	23.9	22.0
Peru	26.7	20.2	20.3	16.8	16.5	18.5	22.0	24.2	23.5
St. Kitts and Nevis	33.3	46.2	42.9	42.9	39.1	44.9	37.8	46.0	46.4
St. Lucia	26.2	24.3	22.8	25.4	24.1	24.8	24.3	19.0	19.0
Suriname	21.2	21.4	21.4	22.3	23.0	21.4	21.3	20.0	20.7
Trinidad and Tobago	26.4	16.6	14.1	16.1	12.3	13.1	13.4	14.2	15.5
Uruguay	16.0	12.2	13.6	13.5	13.3	14.6	13.7	13.1	13.2
Venezuela	21.1	19.3	18.0	18.7	23.7	18.8	13.2	15.9	18.0
Mean	21.9	21.5	21.7	22.0	21.8	22.3	21.3	21.4	21.2
GDP-Weighted Mean	21.1	20.7	20.3	19.7	20.5	20.3	20.8	20.7	20.1
Median	21.6	20.6	20.5	19.6	21.1	21.0	21.3	20.0	20.1

Source: World Bank Development Indicators database and World Bank Staff estimates.

23

TABLE 1.8

Gross National Savings

(As percentage of GDP)

COUNTRY	AVERAGE			1991	1992	1993	1994	1995	1996
	1980–85	1986–90	1991–96						
Argentina	17.7	15.4	15.2	13.1	13.0	15.3	16.3	16.9	16.5
Bolivia	4.8	3.8	8.3	8.6	5.6	5.7	10.7	10.9	8.4
Brazil	16.7	21.7	19.5	19.2	21.2	20.4	20.6	19.2	16.3
Chile	7.8	20.0	25.2	24.8	25.1	24.2	25.5	27.6	24.0
Colombia	14.6	20.2	19.0	22.9	19.1	17.2	18.6	18.1	17.9
Costa Rica	14.8	18.8	22.9	23.4	23.8	21.6	23.6	23.2	21.9
Dominican Republic	16.2	21.1	17.8	15.1	13.2	17.7	19.6	18.6	22.7
Ecuador	17.0	13.8	15.9	16.1	19.5	16.4	14.1	14.6	15.0
El Salvador	8.6	9.7	15.8	11.4	15.2	17.4	18.5	17.7	14.6
Guatemala	9.8	9.2	11.4	12.3	11.6	10.8	10.3	11.4	11.8
Haiti	10.1	12.0	1.1	2.9	1.5	−1.2	1.9	2.4	-1.1
Honduras	8.4	12.8	17.7	17.0	16.2	21.9	15.4	17.1	18.4
Mexico	21.7	19.6	17.5	18.3	17.1	15.2	14.9	19.1	20.4
Paraguay	19.2	20.2	14.8	19.5	13.2	15.3	13.7	12.1	15.0
Peru	23.5	14.2	15.1	13.8	11.7	13.4	16.9	17.0	17.7
Trinidad and Tobago	23.8	15.2	17.1	16.0	14.9	15.5	17.8	19.7	18.5
Uruguay	12.8	12.8	12.1	13.9	12.3	12.1	11.0	11.9	11.7
Venezuela	25.3	20.4	19.4	22.0	17.5	15.4	17.6	18.9	25.2
Mean	15.2	15.6	15.9	16.1	15.1	15.2	15.9	16.5	16.4
GDP-Weighted Mean	18.2	19.6	18.2	18.2	18.2	17.7	18.2	18.8	17.9
Median	15.8	15.6	16.3	16.0	15.1	15.5	16.6	17.4	17.1

Source: World Bank staff estimates.

TABLE 1.9

Rate of Unemployment

(In percent)

COUNTRY NAME	AVERAGE			1991	1992	1993	1994	1995	1996
	1980–85	1986–90	1991–96						
Argentina	4.7	6.5	11.6	6.5	7.0	9.6	11.5	17.5	17.2
Barbados	14.7	16.6	21.1	15.8	22.4	24.2	21.9		
Bolivia	7.1	8.3	4.5	5.8	5.4	5.8	3.1	3.6	3.5
Brazil	6.6	3.8	5.2	4.8	5.8	5.4	5.1	4.6	5.4
Chile	15.9	9.8	7.2	8.2	6.7	6.5	7.8	7.4	6.5
Colombia	11.0	11.5	9.7	10.2	10.2	8.6	8.9	8.8	11.3
Costa Rica	7.8	5.5	4.9	6.0	4.3	4.0	4.3	5.7	
Ecuador	7.6	9.1	8.2	8.5	8.9	8.3	7.8	7.7	
El Salvador	n/a	9.3	7.6	7.9	8.2	8.1	7.0	7.0	7.5
Guatemala	6.8	9.6	5.4	6.4	5.7	5.5	5.2	4.3	
Honduras	9.8	9.9	6.1	7.4	6.0	7.1	4.0	6.0	6.3
Jamaica	26.3	19.2	15.8	15.7	15.7	16.3	15.4		
Mexico	4.9	3.5	4.1	2.7	2.8	3.4	3.6	6.3	5.6
Nicaragua	17.7	12.5	18.1	14.2	17.8	21.8	20.7	18.2	16.1
Panama	11.8	15.8	16.8	19.3	17.5	15.6	16.0	16.2	16.4
Paraguay	5.4	5.8	5.2	5.1	5.3	5.1	4.1	5.5	6.0
Peru	8.1	6.7	8.3	5.9	9.4	9.9	8.8	7.1	8.7
Trinidad and Tobago	11.4	20.4	19.5	18.5	19.6	20.3			
Uruguay	11.4	9.4	9.6	8.9	9.0	8.3	9.2	10.3	11.9
Venezuela	10.2	9.8	9.2	9.5	7.8	6.6	8.7	10.9	11.9
Mean	10.5	10.2	9.4	9.4	9.8	10.0	9.1	8.7	9.6
Population-Weighted Mean	7.4	6.0	6.7	5.9	6.4	6.4	6.4	7.2	7.8
Population-Weighted Mean									
w/o Arg.	7.7	6.0	6.2	5.8	6.3	6.1	6.0	6.3	6.9
Median	9.5	9.7	7.9	8.1	8.0	8.2	7.8	7.1	8.1

Source: ECLAC, *Statistical Yearbook of Latin America and the Caribbean, Balance Preliminar de la Economía de América Latina y el Caribe* ECLAC, Various issues; and World Bank staff estimates.

II
Structural Reform and Economic Progress

IN THE LATE 1980S, AFTER DECADES OF POOR ECONOMIC MANAGEMENT, MANY LATIN AMERICAN countries started a process of economic reform.[1] Although the breadth and depth of this process differed from country to country, its basic principles were similar: fiscal and monetary discipline and reliance on market forces to determine the allocation and distribution of resources. Although much has been accomplished, it has become clear, particularly in the wake of the 1994 Mexican peso crisis, that the reform process has a long way to go in most countries in the region.

The purpose of this chapter is both to assess the state of economic reform and to provide an evaluation of economic progress in areas under reform. Economic reforms follow a complex and multifaceted process, proceeding at different speeds in several areas of public policy. Economic reforms entail policy modifications that, with time, bring about changes in the performance and structure of economic activity. Therefore, reforms can be assessed by examining their corresponding policy measures or their outcomes. In principle, both elements are relevant. In this chapter, however, more emphasis is placed on outcome measures to evaluate the advance of economic reforms. There are two reasons for this approach. The first is data availability: Policy measures are difficult to isolate and quantify objectively, whereas in most cases, outcome indicators of reform are available. The second reason is that the ultimate test for the advance of economic reform lies in its impact on economic activity. Nevertheless, when information is available, policy measures are also included in the analysis.

Naturally, not all economic progress in the last few years can be interpreted as resulting from reforms; this progress can also be the result of the normal process of growth and development. This chapter is not, however, concerned with isolating the portion of economic progress

that is due to reform. Rather, the analysis in this chapter of economic performance fulfills the dual purpose of assessing the state of reform and evaluating general economic development, under the hypothesis that in the recent experience of Latin American countries, economic development is largely a reflection of macroeconomic and structural reforms.

Given that the previous chapter analyzed macroeconomic stabilization throughout the region, this chapter concentrates on five areas of structural reform: international trade openness, financial development, labor market flexibility, proper use of public resources and efficiency of public revenue generation, and good governance. These areas are recognized as key determinants of growth and development and have been emphasized recently in the endogenous-growth literature. According to this literature, long-run economic growth is not the result of exogenous technological progress but the outcome of purposeful investment in human capital, research and development, and public services, activities clearly influenced by government policy.

Each of the following sections analyzes one of the aforementioned five areas of structural reform. The chapter ends with some concluding remarks.

A. International Trade Openness

There is a growing consensus in both policy and academic circles that economies that are more open to international trade have higher rates of growth, due to both higher investment and greater gains in factor productivity.[2] Along with faster growth rates, trade openness brings about industrial transformation and changes in the structure of employment.

The literature points out five channels through which trade affects economic growth.[3] First, trade leads to higher specialization and, thus, to gains in total factor productivity (TFP), because it allows countries to exploit their areas of comparative advantage. Second, it expands potential markets, which allows domestic firms to take advantage of economies of scale, thus increasing their TFP. Third, trade diffuses both technological innovations and improved managerial practices through stronger interaction with foreign firms and markets. Fourth, freer trade tends to lessen anti-competitive practices of domestic firms. Finally, trade liberalization reduces the incentives for firms to conduct rent-seeking activities that are mostly unproductive.

The empirical evidence indicates that the estimated relationship between economic growth and openness is indeed positive and significant. This is the case even after controlling for other determinants of growth, determinants that in turn may be positively affected by trade openness. Furthermore, this result is robust to the use of various proxies or indicators for openness. Regarding the direction of causality, the evidence points in favor of a "virtuous cycle," by which higher openness produces growth

improvements and vice versa.[4] As to the channels through which openness affects economic growth, empirical studies show that this mechanism not only works through raising domestic investment, but also, most importantly, through efficiency gains (growth in total factor productivity).[5] Countries with more open and less distorted foreign trade sectors exhibit faster TFP growth rates over the long run. Furthermore, TFP growth improves after trade-liberalization reforms. However, the evidence also points out that the degree of improvement is not homogeneous, as some countries (for example, Chile) benefited from trade liberalization more than others (Mexico), possibly because the extent of trade liberalization and the depth of other structural reforms were greater in the former group of countries.

In this section, two sets of indicators of openness to international trade are presented, namely, policy-instrument indicators and outcome-based indicators.

1. Policy indicators of trade liberalization

Policies that present obstacles to trade are of two broad categories: tariff (and para-tariff charges) and quantitative restrictions. Both should be evaluated together, given that one type of restriction has often substituted for the other. The higher the average level and dispersion of tariffs and para-tariffs (for example, duties and customs fees), the more distorted the trade outcome. As recommended by the literature, the measure used to evaluate the level of tariffs and para-tariffs is the *weighted average rate of tariff and para-tariff charges, using as weights their respective shares in world*

TABLE 2.1

Indicators of Trade Openness

	WEIGHTED MEAN TARIFFS AND PARA-TARIFFS			WEIGHTED INCIDENCE OF NON-TARIFF MEASURES			STANDARD DEVIATION OF TARIFFS AND PARA-TARIFFS			TRADE INDEX[1]		
	1984–87	1988–90	1991–93	1984–87	1988–90	1991–93	1984–87	1988–90	1991–93	1984–87	1988–90	1991–93
Argentina	38.6	26.8	16.6	21.2	29.6	3.1	21.0	15.0	7.0	−0.27	−0.10	1.01
Bolivia	19.5	16.5		32.1	3.5		4.5	2.0	1.0	0.31	1.18	
Brazil	75.2	28.4	16.9	44.1	22.2	14.3	30.0	23.0	15.0	−1.77	−0.22	0.44
Chile	20.2	18.3	21.2	16.1	20.7	0.4	2.0	1.0	1.0	0.81	0.75	1.23
Colombia	73.7	43.5	11.7	76.9	80.4	2.3	17.0	16.0	6.0	−2.14	−1.72	1.15
Ecuador	39.1	37.4	10.2	51.0	52.2		39.0	29.0	6.0	−1.68	−1.36	
Mexico	13.4	9.5	15.8	24.1	22.2	19.0	14.0	6.0	4.0	0.28	0.68	0.71
Paraguay	63.6		12.9	22.5		4.6	15.0	14.0	8.0	−0.52		1.02
Peru[2]	63.0	68.0	18.0		20	0.0	26.0	25.0	4.0		−0.87	1.17
Venezuela	31.4	31.4	16.2	46.1	11.7	2.8	30.0	24.0	6.0	−1.13	−0.03	1.06

Source: UNCTAD (1994); IDB (1996); and Echavarria (1997) (OAS, Trade Unit).
[1]Estimation: Index includes the following indicators: weighted non-tariff measures, weighted tariffs and para-tariffs, and standard deviation of tariffs and para-tariffs. The index is a weighted average of the principal components of its corresponding indicators, where the weights are given by the share of the indicators' variance explained by each principal component.
[2]Simple averages taken from Echavarria (1997) (OAS, Trade Unit).

FIGURE 2.1

Trade Liberalization Index

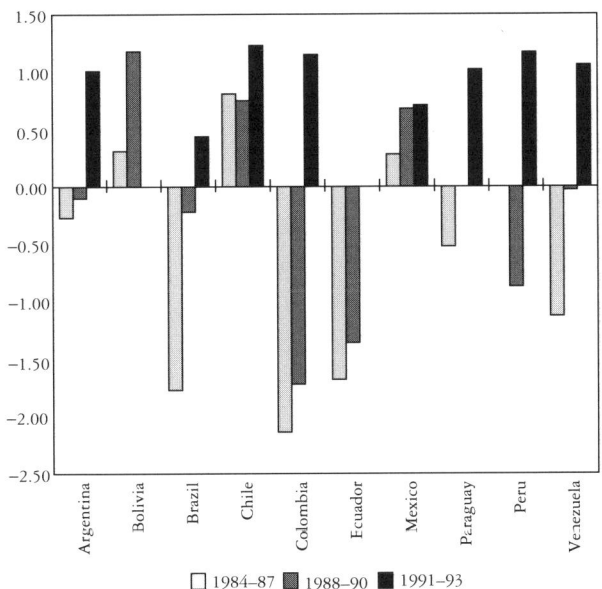

Source: UNCTAD (1994); IDB (1996); and Echavarria (1997) (OAS).
Estimation: Index includes the following indicators: weighted non-tariff measures, weighted tariffs and para-tariffs, and standard deviation of tariffs and para-tariffs. The index is a weighted average of the principal components of its corresponding indicators, where the weights are given by the share of the indicators' variance explained by each principal component.

imports.[6] By the same token, the measure used to evaluate the level of nontariff restrictions is the *weighted percent of tariff-code lines covered by various types of non-tariff barriers (licenses, quotas, prohibitions) as a percentage of all tariff code lines, using as weights the respective shares in world trade.* The dispersion of tariff and para-tariff rates is measured by their simple standard deviation. Table 2.1 presents data on each of these indicators for the periods 1984–87, 1988–90, and 1991–93. Unfortunately, only ten countries could be included in the table; they are the largest countries in South America and Mexico. For most of the smaller countries in the region, UNCTAD's *Directory of Import Regimes,* the main data source, does not report historical figures for the indicators on trade restrictions.[7]

A summary index was computed to measure the degree of trade liberalization.[8] This index was constructed in such a way that comparisons over time and across countries are possible. This policy-based index of trade liberalization is presented in Figure 2.1. It shows that Chile, the pioneer of trade liberalization in the 1970s, has also led the process in the late 1980s and early 1990s. Bolivia, Mexico, Venezuela and, to a lesser extent, Brazil, made considerable progress in trade reform in the late 1980s; all of the remaining countries conducted major trade reforms in the early 1990s. Whereas Brazil and Venezuela liberalized their tar-

FIGURE 2.2
Weighted Tariffs and Para-Tariffs

Weighted Incidence of Non-Tariff Measures

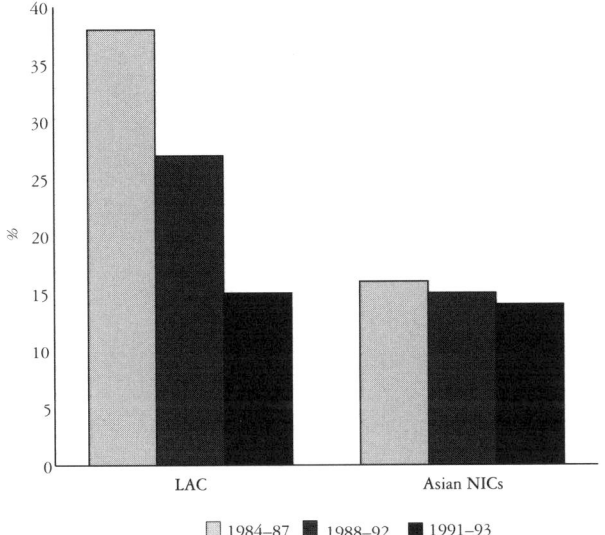

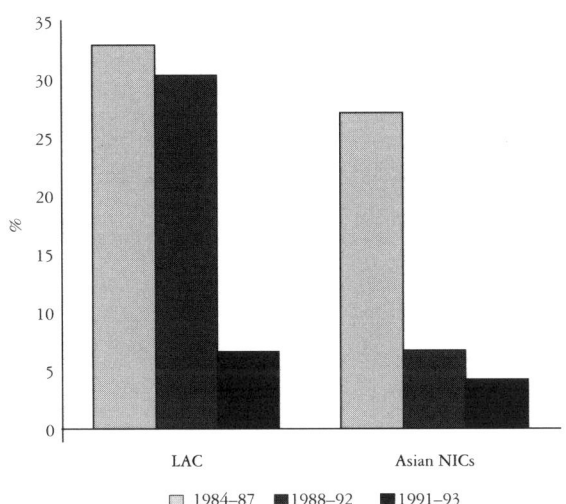

Source: UNCTAD (1994).

TABLE 2.2

Trade Regime

COUNTRY	NON-WEIGHTED MEAN TARIFF RATE %		STANDARD DEVIATION OF TARIFF RATES		ITEMS COVERED BY NON-TARIFF BARRIERS %
	1990–93	1995	1990–93	1995	1990–93
Argentina	9.9	13.9	6.9	7.4	0.2
Barbados		14.1		13.1	
Belize		14.3		13.3	
Bolivia	9.7	9.7	1.2	1.2	2.0
Brazil	11.1	12.7	6.3	9.8	1.5
Chile	11.0	11.0	0.7	0.7	0.1
Colombia	13.3	11.4	4.9	6.5	1.7
Costa Rica	21.1	10.2		7.7	0.8
Dominican Republic	..				
Ecuador	12.3	11.2	5.5	6.5	63.6
El Salvador	21.1	10.2		7.6	19.2
Guatemala	22.8	10.2		7.4	7.4
Guyana		15.0		15.1	
Haiti	11.6				30.8
Honduras	10.1	10.1	6.5	7.5	
Jamaica	17.3	14.0	..	12.5	6.6
Mexico	12.6	14.2	5.4	12.5	3.9
Nicaragua	10.7	10.1	17.8	7.5	
Panama	..		..		
Paraguay	9.3	9.5	6.9	7.5	1.8
Peru	17.6	16.3	4.4	3.4	0.0
Suriname		14.0		12.7	
Trinidad and Tobago	18.7	14.1	15.3	12.7	23.4
Uruguay	9.3	9.6	7.1	7.6	..
Venezuela	13.4	11.8	4.8	6.2	2.4
LAC	**13.8**	**12.2**	**6.7**	**8.5**	**10.3**

Source: World Development Indicators Database (1997): for mean tariff rates, standard deviation of tariff rates and non-trade barriers from 1990–93. IDB (1996): for mean tariff, standard deviation of tariff rates for 1995 and non-trade barriers only for Peru.

iff regimes over a few years, Argentina, Colombia, and Peru conducted faster trade liberalizations. (Although not included in the index for lack of comparable data, countries such as Uruguay and Costa Rica in the late 1980s, and El Salvador, Guatemala, Nicaragua, and the members of the Caribbean Community in the early 1990s also conducted important trade liberalizations.)[9] Closer examination of the components of the index (see Table 2.1) reveals that the process of trade liberalization was accomplished through a balanced reduction of all trade restrictions, that is, a decrease in the level and dispersion of tariffs and para-tariffs and sharp reductions (even elimination, as in Chile and Peru) of nontariff barriers. To appreciate the forcefulness of trade liberalization in Latin America, it is illustrative to compare the regional average of both the rate of tariff and para-tariff charges and the incidence of nontariff measures with those of the Asian NICs. Figure 2.2 shows that the enormous differences in trade barriers between the two groups of countries that existed in the 1980s were reduced considerably in the early 1990s.

Table 2.2 reports simple mean tariff rates and their standard deviations for the periods 1990–93 and 1995 for a larger group of countries. This table should provide an idea (albeit imperfectly, given that para-tariffs are excluded and averages are unweighted) of how most countries in the region compare to each other in terms of trade policy. It shows that by 1995, there was considerable uniformity across countries in the region in the level and dispersion of tariff rates.

2. Outcome indicators of trade liberalization

Trade policy reform is effective to the extent that it encourages undistorted and (almost always) larger volumes of trade. The first two outcome indicators presented below are related to, respectively, changes and levels of trade intensity.[10] Their usefulness as indicators is based on the proposition that trade liberalization leads to larger flows of

[handwritten: One of the most painful arguments to make.]

TABLE 2.3

Percentage Change in the Ratio of the Volume of Trade, relative to GDP

	1986–89	1990–94
Argentina	0.42	8.86
Bahamas	–9.44	0.29
Barbados[1]	–5.98	–1.01
Belize[1]	3.86	–2.10
Bolivia	3.72	2.71
Brazil	2.89	7.16
Chile	5.40	3.83
Colombia	1.57	7.98
Costa Rica	6.84	3.97
Dominican Republic	0.51	2.70
Ecuador	1.40	2.96
El Salvador	–3.46	8.93
Grenada[1]	0.38	0.68
Guatemala[1]	2.56	4.17
Gyuana	–6.40	3.44
Haiti[1]	–0.65	1.32
Honduras	–0.67	0.42
Jamaica[1]	1.82	–2.07
Mexico	7.52	5.03
Panama[1]	0.95	1.26
Paraguay	10.36	12.18
Peru	–0.86	5.30
Trinidad and Tobago	–1.12	11.72
Uruguay	2.99	5.17
Venezuela	–0.32	2.39
LAC Average	1.0	3.7
OECD Average	2.85	2.77
Asian NICs Average	2.20	2.10

Source: Staff estimations based on International Economics Department Database, World Bank; and International Financial Statistics Database, IMF.
Estimation: Real imports plus real exports over real GDP, except for Barbados, Costa Rica, and Suriname, for which nominal figures were used.
[1]Computed using latest available years.

imports and exports relative to GDP. The third indicator, the black market premium on foreign exchange, measures the inadequacy of regulations governing foreign-exchange markets; as such, it serves as a proxy for price distortions present in both current- and capital-account transactions.[11]

Using the *percentage change in the ratio of real imports plus real exports to real GDP* as an outcome indicator of trade reform rests on the assumption that average changes in this ratio that occur in the medium-term (say four to five years) are mostly caused by policy changes.[12] Under this assumption, this indicator can be used to compare improvements in trade openness over time and across countries (to the extent that initial trade openness is similar across countries).[13] Table 2.3 reveals that, in the case of the early reformers, among them Bolivia, Chile, Costa Rica, and Mexico, the expansion of trade as a share to GDP occurred mostly in the 1986–89 period. In the 1990s, the MERCOSUR countries—Argentina, Brazil, Paraguay, and

Uruguay—experienced very high growth rates in the volume of trade. While Colombia, El Salvador, Guatemala, and Peru saw their respective trade intensities increase rapidly in the early 1990s (surely as result of liberalization), the oil-exporting economies of Ecuador and Venezuela experienced less improvement, despite liberalization programs similar to those of the former countries (especially to Colombia's).[14] *[handwritten: enclave economies]*

The *structure-adjusted trade intensity (SATI)* consists of the ratio of real imports plus real exports to real GDP, corrected for certain structural characteristics that determine a country's trade, such as its size (both area and population) and transport costs.[15] This indicator proxies for the level of trade explained by trade policy, and therefore allows for comparisons across countries with different structural characteristics. Figure 2.3 graphs the structure-adjusted trade intensity of most countries in the region for the period 1985–95. It shows Chile and Paraguay as the region's leaders in trade openness, considering both the level and rate of growth of their structure-adjusted trade intensity. Costa Rica also stands out as a country that has improved remarkably its openness standing in the region since the mid-1980s. This is true also, albeit to a lesser extent, of Mexico and Colombia. The general trend in the region is *[handwritten: 2 of most democratically backwards countries]*

TABLE 2.4

Black-Market Premium on Foreign Exchange

	1985	1989	1995
Argentina	40.00	122.85	0.00
Bahamas	11.00	15.00	5.00
Barbados	11.00	–12.98	0.00
Belize	62.50	23.50	4.50
Bolivia	9.34	0.67	–0.30
Brazil	48.95	173.61	0.72
Chile	16.06	19.38	5.67
Colombia	9.03	14.08	1.76
Ecuador	13.43	15.67	1.93
El Salvador	234.00	4.08	–25.47
Guatemala	88.68	9.41	–0.69
Haiti	66.00	235.00	36.61
Honduras	58.10	49.15	–0.42
Jamaica	18.61	28.09	4.38
Mexico	11.73	28.67	5.99
Nicaragua	104.67	6.61	0.31
Paraguay	53.85	3.54	11.63
Peru		15.92	1.73
Trinidad and Tobago	42.86	56.47	0.05
Uruguay	12.00	11.80	0.52
Venezuela	25.00	13.26	12.07
LAC	46.84	39.70	3.14

Source: IDB (1996); based on International Currency Yearbook, various issues.

[handwritten top right: chart]

FIGURE 2.3

Structure-Adjusted Trade Intensity

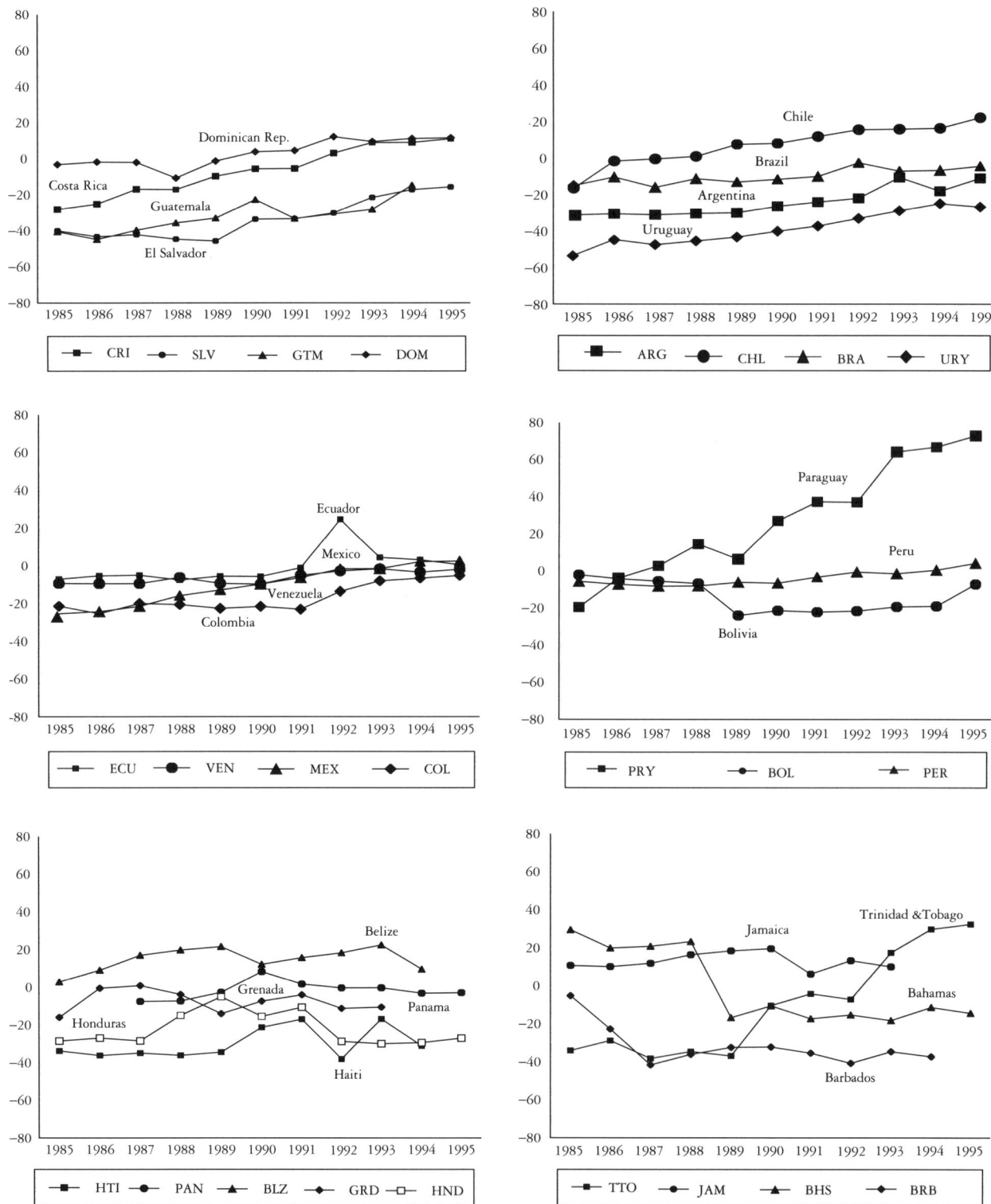

Source: Staff estimations based on the International Economic Department Database, World Bank; and International Financial Statistics Database, IMF.
Estimation: The Structure-Adjusted Trade Intensity is the difference between the actual and the "structural" ratio of exports plus imports to GDP; this structural ratio (STI) is the estimated value of a regression that includes the following variables: Population, Area, FOB/CIF (as a measure of transportation costs), and an industrialized-country dummy. The estimated regression is the following: STI = -7.273* ln (Area) - 5.212* ln (population) + 2.663 (CIF/FOB) * 100 - 14.260 * Ind. country dummy.

FIGURE 2.4

Structure-Adjusted Trade Intensity Comparison by Regions

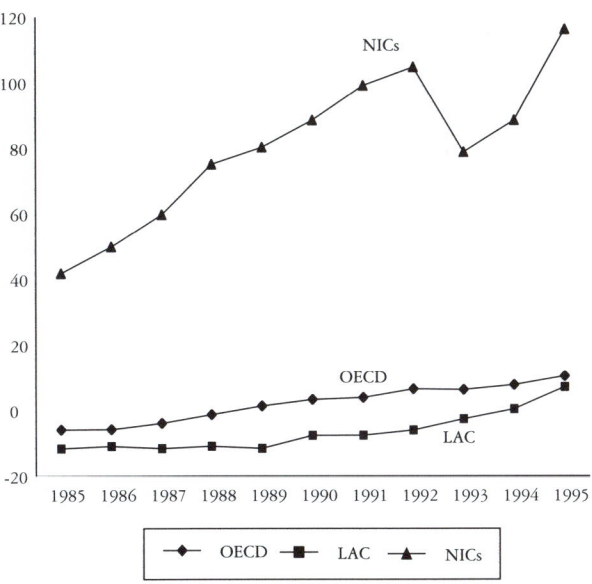

Source: Staff estimations based on the International Economic Department Database, World Bank; and International Financial Statistics Database, IMF.
Estimation: The Structure-Adjusted Trade Intensity is the difference between the actual and the "structural" ratio of exports plus imports to GDP; this structural ratio (STI) is the estimated value of a regression that includes the following variables: Population, Area, FOB/CIF (as a measure of transportation costs), and an industrialized-country dummy. The estimated regression is the following: STI = -7.273* ln (Area) - 5.212* ln (population) + 2.663 (CIF/FOB) * 100 - 14.260 * Ind. country dummy.

quite clear from Figure 2.3: Most countries have experienced, since their period of trade-regime liberalization, a noticeable increase in their trade intensity. This explains why the average (structure-adjusted) trade intensity for the region has risen significantly in the 1990s (see Figure 2.4). This increase has allowed Latin America to approach on average the structure-adjusted trade intensity of OECD countries. It must be noted, however, that in spite of the substantial increase in trade intensity in most Latin American countries, the region on average and even its most open countries still lag behind the Asian NICs in terms of (structure-adjusted) trade intensity, which demonstrates, in part, that the effects of trade policy liberalization on trade intensity need time to take hold.

In general, countries that implemented more liberal trade policies experienced stronger outward orientation, whether measured either by the simple share of trade in GDP or the structure-adjusted trade intensity.

The *black market premium on foreign exchange (BMP)* measures restrictions on the availability of foreign currency,

which are usually imposed in regimes with multiple exchange rates and misaligned official rates. As Table 2.4 shows, by 1995 most countries in the region had negligible black-market premium rates; that is, their official exchange rates equaled their market rates, except for small differentials due to transaction costs. The black-market premium on foreign exchange, persistently large in the 1980s, had dropped dramatically in the early 1990s as restrictions on foreign currency transactions were abolished; mostly, this occurred either because a regime of flexible exchange rates was adopted (as in Peru) or because a fixed exchange-rate system was made credible (as in Argentina). Even Guyana, Haiti, and Suriname, which had BMPs of well over 100 percent in the 1980s and early 1990s, had seen a sharp drop in their respective black-market premiums (to less than 5 percent in the case of Guyana). Of the larger countries, only Venezuela and Paraguay had BMPs of more than 10 percent in 1995.

B. Financial Development

Ample evidence from recent empirical studies, including firm-level, industry-level and country-level studies, indicates that well-functioning financial markets promote long-run economic growth.[16] The relationship between finance and economic activity goes, then, beyond the effect of financial instability on short-term macroeconomic fluctuations. Previous literature had emphasized the recessionary impact of financial crises (currency and bank runs) but had not given to financial development a positive, causal role in long-term economic activity. At present, the growing consensus is that the development of financial institutions and markets promotes more efficient investment, and thus, higher long-run growth.[17]

Well-functioning financial systems impact positively on economic efficiency through different channels. They facilitate the trading, hedging, diversifying, and pooling of risk; they mobilize savings, and thus, allocate resources for investment. Financial systems also monitor managers and exert corporate control by allowing the market to price companies according to their expected performance; and finally, they facilitate the exchange of goods and services, acting as intermediaries between buyers and sellers.

The conclusion that financial development promotes economic growth raises the question of whether public policy can foster growth by inducing the progress of financial institutions and markets. Several studies conclude that improvements in the financial regulatory system, namely, market liberalization accompanied by prudential norms, can indeed lead to the development of sound financial institutions. For instance, the legal system can aid the development of capital markets by advocating the rights of corporate shareholders and establishing clear bankruptcy rules;[18] also, a competitive banking environment may be induced by allowing international banks to participate in the domestic market and eliminating subsidies to domestic banks, as well as by enforcing accounting rules that make transparent the financial position of all banks.

The most common pattern of financial reform in Latin America has been, first, radical liberalization, and second, implementation of prudential norms that moderated the initial liberalization. The policy changes related to the financial system (namely, the removal of interest-rate controls, elimination of mandated credit to "priority" sectors, privatization of state banks, liberalization of the foreign investment regime, and more recently, improvements in the regulatory framework) have improved both the banking system and the stock market. In the banking system, financial reform has led to greater depth in banking intermediation of medium- and long-run instruments and more active participation of the private sector in both allocating and receiving credit. In stock markets, the result of financial reform has been an increase in stock-market capitalization relative to GDP, an even stronger increase in value traded in the stock exchange, and a decline in market concentration—in other words, the creation of larger and more active and liquid stock markets.

Rather than presenting the actual changes in financial policy, this chapter studies progress in financial development by analyzing several of its outcome indicators. The indicators presented below shed light on different aspects of financial markets and must be considered both separately and as a whole. Studying these indicators jointly is important because different financial institutions and markets often complement and substitute for each other; that is, the fact that the pattern of development of stock markets, banking, and other financial institutions varies across countries must be taken into account. For example, it would be a mistake to consider countries with low stock-market capitalization as financially backward if, for instance, they allocate a large amount of credit to private enterprises through the banking sector.

Using the methodology outlined in the previous section, two indices are presented to measure the degree of a country's financial development. They were constructed in a way such that comparisons over time and across countries are possible. Each index consists of indicators that quantify different aspects of the performance of the financial system. The first index is closely linked to the development of the banking sector. The second is related to stock markets. In order to obtain information about long-term financial development from the following financial indicators, it is important to focus on their long-run trends. Their temporary fluctuations, which may be rather large, are mostly determined by the business cycle and one-time events, such as the privatization of public enterprises.[19]

1. Banking sector development

The first element to consider in assessing the development of the banking sector is the depth of a nation's financial system relative to the size of its economy. This can be measured by *quasi-liquid liabilities of the financial system relative to GDP*, that is, $(M3-M1)/GDP$.[20] Currency and highly liquid demand deposits (M1) are excluded because they are rather volatile and do not represent long-term investments in financial intermediaries. Another element to consider is the participation of private institutions in providing credit. This is important because private institutions have clearer incentives to mobilize savings toward profitable projects, exert corporate control, and facilitate risk diversification. To proxy for the participation of private institutions in the provision of credit, this chapter uses *the ratio of credit allocated by deposit money banks to GDP*.[21] The last indicator of banking sector development considers the issue from the point of view of the recipients of credit: financial systems that allocate more credit to the private sector are more actively engaged in researching firms, monitoring managers, and facilitating risk management. To measure this indicator, *the ratio of credit allocated to the private sector to GDP* is used.

The index on banking development for the period 1985–95 is presented in Figure 2.5. Revealing the importance of the banking industry in their economies, Panama and the English-speaking Caribbean countries of the Bahamas and Barbados were the leaders in banking development in the region. Chile, despite a moderate setback in the second half of the 1980s, has remained the banking development leader in South America. At the other end of the scale, Venezuela and Guyana, which by the mid-1980s

FIGURE 2.5

Banking Development Index

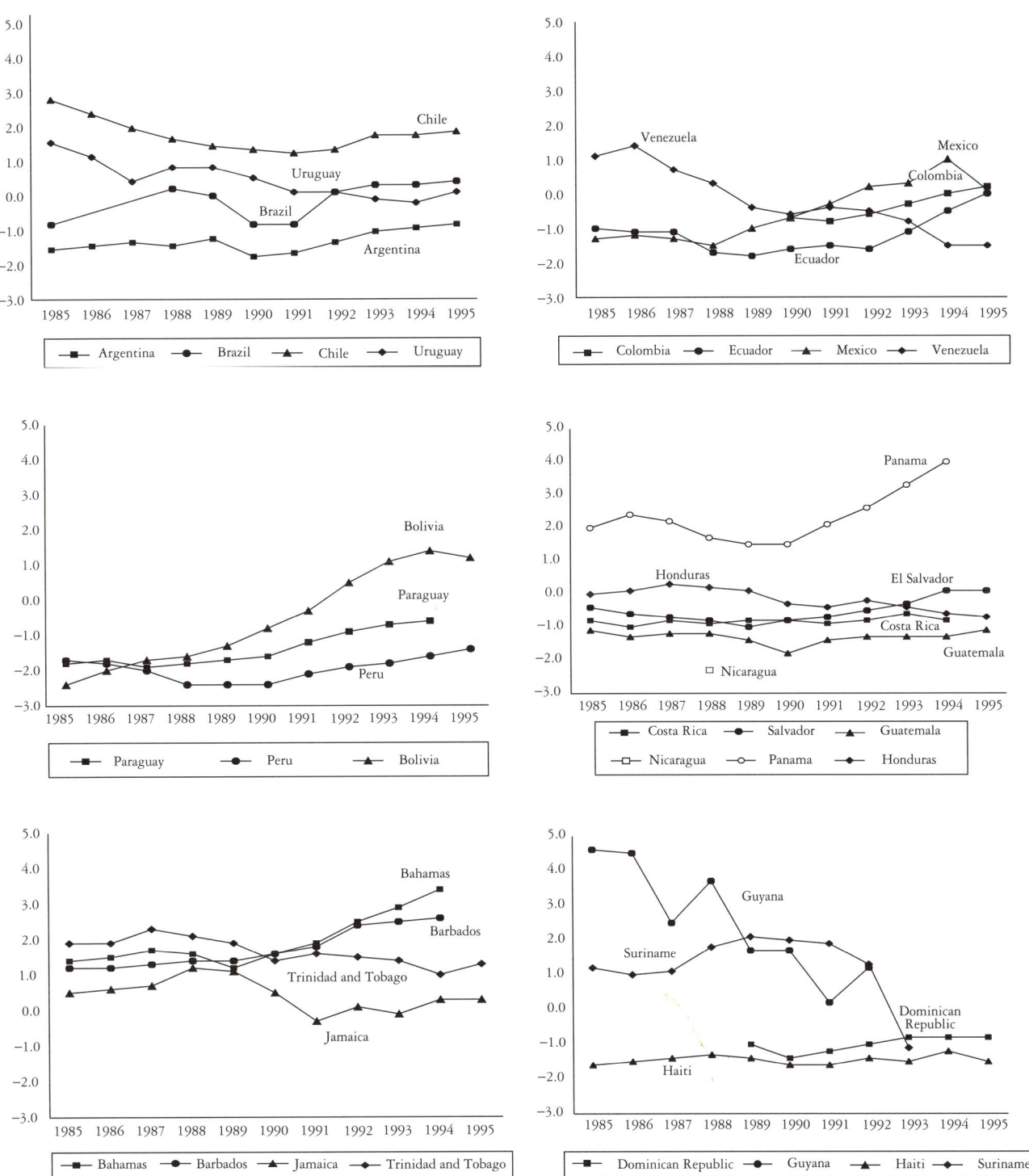

Source: Staff estimations based on the International Financial Statistics Database, IMF.
Estimation: Index includes the following indicators: the ratio of quasi-liquid liabilities to GDP, the ratio of credit allocated to private sector to GDP, and the ratio of credit allocated by deposit money banks to GDP. Index is a weighted average of the principal components of its corresponding indicators, where the eights are given by the share of the indicators' variance explained by each principal component.

appeared to be among the most advanced in the region, have since then suffered a remarkable deterioration in this area. In the case of Venezuela the decline in the banking index was exacerbated by the nation's macroeconomic crisis in the 1990s. Thanks to the financial reforms introduced in Bolivia in 1985 and enlarged in 1991, this country has been able to achieve rapid and sustained progress in banking development since the mid-1980s. Also benefiting from financial reform and macroeconomic stability, most other countries—particularly Argentina, Brazil, Colombia, Ecuador, Peru, and Paraguay—experienced gradual progress in banking development in the 1990s. Mexico shared that trend until 1995, when its banking index fell sharply, due mainly to a decline in both credit allocated to private enterprises and credit provided by private banks relative to GDP.

2. Stock market development

This chapter considers five indicators of stock-market development. The first one, *the ratio of average stock-market capitalization (the value of listed shares on the country's exchange) to GDP,* measures the size of stock markets relative to the overall economy. The second indicator, *the value-traded ratio (total value of shares traded in a year divided by GDP),* reflects liquidity on an economy-wide basis. The third indicator, *the turnover ratio (total value of shares traded in a year divided by average stock-market capitalization),* also measures liquidity but on the basis of the size of the stock market, thus reflecting the activity of the market. A high turnover ratio is usually associated with low transaction costs. The fourth indicator, *the share of market capitalization accounted for by the ten largest stocks,* measures the degree of market concentration, which may adversely affect the degree of free competition of the stock market. Finally, to measure regulatory and institutional features of these emerging stock markets, an indicator of *regulatory efficiency* is constructed from information published by the International Financial Corporation (IFC). This indicator considers whether firms listed in the stock market publish price-earnings information, the quality of accounting standards, the quality of investor protection laws, whether the country has a securities and exchange commission, and whether foreigners face restrictions on domestic investment or on dividend and capital repatriation.

These indicators complement each other. For instance, a small but active market will have low market capitalization but a high turnover ratio; this is the case, for example,

FIGURE 2.6

Stock Market Development Index I

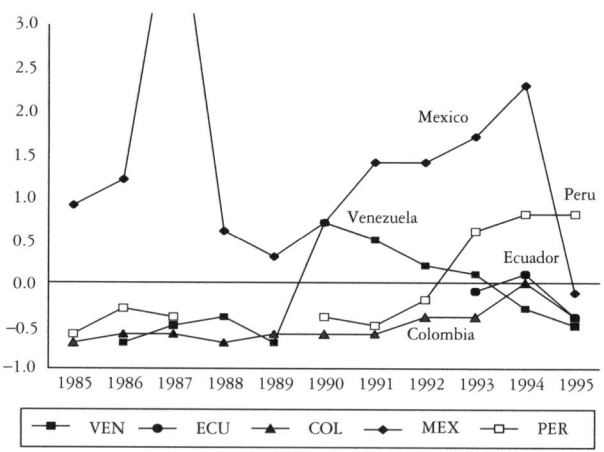

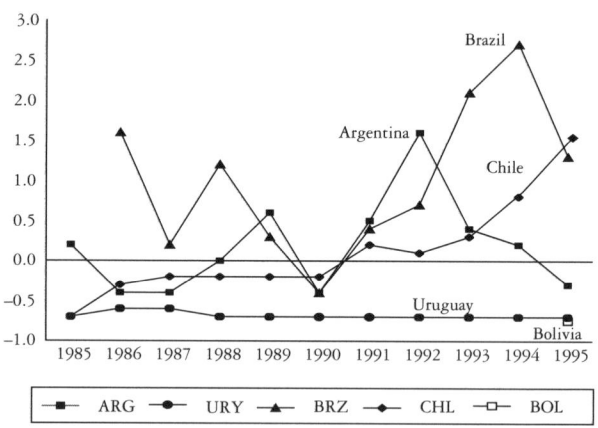

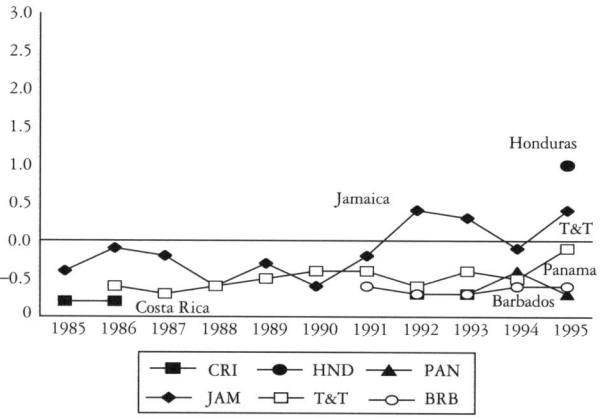

Source: Staff estimations based on the *Emerging Stock Markets Factbook,* IFC, various issues; World Development Indicators Database, World Bank; and International Financial Statistics Database, IMF.
Estimation: Index includes market capitalization as a percentage of GDP, value traded as a percentage of GDP and turnover ratio. The index is a weighted average of the principal components of its corresponding indicators, where the weights are given by the share of the indicators' variance explained by each principal component.

of Norway, India, Brazil, and Argentina; conversely, Chile's market capitalization is well above the average of the sample reported by the IFC, whereas its turnover ratio is one of the smallest. Another instance of complementarity is between the indicators of market concentration and regulatory efficiency. For example, although Argentina, Colombia, and the Philippines present quite concentrated stock markets by international standards, they are above average in terms of the quality of regulatory efficiency.

Given that the indicators on market concentration and regulatory efficiency have a rather limited country coverage, two sub-indices on the development of stock markets are presented: The first one includes only the indicators on market capitalization and liquidity, and the second one adds to the first the market-concentration and regulatory-efficiency indicator.

Figure 2.6 presents the first index on stock-market development for the period 1985–95. In this regard, Chile showed steady improvement since 1985. Brazil, Mexico, and Peru evidenced noteworthy progress in the 1990s. By contrast, Venezuela's index declined in the same period

FIGURE 2.7

Stock Market Development Index II

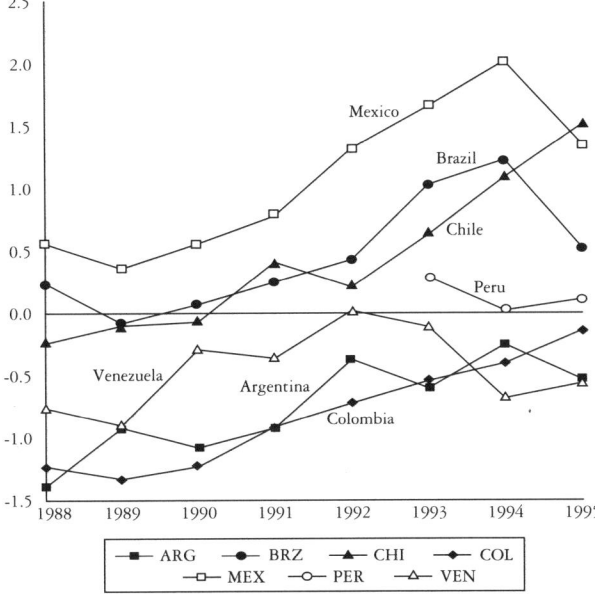

Source: Staff estimations based on the *Emerging Stock Markets Factbook,* IFC, various issues; World Development Indicators Database, World Bank; and International Financial Statistics Database, IMF.
Estimation: Index includes market capitalization as a percentage of GDP, value traded as a percentage of GDP, turnover ratio, market concentration, and an institutional index. The index is a weighted average of the principal components of its corresponding indicators, where the weights are given by the share of the indicators' variance explained by each principal component.

after climbing rapidly in the late 1980s; this decline was due in part to the unraveling of the first wave of reforms in that country and the ensuing macroeconomic crisis in the 1990s. Mexico during 1987 and Argentina during 1991–92 presented temporary sharp rises in their respective indices due to their privatization programs. Peru's improvement in this regard since 1993 (and to some extent Colombia's and Brazil's) might also reflect the partially temporary effect of a privatization program. With the exception of Jamaica, Central American and Caribbean countries are less developed in this respect than the other countries in the region.

Figure 2.7 presents the second index on stock-market development for the period 1988–95. This second index combines the indicators included in the first index with those on market concentration and regulatory efficiency. It generally agrees with the first index that Chile, Brazil, and Mexico had an outstanding performance during this period, and that Venezuela's performance after 1992 was rather disappointing. Argentina and Colombia also showed marked improvement, mainly due to a sharp decrease in their market concentration and enhancements in their regulatory efficiency. It is noteworthy that not only the stock-market index of Mexico, but also that of Brazil, and to a lesser extent, Argentina, suffered a drop in 1995 in the aftermath of the Mexican currency crisis. In this respect, Chile, Colombia, and Peru seem to have escaped the "tequila" effect.

Figure 2.8 and 2.9 compare the averages of Latin American and the Caribbean with those of OECD countries and Asian NICs for the banking and stock-market indicators, respectively.[22] Although many countries in the region have made considerable progress in both aspects of financial development, the region in general and even the most advanced Latin American countries lag substantially behind OECD and the newly industrialized Asian countries. In 1995, the Latin American average for each banking development indicator was between one-fourth and one-fifth of the corresponding indicator for the Asian NICs. The differences are no less marked in terms of stock-market size, market activity, and market liquidity.

C. Labor Market Liberalization

The problem of high and persistent unemployment rates in many European and some Latin American countries, such as Argentina, as well as the continuous presence of infor-

FIGURE 2.8

Banking Development Indicators

Domestic Credit Provided by Deposit Money Banks

(as a percentage of GDP)

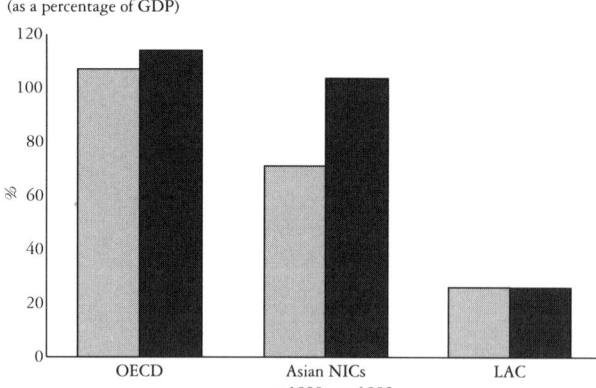

Source: World Development Indicators Database, World Bank; and staff estimations based on International Financial Statistics Database, IMF.
Estimation: Credit allocated by deposit money banks as a percentage of GDP.

Domestic Credit to Private Sector

(as a percentage of GDP)

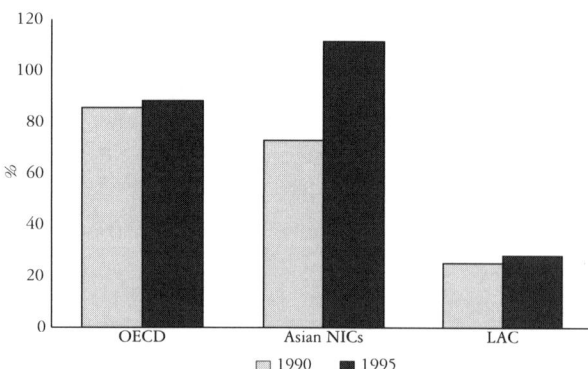

Source: World Development Indicators Database, World Bank; and staff calculations based on the International Financial Statistics Database, IMF.
Estimation: Claims to the private sector as a percentage of GDP.

Quasi-Liquid Liabilities

(as a percentage of GDP)

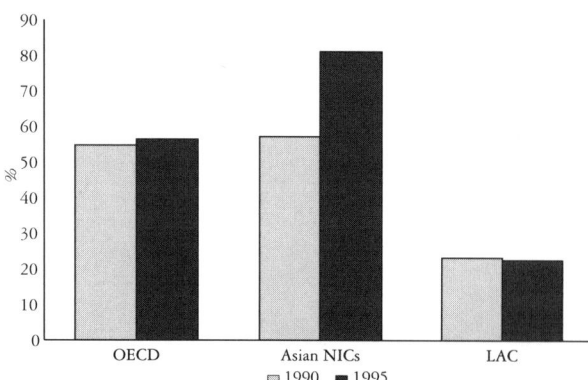

Source: World Development Indicators Database, World Bank; and staff estimations based on International Financial Statistics Database, IMF.
Estimation: Quasi-liquid liabilities (M3-M1) as a percentage of GDP.

mal employment in Latin America and its rising level in Eastern Europe have made labor market liberalization an important reform issue around the world. Labor market liberalization would remove the distortions, many of them induced by government regulations, that make labor too costly and risky in relation to its relative abundance in the economy. Undistorted labor markets enjoy greater flexibility that allows the economy to adjust efficiently to changes in aggregate demand coming from either external or internal sources.[23] In times of negative shocks, a flexible labor market minimizes the rise of unemployment, thus promoting a timely output recovery. In times of booming economic activity, labor market flexibility guarantees that output growth is accompanied by full employment and rising real wages.

Undistorted labor markets are important not only for the short-term adjustment to shocks, but also for ensuring a "broad-based" long-run growth, the kind of growth that brings about a rise in income not only to the owners of physical capital, but also to most workers. When firms perceive that labor is too costly or risky, they will choose investment strategies that are excessively capital-intensive; this is particularly problematic for developing countries, given that they are relatively abundant in labor. This excessive capital intensity in the formal economy (relative to the country's factor endowments) implies a segmentation of firms, under which a formal, industrialized sector coexists with an informal sector, in which enterprises tend to be smaller and the technology rudimentary. This segmentation also applies to the labor force, as workers in the formal sector receive a higher wage than in the informal sector, given that the capital-labor ratio (and thus, labor productivity in the formal sector) is higher.[24] In this condition of high perceived labor costs and the resulting segmentation of the economy, growth will tend to be concentrated in the industrialized sector, and this growth will be reflected in higher capital profits and higher wages for only some workers in the economy. If growth in the industrialized sector continued, and the distorted costs of labor employment did not rise more rapidly, eventually the market segmentation would disappear; nonetheless, before that point, economic growth would not have been broad-based.[25]

In contrast to the focus of the other sections of this chapter, the indicators of labor market liberalization involve policy instruments or institutions rather than outcome indicators, such as the employment response to

FIGURE 2.9

Stock Market Development Indicators

Market Capitalization

(as a percentage of GDP)

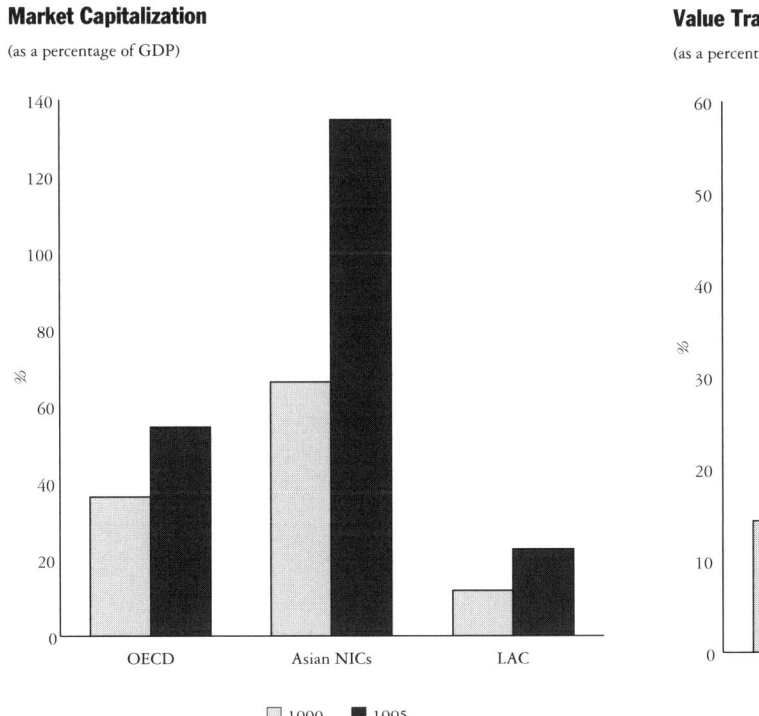

Value Traded

(as a percentage of GDP)

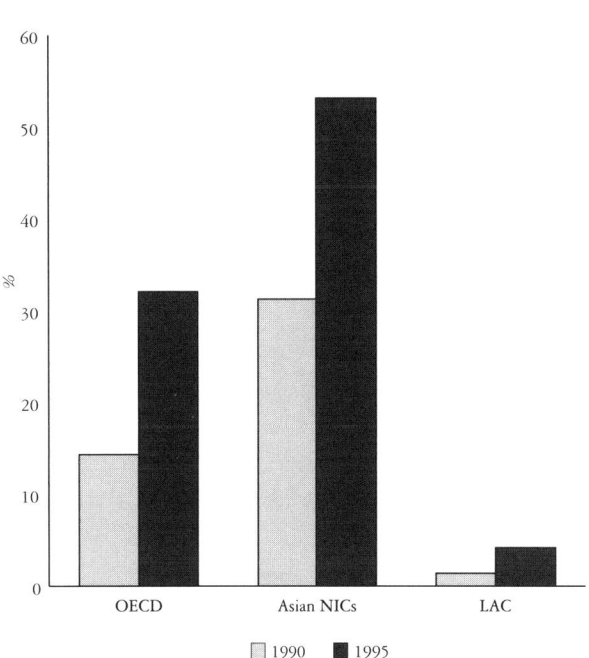

Turnover Ratio

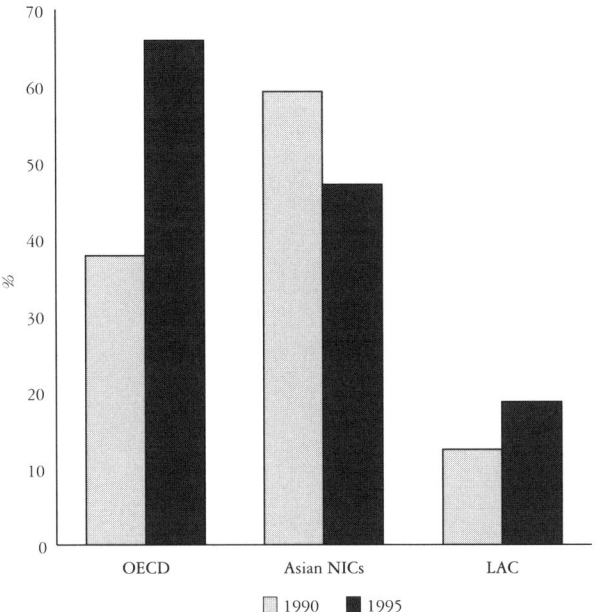

Estimation: Value traded as a percentage of market capitalization.

Market Concentration

*(share of market capitalization
held by the ten largest stocks.)*

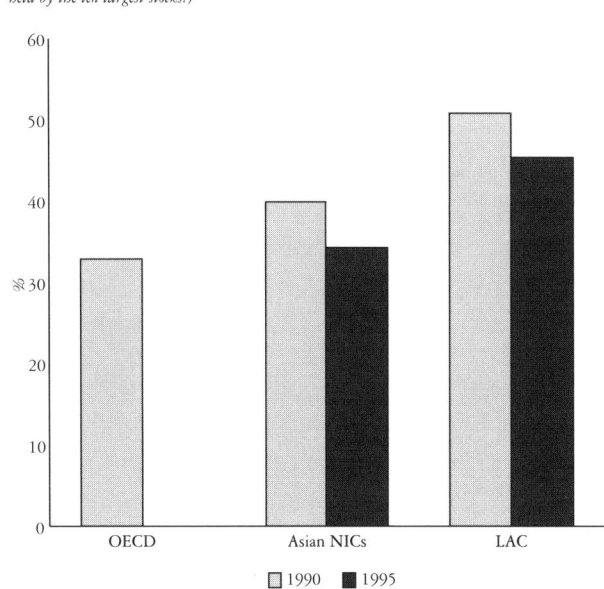

Estimation: Percentage of total market capitalization accounted for by the ten
largest stocks based on end-of-year estimates.

Source: World Bank Indicators Database, World Bank; and staff estimations based on the *Emerging Stock Markets Factbook*, IFC, various issues; and International Financial Statistics
Database, IMF.

TABLE 2.5

Indicators of Labor-Market Reforms

	ECONOMIC DIFFICULTIES AS A JUST CAUSE DISMISSAL[1]		SEVERENCE PAYMENT AS DEFERRED REMUNERATION[2]		FLEXIBILITY ON TEMPORARY CONTRACTS[3]		COMPENSATION FOR DISMISSAL AT ONE-YEAR SENIORITY[4]		COMPENSATION FOR DISMISSAL AT TEN-YEAR SENIORITY[5]		SOCIAL SECURITY CONTRIBUTION-BENEFIT LINK[6]	
	1990	1995	1990	1995	1990	1995	1990	1995	1990	1995	1990	1995
Argentina	0	1	0	0	0	0.5	3.0	3.0	12.0	11.0	0	1
Bahamas	1	1	0	0	1	1	0.5	0.5	1.0	1.0	0.5	0.5
Barbados	0	0	0	0	1	1	1.0	1.0	1.5	1.5		
Belize	0	0	0	0	1	1	0.5	0.5	0.5	0.5	0.5	0.5
Bolivia	0	0	0.5	0.5	0	0	4.0	4.0	3.0	3.0	0	0
Brazil	0	0	0	0	0.5	0.5	2.4	2.4	15.0	15.0	0	0
Chile	1	1	0.5	0.5	0.5	0.5	2.0	2.0	6.0	6.0	1	1
Colombia	0	0	0	1	0.5	1	1.5	1.5	10.5	13.5	0	1
Costa Rica	0	0	0	0			2.0	2.0	9.0	9.0		
Dominican Republic	0	0	0	0	0	0	0.5	0.5	6.9	6.9	0	0
Ecuador	0	0	1	1	0	0.5	4.3	4.3	13.5	13.5	0	0
El Salvador	0.5	0.5	0	0	0	0	1.0	1.0	10.0	10.0	0.5	0.5
Guatemala	0.5	0.5	0	0	0	0	1.0	1.0	10.0	10.0	0	0
Guyana	1	1	0	0	1	1	1.0	1.0	6.7	6.7	0.5	0.5
Haiti							1.0	1.0	3.0	3.0		
Honduras	0	0	0	0	0	0	1.0	1.0	10.0	10.0	0.5	0.5
Jamaica	1	1	0	0	1	1	0.5	0.5	1.5	1.5	0.5	0.5
Mexico	0	0	0	0	0	0	4.0	4.0	10.7	10.7	0	1
Nicaragua	0	0	0	0	0.5	0.5	3.0	3.0	21.0	21.0		
Panama	0	0	0	0	0	0.5	1.9	1.9	8.5	8.5	0.5	0.5
Paraguay	0	0	0	0	0.5	0.5	1.3	1.5	4.3	6.0		
Peru	0	1	0	1	0	0.5	3.0	1.0	30.0	10.0	0	1
Suriname												
Trinidad and Tobago	0	0	0	0	1	1	2.5	2.5	9.5	9.5		
Uruguay	0	0	0	0	0	0	1.0	1.0	6.0	6.0	0	1
Venezuela	0	0	0	0	0	0	1.3	1.3	10.3	10.3	0.5	0.5

[1]Are dismissals resulting from economic difficulties of the firm considered justified? Estimation: 1=Yes; 0=No; 0.5=Partially

[2]Are Severance Payments periodically deposited in accounts in the name of the workers? Estimation: 1=Yes; 0=No; 0.5=Partially

[3]Are there restrictions on contemporary contracts? Estimation: 1=Unrestricted; 0.5=Somewhat restricted, limited renewal but contracts do not generate same obligations as workers with indefinite contracts, 0 = not contemplated by law, restricted or when they generate same obligations as workers with indefinite contracts.

[4]Compensation for dismissal, excluding amount that would have been paid in the event of worker's resignation with one year of seniority. Estimation: Severance payments were calculated adding the cost of the required period of prior notice plus payments for dismissal without just cause minus the compensation for termination by worker.

[5]Compensation for dismissal, excluding amount that would have been paid in the event of workers resignation after ten years of seniority.

Estimation: Severance payments were calculated by adding the cost of the required period of prior notice plus the payments for dismissal without just cause minus the compensation for termination by worker.

[6]To what extent contributions made by workers are linked to the benefits received. Estimation: 0=Pension system is mostly pay-as-you-go; that is, less than 25% of its revenues come from income derived from pension-fund investment; 0.5 = Pension system financed partly by investment income (at least 25% of revenues); 1 = Pension system is mostly a capitalization system based on individual retirement accounts managed by private companies.

aggregate demand shocks or the degree of labor market segmentation. Evaluating these outcome indicators involves a level of specialized analysis that is beyond the scope of this document.

The indicators of government-induced labor-market distortions to be considered are divided into four groups.[26] Most of these indicators are qualitative and based on comparisons across countries in the region. (See Table 2.5.) The first group of indicators refers to *constraints on the hiring and firing of workers.* If this process is burdensome, employing labor becomes more costly and risky, especially if economic conditions are uncertain, and the ability to match workers' characteristics with the needs of the firm is limited. These constraints on hiring and firing have several aspects; in what follows, an indicator is presented for some of the most important of them. (See Table 2.5.) The first aspect is whether labor legislation considers dismissals caused by economic difficulties of the firm to be unjustified, thus ignoring that in an active economy, some firms and sectors shrink as others expand. The second aspect is whether at

TABLE 2.5

Indicators of Labor-Market Reforms (Cont.)

	CONTRIBUTION-BENEFIT LINK 2[7]		SOCIAL SECURITY TAX RATE[8]		LABOR DISPUTES[9]		EMPLOYMENT PUBLIC SECTOR[10]		INDEX 1[11]		INDEX 2[12]	
	1990	1995	1990	1995	1988–91	1993–95	1990	1995	1990	1995	1990	1995
Argentina	0	1	47.0	45.4			19.3	19.3	−3.2	−1.1		
Bahamas	0	0	8.8	8.8					4.0	4.0		
Barbados	0	0	11.6	11.6					2.1	2.1		
Belize	0	0	7.7	7.7					2.7	2.7		
Bolivia	0	0	23.5	23.5		1.4	16.5	11.4	−0.6	−0.6		0.6
Brazil	0	0	31.0	31.0	16.2	12.4	11.0	9.6	−2.3	−2.3	−5.5	−3.8
Chile	1	1	24.7	24.7	1.5	1.1	7.0	7.7	2.0	2.0	13.6	13.4
Colombia	0	1	21.1	33.0	0.9	1.4	9.6	8.4	−0.7	1.1	5.6	6.9
Costa Rica	0	0	27.0	27.0	1.7	1.4	22.0	17.9				
Dominican Republic	0	0	12.5	12.5					0.0	0.0		
Ecuador	0	0	17.6	17.6	2.6	0.5	17.6	13.4	−1.4	−0.7	−7.6	−3.2
El Salvador	0	0	13.5	13.5	9.1	5.0			−0.1	−0.1		
Guatemala	0	0	14.5	14.5					−0.1	−0.1		
Guyana	0	0	12.5	12.5					2.6	2.6		
Haiti	0	0	11.0	11.0								
Honduras	0	0	10.5	10.5			14.9	12.5	−0.8	−0.8		
Jamaica	0	0	5.0	5.0	0.6	1.7			4.0	4.0		
Mexico	0	1	23.8	26.0	1.4	1.6	25.0	22.5	−3.0	−3.3	−10.1	−6.81
Nicaragua	0	0	15.0	15.0					−3.3	−3.3		
Panama	0	0	11.7	11.7	0.0	0.1	32.0	23.4	−1.0	−0.3	−3.4	2.6
Paraguay	0	0	22.5	22.5			12.2	11.9	0.5	0.1		
Peru	0	1	24.6	25.6	5.3	0.7	11.6	8.9	−5.8	2.9	−12.9	13.1
Suriname												
Trinidad and Tobago	0	0	8.4	8.4	0.4	0.4			−0.1	−0.1		
Uruguay	0	1	40.5	40.5			20.1	17.7	−0.8	−1.0		
Venezuela	0	0	25.5	25.5	6.8	0.1	22.3	19.5	−1.3	−1.3	−2.7	0.4

[7]To what extent contributions made by workers are linked to the benefits received. Estimated: 0 = Pension system is mostly pay-as-you-go; that is less than 25% of its revenues come from income derived from pension-fund investment; 1 = Pension system is mostly a capitalization system based on individual retirement accounts managed by private companies.
[8]Social security related contributions as a % of basic wages. Comprises old age, disability, death, sickness, maternity, work injury, unemployment, and family allowances.
[9]Number of annual hours not worked per worker as a result of strikes.
[10]Public sector employment as a percentage of total nonargricultural employment.
[11]Index 1 includes indicators 1 to 5 and 7 and 8.
[12]Index 2 includes indicators 1 to 6 and 8 and 9.

Source: Staff calculations based on Lora and Pages (1996); IDB (1995); International Labor Office for Latin America and the Caribbean; U.S. Government (Dept. of Health and Human Services) 1990, 1995.

least a portion of severance payments are periodically deposited in accounts in the name of the workers, so that these funds and their associated market yields are available to workers even if they resign from the firm. The existence of these funds signals that labor legislation considers severance payments to be deferred compensation rather than penalties designed to prevent firms from shedding labor. The third aspect relates directly to the monetary compensation for dismissal that represents an actual cost to the firm, that is, excluding what would have been paid even in the event of a worker's resignation; the corresponding indicator, measured as multiples of the last monthly wage, varies with the level of workers' seniority and across countries. To account for this fact, it is presented at one-year and ten-year seniority levels. High compensation for dismissal is especially distortionary for the labor market and costly to the firm if economic difficulties are treated as unjustified causes for dismissal. In this case, firms find themselves trapped in a situation in which downsizing may be the only way for them to manage their economic difficulties but is too expensive to undertake. The fourth aspect to be considered is restrictions on temporary contracts; this type of contract is needed to fulfill particular needs of the firm and when, as result of an active economy, new and rather uncertain ventures frequently appear. In economies in which rigid constraints on the hiring and firing of permanent workers exist, temporary contracts may provide a way, albeit imperfectly, to make labor markets more flexible. It is important that when temporary contracts become less restricted, permanent contracts be also liberalized. Otherwise, the prevalence of temporary workers will be abnormally large, creating labor segmentation within the firm that lowers the incentives for it to invest in the training of workers. Moreover, to the extent that temporary workers are not represented in the firm's trade union, labor segmentation induces unions to demand pay raises that are inconsistent with the job stability of temporary workers.

The second group of indicators of government-induced labor-market distortions is related to *payroll taxes*. These taxes are social security-related contributions, comprising old age, disability, death, sickness, maternity, work injury, unemployment, and family allowances. If there were a strong link between contributions and benefits from the perspective of the individual, then these taxes would not be distortionary but would represent a form of remuneration to the worker. As such, these contributions (including the share paid by the firm) would be taken into account when firms and workers negotiate on the remuneration package. Unfortunately, in Latin America and the Caribbean, as well as in most other regions, the link between social security contributions and benefits at the individual level is, in general, rather weak. The clearest example of this weak relationship is old-age pension systems, which in this region are mostly of the pay-as-you-go kind. Generally, what is paid into this type of pension system during work years bears little relation to what is received at retirement. Following this discussion, two indicators are used to measure labor market distortions due to payroll taxes. The first is the rate of social security contributions, paid both by employers and employees, expressed as a percentage of basic wage. The second indicator attempts to control for the degree to which contributions and benefits are connected. Focusing on old-age pension systems, this indicator grades countries according to the extent that their pension regimes are based on a capitalization system. The highest score is given to pension regimes that feature a

fully-funded capitalization system with individual accounts managed by private companies; these are present in countries that have undertaken major pension reform, namely, Chile in 1981, Colombia in 1993, Peru in 1993, Argentina in 1994, and Mexico in 1996. The lowest score is given to pension regimes that are mostly based on a pay-as-you-go system, and an intermediate score is given to systems that, although not fully funded, receive at least 25 percent of their revenues from investment income from established pension funds.

The third category of indicators on labor market distortions concerns the *lack of mechanisms for peaceful resolution of labor disputes*, measured by the amount, per worker, of annual hours not worked due to strikes in the modern sector.[27] The prevalence of labor strikes indicates not only that labor legislation does not provide the means to settle labor conflicts, but also that such legislation may induce labor stoppage by making one party (usually the firm) bear most of its costs. For instance, in countries such as Ecuador and Nicaragua, legislation requires that workers be paid even when they are on strike. Both workers and firms should have something to lose if delays in reaching agreement occur; in this way, the bargaining process will move more speedily toward compromise.[28]

The last category of labor market distortions is related to the prevalence of *public employment* in the economy, measured by the ratio of public to total employees in the nonagricultural sector. In most Latin American countries, public employment has traditionally been used both as a way to solve unemployment problems during economic downturns and as a political tool to reward allegiance to the governing party; therefore, the process of hiring public employees has often neglected to adequately match workers to the needs of public administration. This overstaffing and excessively high remuneration in public administration (relative to productivity) has bid up labor costs in the private sector; the ensuing welfare loss is caused by the fact that the marginal productivity of labor in the public sector has not equaled that in the private sector. Apart from this static distortion, low productivity in the public sector has had harmful consequences on the development of human capital of those employed by the state. Generally, public employees have lacked incentives to remain well-trained, so their preparation and training have soon become obsolete and this has made them unfit to compete with their private-sector counterparts. This contention is supported

FIGURE 2.10

Labor-Market Liberalization Index I

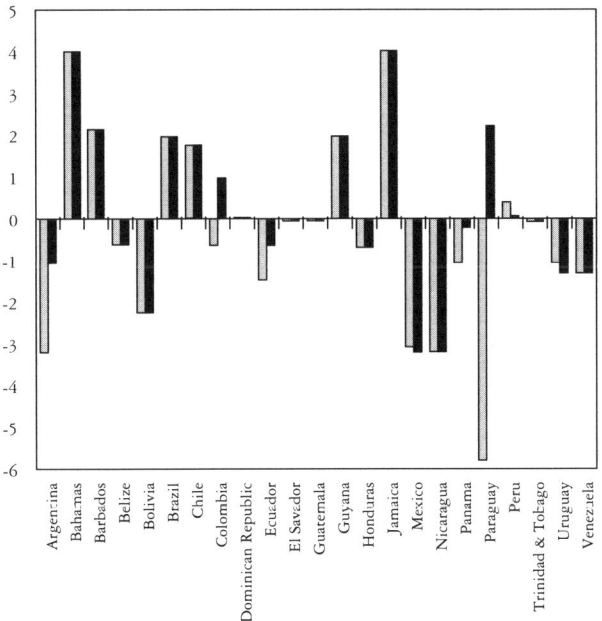

Source: Staff calculations based on Lora and Pages (1996); IDB (1996); and International Labor Office for Latin America and the Caribbean.
Estimation: Index includes economic difficulties as just cause, severance payment as deferred remuneration, flexibility of temporary contracts, compensation for dismissals with one and ten years of seniority, social security contribution-benefit link, and social security tax rate. The index is a weighted average of the principal component of its corresponding indicators, where the weights are given by the share of the indicator's variance explained by each principal component.

FIGURE 2.11

Labor-Market Liberalization Index II

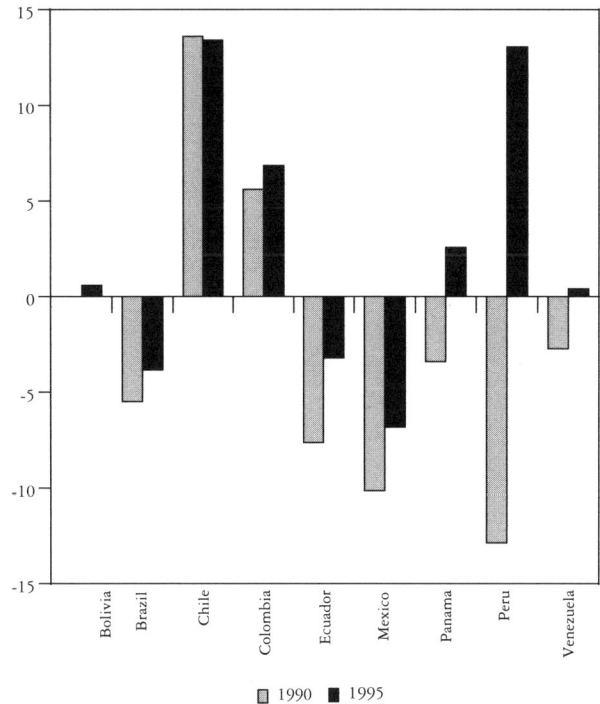

□ 1990   ■ 1995

Source: Staff calculations based on Lora and Pages (1996), IDB (1995), and International Labor Office for Latin America and the Caribbean.
Estimation: Index includes economic difficulties as just cause, severance payments as deferred remuneration, flexibility of temporary contracts, compensation for dismissals with one and ten years of seniority, social security contribution-benefit link, social security tax rate, labor-disputes, and employment in the public sector. The index is a weighted average of the principal component of its corresponding indicators, where the weights are given by the share of the indicator's variance explained by each principal component.

by preliminary findings of studies on public downsizing;[29] these studies indicate that former public employees find it hard to adjust to the demands of the private sector, even when their human capital is generally sufficient to be applied to both private- and public-sector jobs.

Table 2.5 presents information on each of these indicators of labor market liberalization for most countries in Latin America and the Caribbean. In order to provide a summary measure of progress in this area, two indices were computed. The first, presented in Figure 2.10, includes only the first two groups of labor market distortions (constraints on hiring and dismissal and payroll taxes) in order to cover a larger range of countries. The second index, which also includes information on labor dispute resolution and public employment, has a more limited country coverage. (See Figure 2.11.) Following the common law tradition, the English-speaking countries of the Caribbean, especially the Bahamas, Belize, and Guyana, are the least rigid in the region, particularly in regard to monetary compensation for dismissal, constraints on temporary con-

tracts, and the rate of payroll taxes. Among the other Latin American countries, Chile has been the leader in labor market liberalization, even since the 1980s. Of the countries that undertook labor market reforms in the early 1990s, Peru's endeavors towards an undistorted labor market are impressive; it has made progress in all aspects of labor market liberalization, and even its mild increase in payroll taxes cannot be regarded as distortionary, given that the contribution-benefit link of social security was strengthened by the adoption of a fully-funded pension system. The progress of the other reforming countries has been more limited. Argentina reduced distortions in its labor market by introducing legislation that distinguishes between unjustified dismissals and those produced by economic difficulties of the firm, by adopting a fully-funded pension system, and by easing some constraints on temporary contracts. Nevertheless, Argentina's payroll tax rate remains the highest in the region, and its mandated compensation for dismissal has rates double those in neighboring Chile. Furthermore, some additional downsizing of public-sector employment is still needed at the provincial level. Colombia also experienced progress in labor market flexibility; however, its strengthening of the link between social security benefits and contributions was to some extent reversed by the steep rise in the social security contribution rate, from 21.1 percent to 33 percent of wages. Countries that also made progress in this area are Ecuador, Panama, and Venezuela. Finally, Brazil and Mexico are two of the most distorted labor markets in the region; in the case of Brazil, this is due to a high compensation for dismissal, without distinguishing between unjustified and economic reasons; and a high incidence of labor conflict. In the case of Mexico, the large presence of public-sector employment in the economy contributes to the country's lack of progress regarding labor market liberalization.

In closing this section, it is important to note that the indicators of labor market distortions used in this document are policy instruments rather than outcome indicators. This clarification is important, for there may be cases in which labor markets remain undistorted, despite having potentially distortionary policies, because those policies are not enforced (or not binding).

D. Proper Use of Public Resources and Efficiency of Revenue Generation

The previous chapter studied the effects of public deficits on macroeconomic stability. In this chapter, the analysis emphasizes how government obtains its revenues and allocates its expenditures, and their impact on economic development. Effective management of government resources is linked to both good governance (to be analyzed in the following section) and good policies. On the expenditure side, good policies attempt to allocate expenditures so as to promote human capital development and provide essential public goods. An important lesson learned from failed populist regimes is that public resources cannot be used properly when government intervenes directly in market activities, except when it serves as a regulator in cases where clear externalities exist. Another aspect of the same lesson is that the private sector should be encouraged to participate in providing public services. Following this logic, the recent privatization of public enterprises, including public utilities, represents

an improvement in the way governments use public resources. On the revenue side, an efficient system of revenue generation seeks to minimize the distortionary effect of taxation, while securing enough revenues both to avoid unmanageable deficits and to finance essential public goods and services.

1. Indicators on the proper use of public resources

The historical paradox of Latin American governments is that, while they have been almost omnipresent in the economy, they have also been weak.[30] Their weakness consisted of being unable to provide essential public services and being easily manipulated by particular interest groups. The challenge Latin American governments face is to become strong by specializing in economically essential areas in which the private sector does not perform or performs poorly. A successful response to this challenge requires a reform of government institutions and the way they manage their resources. The next section, titled "Governance," evaluates progress achieved in the area of institutional reform. This section deals with the way governments manage their resources.[31] In this respect, Latin American countries have generally had two deficiencies, which the current wave of reforms are attempting to remedy. The first is that a large share of government resources was spent on a bloated and ineffective bureaucracy. Public employment was used to reward political loyalties, and in order to accommodate the surplus of employees, new government departments were created, tasks were duplicated, and bureaucratic paperwork was made more lengthy and complicated. The recent empirical-growth literature provides substantial evidence that in countries whose government spends a large share of its revenues to maintain a large bureaucracy, economic-growth performance suffers. Using pooled cross-country and time-series information, these empirical studies find that an increase in government consumption, of which wages and salaries to public employees are the largest component, negatively affects the rate of per capita GDP growth.[32] In order to measure the progress achieved by Latin American countries in this respect, the *ratio of wages and salaries of government employees to primary expenditures* is considered. The level of government used in the evaluation is the central government, except in the case of Argentina, Brazil, and Colombia, for which the general government is used. Given the decentralized nature of these countries' governments, and the fact that fiscal

FIGURE 2.12

Wages and Salaries as a Percentage of Primary Expenditures

Latin America and the Caribbean[1]

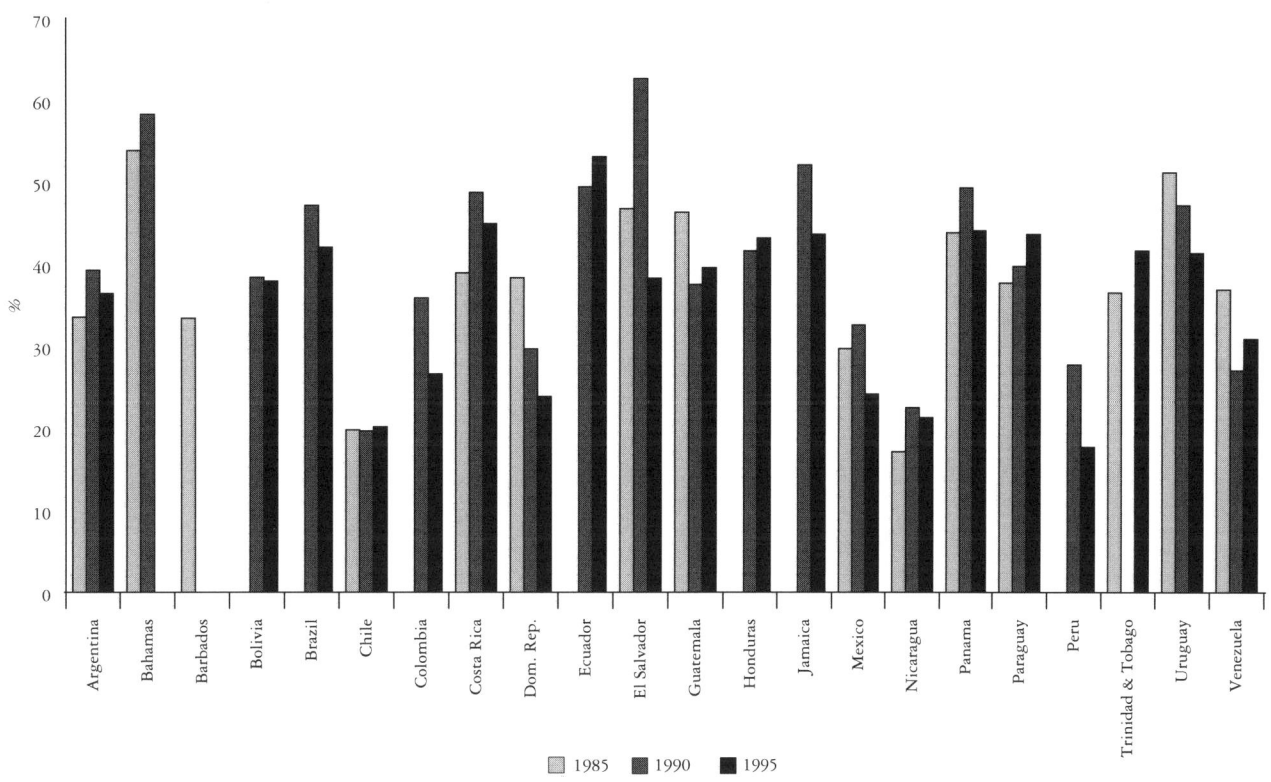

Source: Staff estimations based on World Development Indicators Database, World Bank; Government Finance Statistics
Database and Recent Economic Development Country Reports, IMF.
Estimation: Wages and salaries as a percentage of primary expenditures in the consolidated central government, except in the following cases: For Argentina,
Colombia and Brazil, figures corresponding to general government are used; For Ecuador, El Salvador, Guatemala, and Trinidad and Tobago, figures corresponding
to budgetary central government are used; For Uruguay, primary expenditures net of transfers to social security are used.
[1]Used 1994 figures when data for 1995 was not available.

Comparison by regions

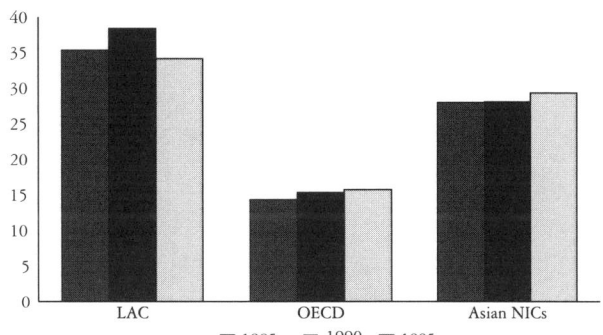

Source: Staff estimations based on World Development Indicators Database, World
Bank; Government Finance Statistics Database and Recent Economic Development
Country Reports, IMF.
Estimation: Wages and salaries as a percentage of primary expenditures.
[1]Used 1994 figures when data for 1995 was not available.

reform in local governments there is not proceeding at the same pace as in the central government, it is essential to consider general government as the unit of analysis for those countries.

As Figure 2.12 shows, a few countries in the region—namely, Colombia, the Dominican Republic, El Salvador, Peru, and Uruguay—have shown in the last ten years a clear tendency to spend less for the services of the bureaucracy. Figure 2.12 also shows that there is considerable variation in the share of government primary expenditures devoted to public employees' salaries, from nearly 50 percent in the Bahamas, Costa Rica, and Ecuador in the mid-1990s to below 20 percent in Chile, Nicaragua, and Peru in the same period. Clearly, the salary-to-expenditure ratio in public administration depends not only on whether the bureaucracy is bloated, but also on structural characteristics such as whether the government is required to specialize in providing labor-intensive services. Nevertheless, it is interesting to note that the Chilean public administration, which enjoys a strong reputation for efficiency in the region (as described in the section on governance), has been absorbing a share of primary expenditures that is among the lowest in Latin America in the last ten years. Also worth noting is the marked difference in this respect between government levels (federal, state, and local) in Argentina and Brazil, the two most seriously decentralized countries in the region; in both countries, the ratio of salaries to primary expenditures is significantly higher at the state (or provincial) level than at the federal level. In Argentina in 1995, this ratio was 23 percent for the federal government and 54 percent on average for provincial governments; in Brazil, the corresponding figures were 28 percent and 49 percent. These numbers support the notion that the fiscal problems of expenditure control and deficit reduction in Argentina and Brazil mainly reside at the provincial (or state) level of government. Comparing the percentage of primary expenditures that go to the bureaucracy in Latin America, the OECD, and the Asian NICs, Latin America on average remains closer to, say, Malaysia (36 percent) than to Korea (12 percent).

The second deficiency in the use of public resources in Latin American concerns the pervasiveness of public enterprises. By the mid-1980s in most countries in the region, public enterprises performed quite poorly, which meant that they not only provided deficient public services, but they also incurred major loses that imposed a heavy burden

TABLE 2.6

Proceeds from Privatization

(as a percentage of GDP)

	1988–1989	1990–1995
Argentina	0.02%	1.48%
Barbados		1.04%
Belize	4.57%	
Bolivia		3.48%
Brazil	0.04%	0.35%
Chile	1.11%	0.59%
Colombia		0.34%
Ecuador		0.29%
Guatemala	0.16%	
Honduras	0.33%	0.44%
Jamaica	1.85%	1.59%
Mexico	0.79%	1.60%
Nicaragua		1.41%
Panama		0.30%
Paraguay		0.28%
Peru		1.73%
Trinidad and Tobago		3.08%
Uruguay		0.06%
Venezuela		0.77%

Source: Staff estimations based on International Finance Division Privatization Database and World Development Indicators Database, World Bank.

on government finances, thus exacerbating the fiscal imbalance that resulted in high inflation.[33] To address this deficiency in the use of public resources, many Latin American governments have included privatization of public enterprises in their process of reform. Privatization of public enterprises is advocated on two grounds. The first is that public enterprises are generally loss-making, due to both poor management and improper pricing policies, thus draining fiscal resources that could be applied to more productive uses. The second reason in favor of privatization is that substituting private for public firms in areas of economic activity inclusive of natural monopolies creates higher productivity, meaning better products and services at a lower cost. Privatization also results in better public infrastructure and utility services, because it allows the government to concentrate on its role as an efficient regulator.

In order to evaluate progress in this area, two indicators are used. The first, *privatization proceeds as a ratio to GDP*, measures privatization effort; this indicator is clearly imperfect because it implicitly assumes that all countries start from similar levels of public-enterprise participation in the economy. Privatization proceeds as a ratio to total initial value of public enterprises would be a better indicator of privatization effort; unfortunately, data on the initial *market* value of the public enterprise sector is unavailable.

FIGURE 2.13

Private Investment as a Percentage of Gross Domestic Investment

Latin America and the Caribbean[1]

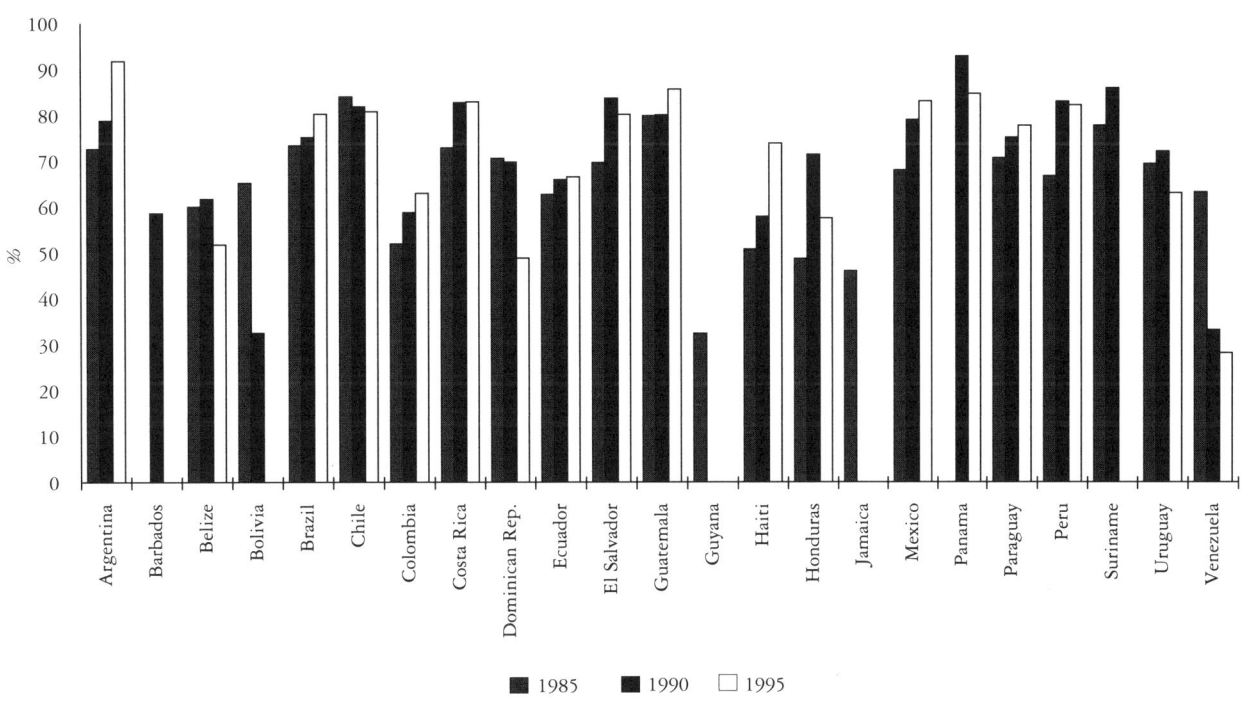

■ 1985   ■ 1990   □ 1995

Comparison by regions

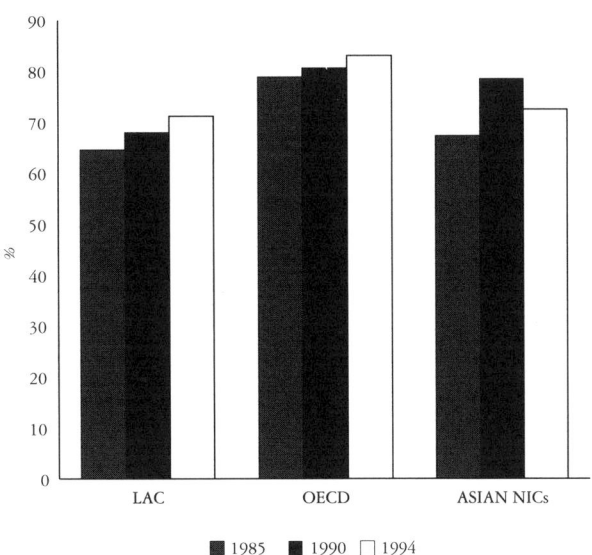

■ 1985   ■ 1990   □ 1994

Source: Staff estimations based on World Development Indicators Database and Savings Research Project Database, World Bank; Government Finance Statistics Database, IMF. Estimation: Ratio of gross domestic investment minus general government and public enterprise investment to gross domestic investment, except for OECD countries, for which "private investment" includes public enterprise investment.
[1] Used 1994 figures when data for 1995 was not available.

Table 2.6 presents proceeds from privatization as a percentage of average GDP for the periods 1988-89 and 1990-95. It shows that most countries in the region participated in the process of privatization. The most significant cases are Argentina, Belize, Bolivia, Chile, Jamaica, Mexico, Nicaragua, Peru, Trinidad and Tobago, and Venezuela. Brazil, Colombia, and Honduras entered the process rather timidly. As of 1995, the remaining countries, among them, Ecuador, Guatemala, Panama, Paraguay, and Uruguay remained outside the privatization effort.

The second indicator, the *ratio of private to total investment*, attempts to measure the reaction of the private sector following privatization, that is, whether the private sector, enlarged by newly privatized enterprises, becomes more active in capital formation. This is especially important in the area of infrastructure and public utilities, for which one of the main objectives of privatization was to promote fresh investment. In order to assess this particular point, it would have been preferable to use as an indicator the ratio of private investment in infrastructure and utilities to total investment in the same activities; however, data on private investment in infrastructure is as yet unavailable. At any rate, since the privatization effort has included all kinds of enterprises, from mining firms and commercial banks to power-generation companies and port authorities, it is informative to examine the behavior of total private investment before and after privatization.

Figure 2.13 presents gross private investment—that is, gross domestic investment minus general government and public enterprise investment—as a percentage of gross domestic investment for most countries in Latin America and the Caribbean. In most countries that conducted a major privatization program in the 1980s or early 1990s, the private investment share of total investment became more than 80 percent by the mid-1990s. This was the case for Chile, Argentina, Mexico, and Peru. Having pioneered privatization in the 1980s, Chile's private investment share remained high and stable in the late 1980s and early 1990s; the other three countries experienced an increase in private-sector participation in total domestic investment of more than ten percentage points over the same period. Brazil and Colombia also experienced an increase in their private investment shares, an increase that accorded with the small size of their privatization programs. Bolivia's experience is a rather disappointing one, for despite a strong privatization effort, its private investment share

actually dropped from its 1985 level and then remained about half as large as that of other countries with a similar privatization effort. The decline of Venezuela's private investment share in the ten years after 1985 cannot be associated with its privatization program, which started only recently; rather, this significant drop was initially due to macroeconomic instability, and subsequently, to an adjustment program. It is interesting to note that some of the countries that did not initiate a privatization effort already had private investment shares in the 1980s of around 80 percent. It is likely that for these countries, namely, Guatemala, Panama, and Paraguay, privatization was not needed as much as in other Latin American countries. Finally, a comparison with the Asian NICs reveals that, for the Latin America and Caribbean region on average, private-sector participation in investment is still below that of the NICs.[34] The difference in this respect between the two groups of countries (five percentage points on average in the 1990s) is larger than it seems because, in general, the productivity of *public* investment is much greater in the Asian NICs than in Latin American countries.

2. Indicators on the efficiency of revenue generation

Clearly, the ability of the state to undertake an expenditure program without incurring an unmanageable deficit depends on efficient revenue generation. Latin American countries have relied excessively on trade taxes and seigniorage through money creation to finance their spending programs. High tax rates coupled with a weak tax administration induced many firms to become part of the informal sector. This undermined the ability of the state to generate revenues from income and domestic sales taxes, prompting the state to obtain revenues through both the inflation tax and taxes on imports and exports, which can be more easily monitored. In the late 1980s, many countries reformed taxes to diminish the distortionary effects of taxation and to increase revenue, thus allowing trade liberalization and disinflationary policies and reducing the tax burden on the formal sector.

The specific measures of tax reform varied across countries but had in common the following three principles: first, tax-rate unification and lower marginal rates; second, de-emphasis of steeply progressive rate structures of income and property taxes in favor of broadly based, low-rate taxes on domestic consumption, such as the VAT; and, third, strengthening of the tax administration.[35]

FIGURE 2.14

FIGURE 2.14
Total Tax Revenue as a Percentage of GDP

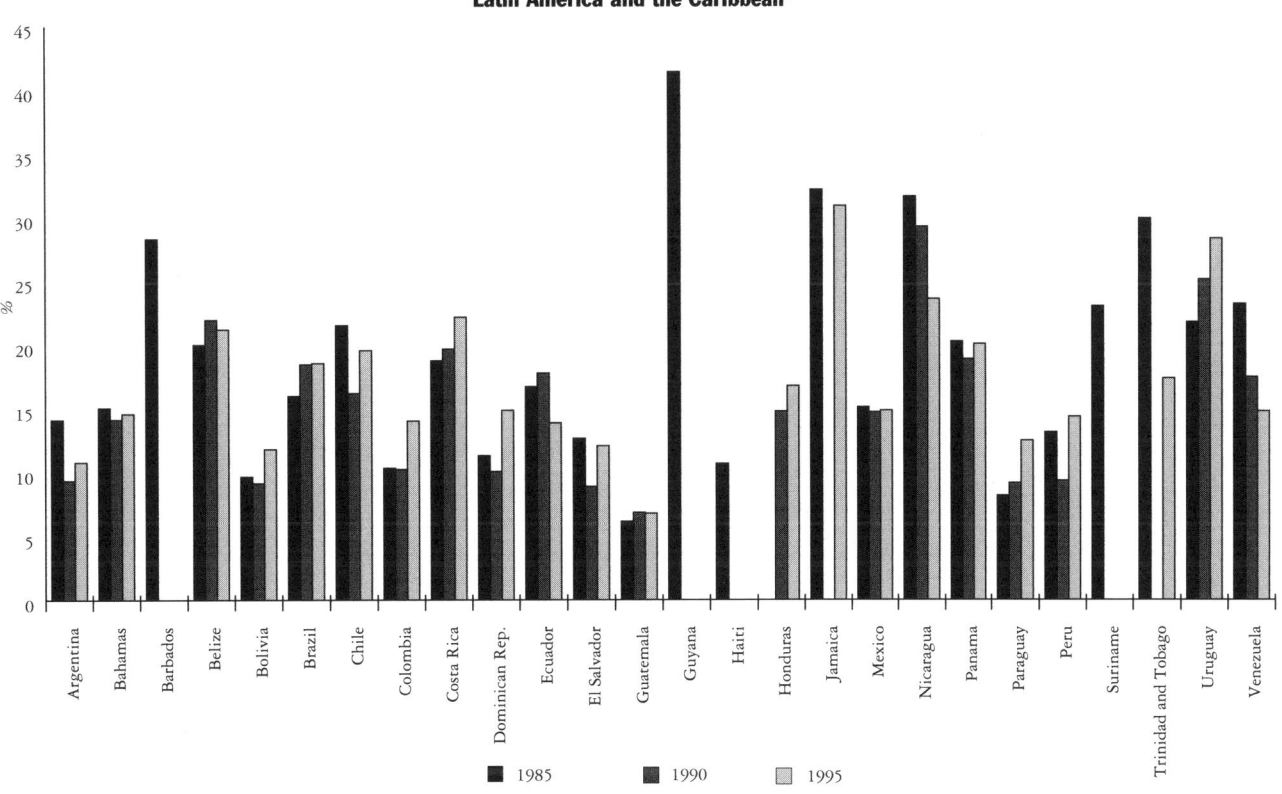

Total Tax Revenue as a Percentage of GDP

Latin America and the Caribbean[1]

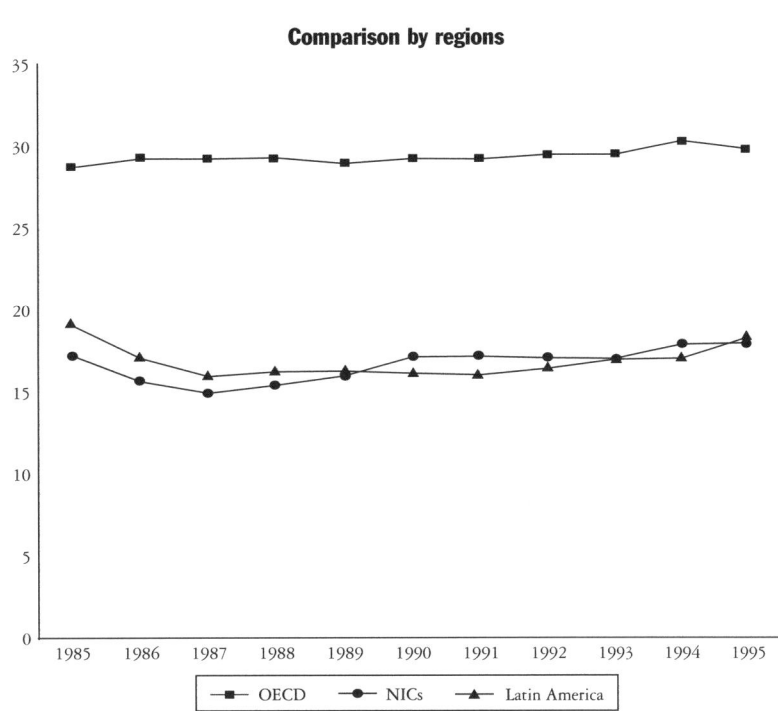

Comparison by regions

Source: Staff estimations based on Government Finance Statistics, IMF; World Development Indicators Database, World Bank.

Estimation: Consolidated central government tax revenue except for Belize, Ecuador, El Salvador, Guatemala, and Trinidad and Tobago, for which budgetary central government figures were used.

[1]Figures for 1995 correspond to latest years where data was available.

FIGURE 2.15

Trade Taxes as a Percentage of Total Tax Revenue

Trade Taxes as a Percentage of Total Tax Revenue

Latin America and the Caribbean[1]

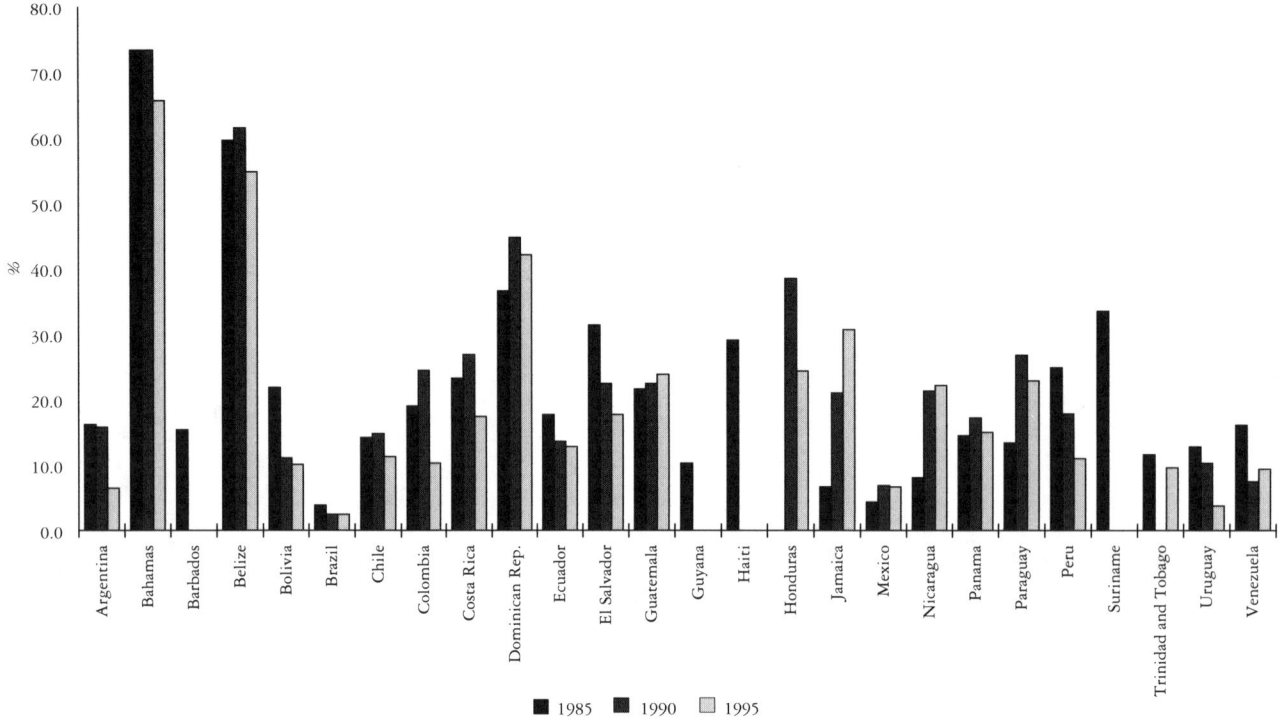

■ 1985   ■ 1990   □ 1995

Comparison by regions

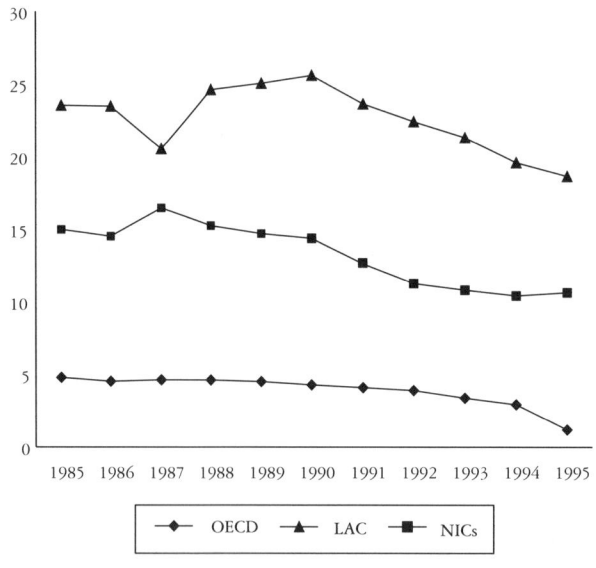

◆ OECD   ▲ LAC   ■ NICs

Source: Staff estimations based on Government Finance Statistics, IMF; Staff Reports, IMF; World Development Indicators Database, World Bank.

Estimation: Consolidated central government tax revenue except for Belize, Ecuador, El Salvador, Guatemala, and Trinidad and Tobago, for which budgetary central government figures were used.

[1]Figures for 1995 reflect latest years where data was available.

In evaluating the efficiency of revenue generation, it is informative to consider the variables that, as outcome indicators, best capture the purposes of tax reform. An increase in the *ratio of tax revenues to GDP* measures, to some extent, the success in raising revenues through noninflationary means; the *ratio of international trade taxes to total tax revenues* evaluates the reliance on the type of taxation that distorts the country's trade position; and, finally, the *VAT revenue productivity ratio* measures the comprehensiveness of the VAT and the strength of the tax administration.[36]

Tax revenue as a ratio to GDP signals government's reliance on taxes, as opposed to debt accumulation, money creation, or transfers from public enterprises, as a way to finance its expenditures. It can not be said, however, that a higher tax-revenue ratio is always better. There is in principle an "optimal" tax rate in which the productivity-enhancing effect of tax-financed public goods just compensates for the negative effect of the tax burden on the economy's net rate of return. The ideal indicator is, therefore, the difference between actual and optimal tax ratios. The determination of this optimal tax ratio for a given country is difficult in practice. Even more difficult is to compare optimal rates across countries, given that an optimal rate's determinants—namely, the efficiency of tax-financed public goods, the extent to which government consumption substitutes for private consumption, and the strength of the tax administration—vary substantially from country to country.

FIGURE 2.16

Adjusted VAT Revenue Productivity Ratio

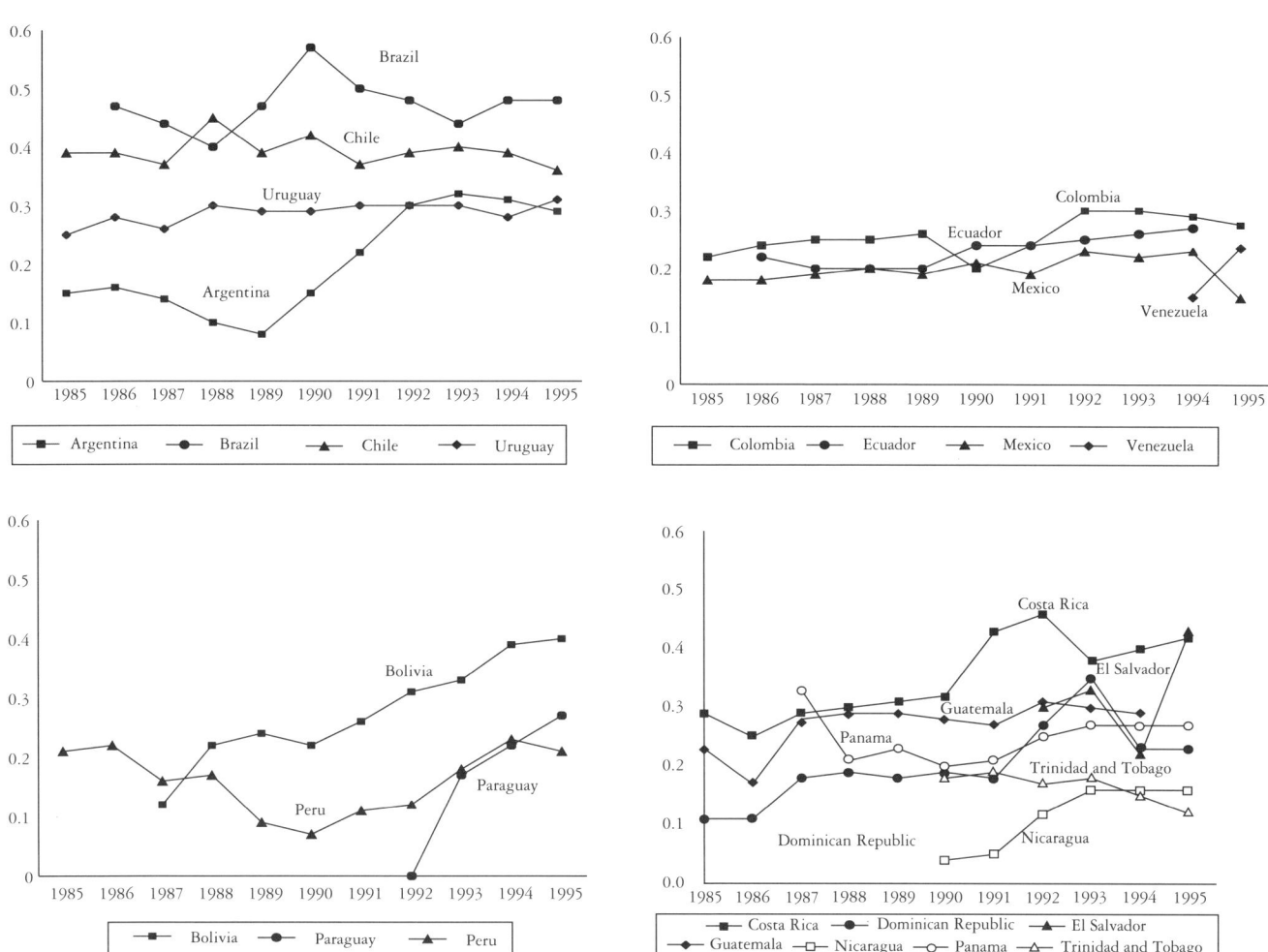

Source: Staff calculations based on IDB, 1996; and International Financial Statistics Database, IMF.
Estimation: VAT revenue productivity ratio minus 0.0025 times the ratio of imports to GDP. The coefficient (0.0025) was estimated in a regression of VAT productivity on the ratio of imports to GDP and a constant.

TABLE 2.7

VAT Indicators for Selected Countries

COUNTRY	YEAR	VAT REVENUE PRODUCTIVITY	VAT TO GDP RATIO	NUMBER OF VAT RATES	AVERAGE VAT RATES
Portugal	1991	0.7	6.4	3.0	9.0
New Zealand	1992–93	0.7	8.4	1.0	12.5
Israel	1992	0.5	9.7	1.0	18.0
S. Africa	1992–93	0.5	5.2	1.0	10.0
Spain	1989	0.5	5.4	4.0	10.5
Chile	1991	0.5	8.8	1.0	18.5
Hungary	1991	0.4	6.1	2.0	14.0
Honduras	1992	0.4	3.1	2.0	7.3
Guatemala	1992	0.4	2.5	1.0	7.0
Panama	1991	0.4	1.8	1.0	5.0
Sweden	1992	0.4	8.0	2.0	23.2
Uruguay	1991	0.3	7.4	2.0	21.6
Argentina	1992	0.3	5.9	1.0	18.0
Canada	1991	0.3	2.2	1.0	7.0
Ecuador	1991	0.3	3.1	1.0	10.0
Mexico	1992	0.3	3.0	1.0	10.0
Bolivia	1990	0.3	3.1	1.0	11.1
Philippines	1992	0.2	2.4	1.0	10.0
Colombia	1991	0.2	2.4	5.0	12.2
Peru	1992	0.2	3.1	1.0	18.0
Average		**0.4**	**4.9**	**1.7**	**12.6**

Source: Silvani and Brondolo (1992).

Although cross-country comparisons are difficult in this respect, the demands on most modern states are such that countries whose tax revenues are below 10 percent of GDP are quite likely to run into financing difficulties. Figure 2.14 shows that several countries in the region found themselves in that predicament around 1990. They were Argentina, Bolivia, Colombia, the Dominican Republic, El Salvador, Guatemala, Paraguay, and Peru. By 1994, however, all countries except Guatemala had a tax-revenue ratio of above 10 percent, with most countries in the region approaching ratios of 15 percent to 20 percent, which, revealingly, are quite similar to the average of the Asian NICs. Nicaragua is an interesting example of a country for which an improvement in tax policy actually meant a decrease in tax revenues relative to GDP from a high level of 32 percent in the mid-1980s to a more moderate 23.6 percent of GDP in 1995.

The behavior of the *ratio of international trade taxes to total tax revenue* also reveals a positive development for the region. A stylized fact revealed by cross-country studies is that as countries develop, international trade taxes represent a smaller share of tax revenues.[37] Largely motivated by tax and trade reforms, this drop in international trade taxes seems to be the Latin American trend in recent years. As Figure 2.15 shows, despite large increases in the volume of trade in most countries, their respective trade tax shares show a decreasing trend, with the exceptions of Guatemala, Jamaica, and Nicaragua. A comparison across countries reveals, not surprisingly, that the countries relying most heavily on trade taxes tend to be those that, because of their small size and location, are more open to international trade. Even including those countries, the share of trade taxes in total tax revenue fell on average for Latin America and the Caribbean below 20 percent; this is a remarkable achievement, especially considering that it did not weaken the countries' fiscal stance. It must be noted, however, that the regional average for the trade-tax share of total taxes is almost eight percentage points higher than that of the Asian NICs.

The *productivity rate of the value-added tax* is arguably the most important indicator of the efficiency of revenue generation in the region. It measures, in part, the success of the recently adopted tax system, for which the VAT is the centerpiece. In a context of weak tax administration, the VAT, with its self-monitoring feature, has become the best option for revenue generation with limited distortions. Its achievements as a revenue generator have allowed the easing of the tax burden on the formal corporate sector and the reduction of trade tax rates. The VAT revenue-productivity ratio contains information on two aspects of the VAT system: the coverage of the VAT, in terms of the share of national expenditure included in the system; and the strength and efficacy of the tax administration in preventing tax evasion. Furthermore, the VAT productivity rate indicates the ability of the state to raise additional revenues from taxes when needed.

Figure 2.16 presents a *trade-adjusted* VAT revenue-productivity rate. Given that imported goods, included in virtually all VAT systems, are the easiest to monitor, an increase in imports relative to GDP will be surely reflected in a higher VAT productivity ratio. In order to analyze the effects of improved tax enforcement or an expansion of VAT coverage on domestic expenditure, which is the purpose of this section, it is necessary to control for the changes in the revenue-productivity ratio explained by import growth.[38] In most countries, especially since 1990, this productivity rate has increased, particularly in Argentina, Bolivia, Costa Rica, Paraguay, and Peru. The recently established VAT systems in El Salvador, Nicaragua, and Venezuela also show remarkable progress with respect to their status at inception. For many countries, however, there is much room for further progress, given that only a few countries (Brazil, Chile, Bolivia, Paraguay, El Salvador, and Guatemala) have achieved trade-adjusted VAT productivity rates of over 40 percent.

Table 2.7 compares VAT revenue-productivity ratios, along with information on tax and collection rates, in a sample of countries from different regions. It shows that even mature tax systems, which mostly rely on income taxes, present VAT revenue-productivity ratios that vary between 0.3 (Canada) and 0.7 (New Zealand and Portugal).

E. Governance

A growing body of literature points to the importance of public institutions and services in originating and implementing welfare-enhancing economic policy. The state can potentially provide the private sector with an environment in which property rights are respected, legal contracts are enforced, and government regulations, rather than complicating business transactions, correct market imperfections. This requires not only a government with enlightened policies, but also one with the ability to implement such policies efficiently and credibly.

There are various interrelated mechanisms through which good governance can affect economic performance. First, the state can act as an efficient protector and guarantor of property and contractual rights. When these rights are infringed, investment decreases sharply and tends to focus wastefully on small and short-term projects in which the need for property and contractual rights is lower.[39] The state can fulfill the role of protector of property rights by having a body of laws and regulations designed to advocate credibly those rights and an autonomous and strong judicial system in charge of supporting and enforcing those laws. Second, the government administration can adequately pro-

vide public services, including making decisions about the types and locations of public infrastructure projects and the awarding of contracts and licenses; protecting public spaces, including the environment; providing a safety net for the poor; and offering police protection for the public. Public institutions can ameliorate adverse social or economic conditions by planning appropriate policies and implementing them effectively. For instance, properly run public institutions can diminish the harmful effects of ethnic conflict and can help disadvantaged people escape the poverty traps of lack of education and health care.[40]

These high responsibilities for government can be achieved only when the public administration behaves both efficiently and honestly. Corruption in government, especially of officials with decision-making power, is detrimental to social welfare because it makes the state pursue public policies and programs that benefit certain groups rather than society in general and because it encourages wasteful rent-seeking activities.[41] Corruption of high-ranking officials is mostly due to both a lack of proper monitoring and clear accountability rules. It must be recognized, however, that corruption among lower ranks of the bureaucracy is linked not only to their ethical strength or the lack of proper monitoring, but most importantly, to the lack of procedural clarity, the complexity of bureaucratic requirements, the imposition of overly restrictive regulations, and excessively high rates of taxes, tariffs, and other public charges.

Good governance is difficult to measure objectively. When analyzing the success of public policies, it is quite hard to isolate the share due to good governance. There is, however, the possibility of assessing the quality of public institutions and services by the way they are perceived by businessmen and economic and political consultants, who deal with various government branches on a daily basis. These subjective indicators are collected by a handful of international agencies, and then sold to prospective international investors. Most of the papers cited above have, in fact, used these subjective indicators as measures of good governance.

This section makes use of the information provided by two independent country-risk evaluators, *International Country Risk Guide* (ICRG) and *Business Environment Risk Index* (BERI), which present ratings for various aspects of governance. The ICRG provides ratings on five variables, including the *rule of law*, measuring the extent to which

FIGURE 2.17
Government Indices

BERI Index

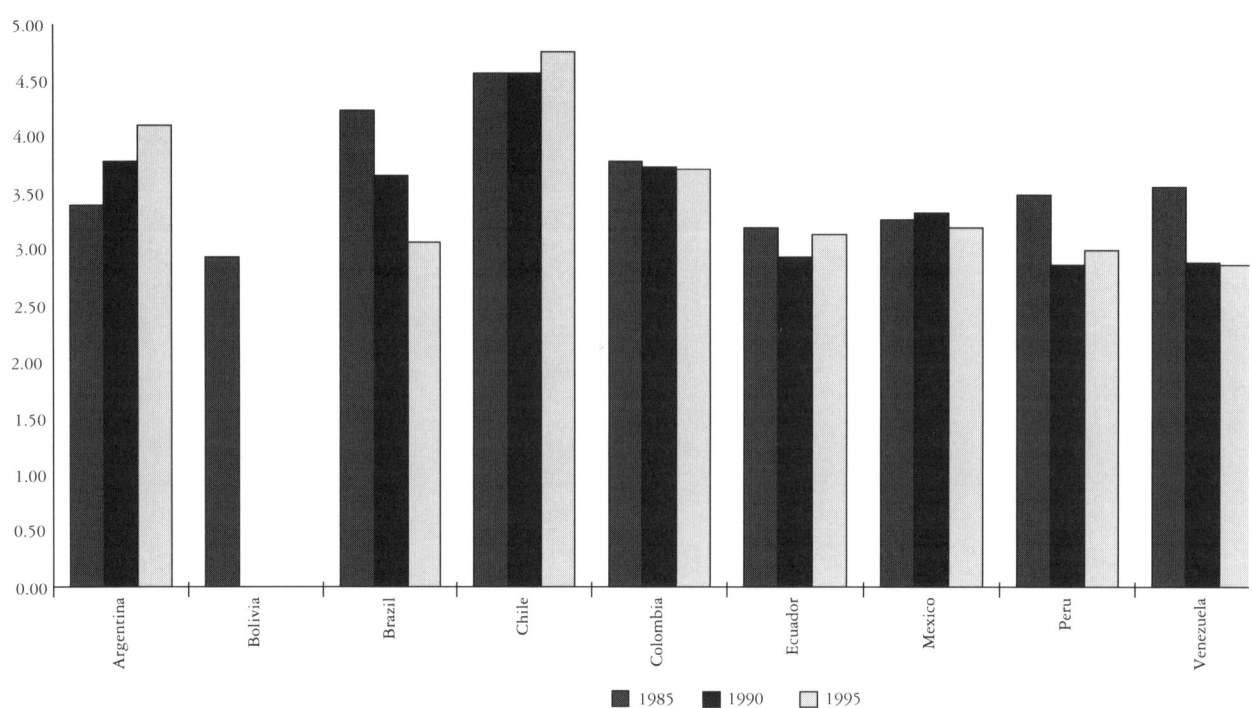

ICRG Index

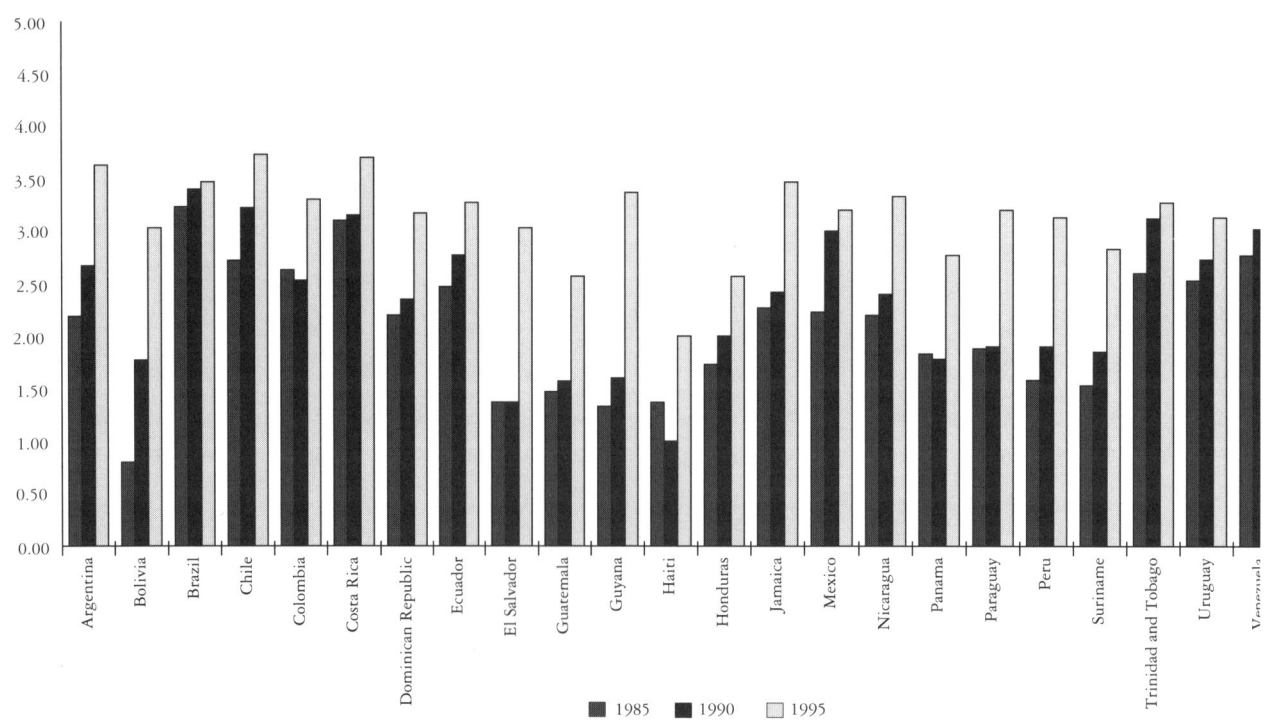

FIGURE 2.17 (continues)

Regional Indices

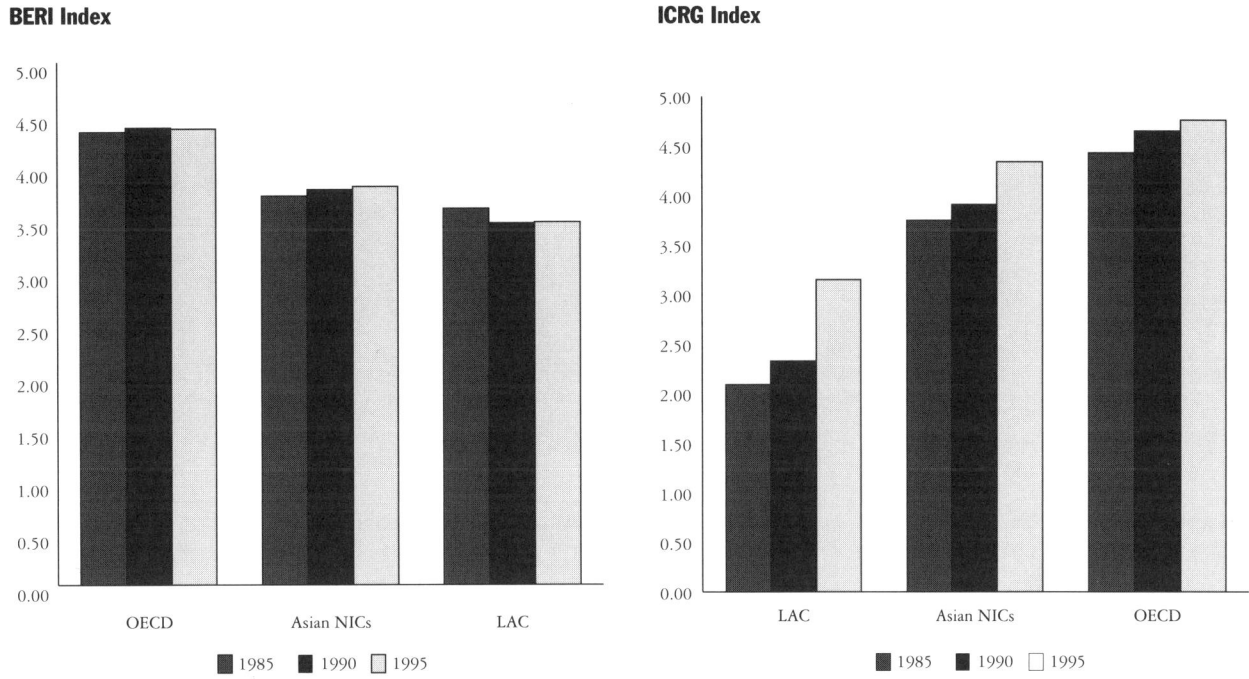

BERI Index

ICRG Index

Source: International Country Risk Guide and Business Environmental Risk Intelligence. Higher score means better governance.

Estimation: ICRG Index includes indicators on: repudiation of contracts, expropriation of private investment, law-and-order tradition, quality of the bureacracy, corruption in government. BERI Index includes indicators on: bureaucratic delays, contract enforeceability, and nationalization risk.

there are mechanisms for peaceful dispute resolution; *expropriation risk,* assessing the risk of nationalization of enterprise equity; and *repudiation of contracts by government,* measuring the state's commitment to fulfill its contractual obligations and proxying for its ability to enforce contracts between private-sector agents. It also analyzes *corruption in government,* evaluating the extent to which bribes to public officials are needed to expedite bureaucratic requirements, to circumvent regulations, to force a change in policy to benefit a given interest group, or to obtain public contracts without a lawful bidding process; and *quality of the bureaucracy,* evaluating both procedural clarity and the technical competence of government officials. Although in principle these ratings measure different aspects of governance, in practice they are highly correlated. Because of this, an overall index is presented here. This index is based on the simple average of the ratings for the five variables. A similar procedure is used with the BERI ratings, which consist of three underlying variables: *enforceability of contracts, nationalization risk,* and *bureaucratic delays.*

The ICRG and BERI indices presented below provide information related to two aspects of good governance. The first is the quality of public institutions (evaluated by the variables *corruption in government* and *quality of the bureaucracy/bureaucratic delays*), which describes the ability of the state to implement its policies through both an appropriate structure of government and honest and technically competent bureaucrats. The second is the quality of public services (evaluated by the variables *rule of law, enforceability of contracts/repudiation of contracts by government,* and *expropriation/nationalization risk*), which determine an environment where contractual obligations are respected both by the state and private agents, where legal disputes are effectively resolved in the judicial system, and where legal rules for investment, employment, and taxation are not arbitrarily modified by the state.

The BERI Index (see Figure 2.17, left panel) shows that Argentina, Chile, Ecuador, and Peru made some progress in the area of governance from 1990 to 1995. For the latter two countries, this meant a recovery toward their 1985

FIGURE 2.18

ICRG Governance Indicators

Repudiation of Contracts

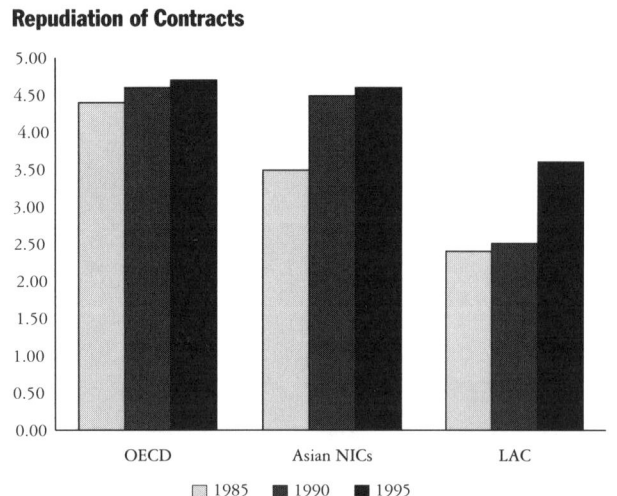

Risk of Expropriation

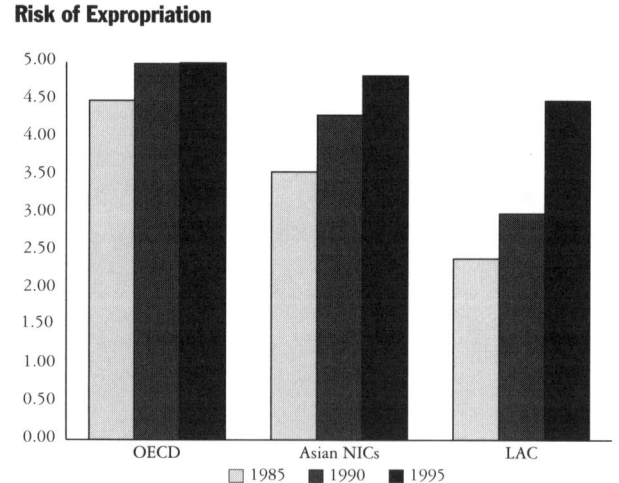

Law-and-Order Tradition

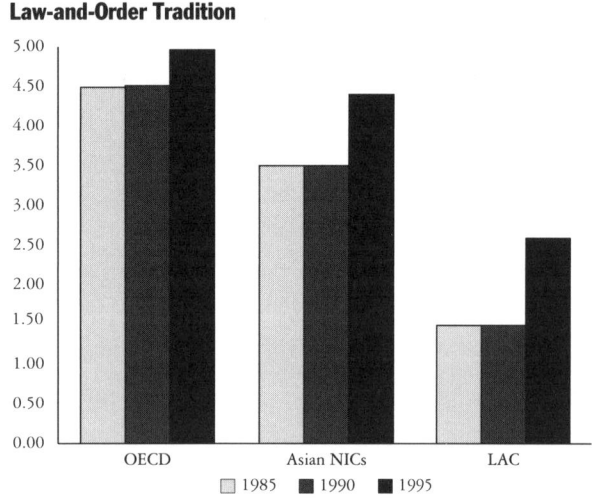

Quality of the Bureaucracy

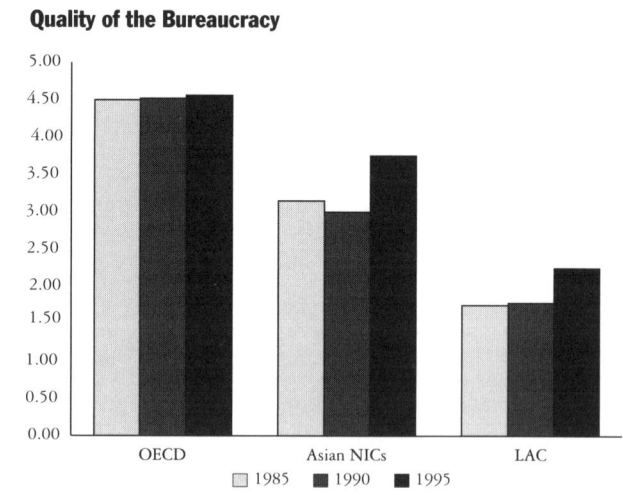

Corruption in Government

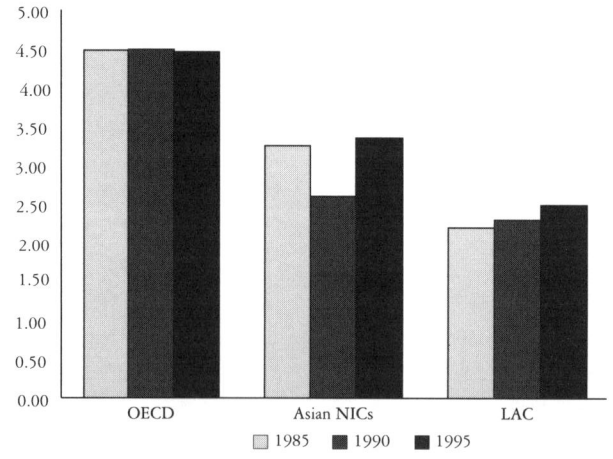

Source: International Country Risk Guide. Higher score means better governance.

level after a fall in the late 1980s. By contrast, governance in Brazil and Venezuela worsened substantially in the same period. In cross-country comparisons, according to BERI, Chile is clearly above all other Latin American countries in the sample, approaching the high level of governance of the OECD and Asian NICs.

The ICRG Index (see Figure 2.18, right panel) presents a more optimistic picture of progress in governance in Latin America and the Caribbean.[42] Although, in general, there are signs of improvement between 1985 and 1990 (especially in Argentina, Bolivia, Chile, and Mexico), outstanding progress only occurs in most countries between 1990 and 1995. The countries of Bolivia, El Salvador, Guyana, and Peru experienced an improvement in governance that is particularly remarkable given their low ratings in the mid-1980s. Of the larger countries, only Brazil, Mexico, and Venezuela present little progress in the same period. According to ICRG, from 1990 to 1995, the region's governance index improved on average by 35 percent. However, despite this general improvement, closer examination of the underlying indicators of the ICRG governance index (see Figure 2.18) reveals that, by 1995, Latin America remained well below the Asian NICs and OECD countries. This gap is particularly large in the area of the rule of law (judicial and police systems) and in the quality of public administration (technical competence and honesty of the bureaucracy, as well as procedural clarity). The difference between Latin America, Asian NICs, and OECD countries is smaller with regard to the risk of nationalization of enterprise equity.

F. Concluding Remarks

The purpose of this chapter has been to examine the experience of structural reform in Latin America and the Caribbean in five areas of economic activity, namely,: international trade, financial markets, labor markets, generation and use of public resources, and governance. The methodological approach used in the study consists of developing quantitative indicators for the corresponding policy reforms and/or their respective outcomes. The result is an empirical characterization of the region's structural reform.

Although the processes of structural reform throughout the region have shared the same principles, both the time of initiation and the depth and content of the reform process have varied from country to country. Similarly, the region as whole has advanced in certain reform areas more than in others.

To review the region's structural reforms in the order of most successful to least successful, one must start with *trade liberalization*. It is in this area that reform has been the deepest and most generalized in the region; in fact, in terms of reducing policy restrictions on trade, the region has come quite close to the Asian NICs. Much has also been accomplished in the areas of *financial development*, particularly in terms of the depth of financial intermediation, of private-sector participation in banking, of the size and activity of stock markets, and of *efficient generation and use of public resources*, notably in terms of the efficiency of the VAT system and the privatization of public enterprises. Reform gains in the area of *governance* have been more modest. In this respect, Latin America remains well behind the Asian NICs and OECD countries, especially concerning the rule of law (judicial and police systems) and the quality of the public administration (the technical competence and honesty of the bureaucracy, as well as procedural clarity). *Labor market reform* is the area of structural reform where the least progress has been made in the region. In most countries, there are still severe constraints on the hiring and dismissal of workers, high payroll tax rates, a lack of mechanisms for nondisruptive labor dispute resolution, and a prevalence of public employment in the economy.

Latin America suffered for several decades from mistaken public policies and weak public institutions, which induced profound distortions in the formation and allocation of physical capital and human talent, and gradually eroded overall efficiency. These deep distortions make it costly and even painful to implement structural reforms (and thus, to alter the modes of production and the system of economic incentives). At the same time, these reforms have the potential to raise substantially the living standards of most people in the economy. There is indeed some evidence that the reforms initiated in most countries in the late 1980s have already borne fruit in terms of improved growth performance. This, however, should not allow anyone to forget that economic reform is a long and arduous process, which requires both political will and social sensibility from the government to be successfully fulfilled.[43]

Notes to Chapter II

1. In this document, the terms "Latin America" and "Latin America and the Caribbean" are used interchangeably.

2. See Balassa (1985), Edwards (1992, 1995), Dollar (1992), and Harrison (1997).

3. See Lederman (1996).

4. See Harrison (1996), and Easterly, Loayza, and Montiel (1996).

5. See Edwards (1995).

6. See Pritchett and Sethi (1993). Actually, the weights are given by the respective shares in total imports of some 120 developing countries in 1985 (see UNCTAD, 1994). Using the country's own import shares as weights leads to an underestimation of the tariff (or quantitative restriction) because these shares are negatively affected by the restrictions.

7. UNCTAD (1994).

8. The methodology used to construct these indices, as well as most indices in this document, is the following. The index is a weighted average of the principal components of its corresponding indicators, in which the weights are given by the share of the indicators' variance explained by each principal component. See Theil (1971), and Demetriades and Luintel (1996).

9. See Edwards (1995).

10. The terms "trade intensity" and "volume of trade as a share to GDP" are used as synonymous with the ratio of real exports plus real imports to real GDP.

11. The black market premium on foreign exchange has also been used in the literature as a proxy for overall price distortions. See Barro (1991).

12. Real, rather than nominal, exports and imports are used in order to abstract from the effect of real exchange rate appreciations on trade measures.

13. Clearly, those countries that were already quite open at the start of the period would also tend to show little change in their volume of trade relative to GDP.

14. As members of the Andean Pact, Colombia, Ecuador, and Venezuela have featured a similar trade regime since the early 1990s.

15. Chenery and Syrquin (1975 and 1989), and Pritchett (1996a).

16. See Levine (1997).

17. See McKinnon (1973), Atje and Jovanovic (1993), Demirguc-Kunt and Levine (1996), Hubbard, Kashyap, and Whited (1995), King and Levine (1993), and Roubini and Sala-i-Martin (1992).

18. See La Porta, Lopez de Silanes, Shleiffer, and Vishny (1996).

19. Of course, the decomposition of any economic variable into its permanent and transitory components is far from trivial. No formal decomposition technique is used in this chapter.

20. The end-of-year nominal quasi-liquid liabilities are deflated by the end-of-year consumer price index (CPI), and nominal GDP is deflated by the yearly average CPI. This deflation is an important correction to the usual practice of taking the ratio of end-of-year liquid liabilities to nominal GDP, practice that renders an artificially high ratio for high inflation countries/periods. In this document, the same deflation procedure is used when dealing with ratios of any end-of-year stock measure (for example, a monetary or capital market aggregate) to a flow measure (for example, GDP).

21. This is the best proxy that is readily available. Clearly, however, it is not perfect. In some countries, notably Brazil, deposit money banks are not completely private but include state-owned commercial banks. Also, this indicator does not consider credit provided by private financial institutions other than deposit banks, credit that may be large in some countries.

22. Regional averages must be analyzed with caution because they mask differences in trends and levels across countries in the region. However, it must be noted that in Latin America, the intraregional dispersion of most indicators, measured by their respective annual standard deviation over the region, has been decreasing in the 1990s.

23. Clearly, labor market flexibility depends also on factors other than regulations. For example, it also depends on the level of education of the labor force, whether firms have proper training mechanisms, and whether technologies across different sectors are similar.

24. See Harris and Todaro (1970), and Fields (1990).

25. See Loayza (1994).

26. An important group of labor-market distortion indicators, not considered in this document for lack of comparable information across countries, refers to the relations between labor and the management of a firm. This would consider issues such as how decentralized and flexible collective bargaining is and whether the government stays out of the negotiation process. It would also analyze how efficient unions are in advocating workers' rights by considering whether labor legislation allows workers, at least in principle, to choose their own union; the freedom to make this choice would generate more efficient worker representation through improved competition, or at least the contestability, of unions.

27. This indicator may also vary as a result of events unrelated to the lack of proper dispute-resolution mechanisms. For example, it could increase in times of political unrest or macroeconomic shocks. At any rate, the fact that strikes can be used as means of political protest reveals excessive union power.

28. See World Bank (1995c).

29. See Rama (1997).

30. Burki and Edwards (1996).

31. The distinction made between appropriate government institutions and policies for proper management of public resources is conceptual, and thus, artificial. The distinction is made here for the ease of exposition and to provide emphasis on different aspects of reform in the public sector.

32. See Barro and Sala-i-Martin (1995), Barro and Lee (1994), Caselli, Esquivel, and Lefort (1996), and Easterly, Loayza, and Montiel (1997).

33. Edwards (1995).

34. Comparison with OECD countries is problematic, given that the available investment figures for this group of countries do not disaggregate corporate investment into its public and private components. Therefore, the "private" investment figures reported for OECD countries in the text and in the appendix include public enterprise investment.

35. See Shome (1992).

36. The VAT revenue-productivity ratio is defined as the ratio of VAT revenues over GDP to the average VAT rate.

37. See Easterly and Rebelo (1993).

38. It must be noted, however, that the simple and trade-adjusted VAT revenue-productivity ratios are very similar to each other; in fact, their correlation coefficient is 0.94.

39. See Knack and Keefer (1995, 1997).

STRUCTURAL REFORM AND ECONOMIC PROGRESS

40. See Easterly and Levine (1996).

41. See Mauro (1995).

42. A note of caution: The optimistic assessment of this rating agency must be viewed with prudence, for there exists the possibility that, despite its efforts to be accurate, reforms in other areas and the ensuing stronger economic investment and growth could be confused with improvements in governance, properly defined. A conservative measure of progress in governance in Latin American countries should be between BERI's and ICRG's assessments.

43. See Easterly, Loayza, and Montiel (1997), Fernandez-Arias and Montiel (1997), and Barrera and Lora (1997).

III
Strategic Priorities for Accelerating Growth

EVEN THOUGH LATIN AMERICA AND THE CARIBBEAN HAS EXPERIENCED AN ECONOMIC recovery during the 1990s, that recovery is still clearly below what is needed to bring about a sharp reduction in the high poverty indices of most countries in the region. An important question, then, is whether LAC will be able to achieve high and sustainable growth rates—above 6 percent annually—as have the high-performing East Asian countries. Chile's track record during the last decade has proven to the rest of the region that such a goal is attainable, even if it is not a foregone conclusion. Hence the real question is: What does it take to get there? This chapter addresses this fundamental question.

Building on the analyses in the previous chapters, the following section briefly assesses the region's growth experience in recent years, especially since the onset of the Mexican peso crisis of December 1994. It also summarily discusses the effects of the economic policy reforms that have been implemented in LAC since the late 1980s. Section B identifies five challenges that the region can meet to achieve high and sustainable growth rates. These challenges focus on key policy areas for the future, including the need to consolidate the region's gains in macroeconomic stability, which was discussed in Chapter 1. Sections C through F discuss in detail the other four strategic priorities and illustrate how they apply to the different subregions of LAC.

A. LAC's Growth in the 1990s

The region experienced an annual rate of growth of approximately 3.2 percent (GDP-weighted mean) between 1991 and 1996, compared with 1.9 percent during 1980–90. (See Table 1.3 in Chapter 1). Due to the Mexican peso crisis of December 1994 and its contagion effect on Argentina, the region as whole experienced a disappoint-

ing growth rate of 0.9 percent (GDP-weighted) in 1995. If we exclude Mexico and Argentina, however, the rest of the region grew at a moderate 4.3 percent. In 1996, Mexico and Argentina experienced significant recoveries, but most of the countries that had grown rapidly in 1995, such as Brazil, Colombia, Peru, and El Salvador, experienced slowdowns. Most countries grew in 1996 at a moderate rate, between 3 percent and 4 percent, and the region's GDP-weighted average was 3.5 percent and the median rate was 3.1 percent. Only Chile and Guyana experienced growth rates above 6 percent, and only Venezuela had a contraction of output in 1996.

Although it is too early to reach a final judgment about the long-term effects of economic policy reforms in LAC, our analysis at the World Bank leads us to believe that they are indeed paying off. Comparisons with the past must be made in per capita terms, and with respect to the rest of the world economy, because LAC growth depends significantly on the performance of world markets.[1] As shown in Figure 3.1, the average per capita growth rate in LAC in the early 1990s (up to 1995) was much higher than in the 1980s. It is particularly noteworthy that in the postreform period

FIGURE 3.1
Per Capita Growth Rates by Region
(annual averages by five-year periods)

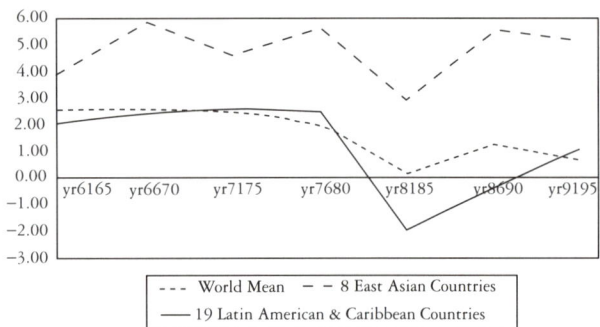

Source: World Bank, International Economics Department Database.

(1991–95), real income per person in the LAC region grew faster than it had during the mid-1980s (1986–90), when the world economy was growing much faster.

Perhaps more important, the improvement in per capita growth rates seems to be largely explained by the positive effects of the region's economic reforms. Recent econometric research conducted at the World Bank and the Inter-American Development Bank has measured the positive effects of the reforms on growth. Table 3.1 shows the results from three newly available studies that measured the increases in the growth rate of LAC's income per capita that can be attributed to the reforms, including macroeconomic stabilization and structural reforms. The consensus seems to be that the package of reforms raised the region's average per capita growth rate by almost two percentage points.

These economic reforms had an important positive effect on domestic investment, on inflows of foreign direct investment, and on export growth. The average annual rate

TABLE 3.1
The Impact of Economic Reforms on LAC's Growth Rates
(percentage change of GDP per capita growth, simple averages)

STUDY	TOTAL IMPACT OF REFORMS	PERMANENT COMPONENT	TRANSITORY COMPONENT
ELM	n.a.	+1.9	considered but not measured
LB	+3.7	+1.6	+2.1
FAM	+1.95	+1.88	+0.07

n.a. = not applicable

ELM = Easterly, Loayza and Montiel (1997)
LB = Lora and Barrera (1997)
FAM = Fernandez-Arias and Montiel (1997)

Sources: ELM, table 4; LB, table 3; FAM, table 2.

of growth of gross domestic investment, measured in constant prices, was 6 percent during 1991–95. This represented a remarkable improvement over the growth rates of GDI during 1980–85 and 1986–89, when the corresponding average annual rates were – 2.1 percent and +2.1 percent, respectively (see Table 3.2). Furthermore, net FDI flows to LAC have risen steadily in the 1990s, from US$8.1 billion in 1990 to a record high of US$21.6 billion in 1996 (see Table 1.2, Chapter 1). Export growth for LAC in the first half of the 1990s was twice as fast as it had been during the 1980s, despite the fact that world trade did not accelerate until 1994–95 (see Table 3.3). Indeed, the full benefits of increased macroeconomic stability, of greater international competition and capital flows, and of the new opportunities for private-sector development, especially in the infrastructure sectors, have probably yet to be felt. These considerations, together with an expected improvement in the growth rate of the world economy, lead us to forecast a growth rate for the LAC region of slightly more

TABLE 3.2
Growth of Gross Domestic Investment in LAC, 1980–1995
(average annual growth rates)

COUNTRY NAME	1980–85	1986–90	1991–95
Argentina	−7.6	−1.3	15.4
Belize	−1.6	18.6	3.5
Bolivia	−18.0	5.7	4.9
Brazil	−2.0	2.0	3.4
Chile	9.0	14.3	12.0
Colombia	2.0	2.6	16.9
Costa Rica	−0.7	8.2	5.3
Dominican Republic	−1.9	7.3	4.4
Ecuador	−2.8	−3.2	7.8
El Salvador	−10.7	9.0	15.1
Guatemala	−8.1	6.2	11.7
Guyana	−12.8	−1.7	7.2
Haiti	3.0	−4.5	−36.7
Honduras	−3.9	7.4	9.9
Jamaica	−0.4	2.1	5.1
Mexico	0.4	2.6	−1.8
Nicaragua	−55.8	−11.8	5.5
Paraguay	1.9	6.7	3.8
Peru	−0.2	6.8	6.8
Trinidad and Tobago	0.2	−14.6	5.5
Uruguay	−14.3	3.9	13.4
Venezuela	−3.6	−5.3	17.6
Mean	−5.9	2.8	6.3
GDP-Weighted Mean	−2.1	2.1	6.0

Source: World Bank, World Development Indicators Database.
Note: GDI in local currency, 1987 prices.

TABLE 3.3

World Merchandise Trade, 1981–1995

(average annual growth rates of trade *volumes,* percentages)

COUNTRY NAME	1981–90	1991–93	1994–95
World Trade Growth*	4.1	4.0	9.2
Export Growth			
LAC	4.4	9.3	8.8
East Asia	9.3	14.1	17.4
South Asia	5.6	10.8	10.1
East Europe	−0.5	−3.8	10.2
OECD	4.6	2.9	8.1
Import Growth			
LAC	−0.3	16.3	3.9
East Asia	7.0	14.6	16.7
South Asia	4.2	5.5	14.9
East Europe	0.7	-5.2	5.4
OECD	4.8	1.8	9.0

*growth rate of the sum of merchandise export and import volumes.
Source: World Bank (1996c, Table 1–5, p. 14).

than 4 percent for 1997, greater than 4.5 percent during 1997–2000, and higher than 5 percent in the first five years of the twenty-first century.

B. Strategic Priorities for Accelerating Growth in LAC

Based on the evidence that was presented in Chapter 2, which analyzed various indicators of progress in economic policy reform, we have no doubt that to sustain growth rates above 6 percent over time, much more must be done—there is no room for complacency. We have identified five strategic areas, including *the consolidation of macroeconomic stability,* which was discussed in Chapter 1. The other four areas are

1. promoting quality investment in human development,
2. accelerating the region's financial development,
3. improving the legal and regulatory environment for private-sector development, and
4. enhancing public-sector efficiency and governance.

There are obvious complementarities and interactions among the efforts in these key areas. For instance, improving the quality of education services requires reforms in the public sector. Similarly, fiscal strengthening and effective regulation of capital markets require efficient and well-governed public sectors. In general, it is clear that institutional modernization is an important ingredient for improving the quality of investment in human development, for strengthening fiscal policies, and for developing healthy financial sectors.

The choice of these strategic areas is inspired both by economic theories and empirical studies of the sources of economic growth, as well as by the fact that, in these areas, LAC countries are seriously lagging behind the industrialized countries of the Organization for Economic Cooperation and Development and the fast-growing East Asian economies, as was made evident in Chapter 2.

In general, growth rates are determined by the rate of change in the level of both physical and human capital and by the efficiency or productivity of these two factors of production.[2] Hence we can address the need to move forward in these priority areas by acknowledging that improvements in these areas will affect the level and efficiency of human and physical capital, and that the present levels of achievement in these areas in LAC countries lag behind those of more advanced or fast-growing economies.

Physical capital is accumulated through investment. Although investment rates in LAC have increased during the 1990s, they are still well below those of the fast-growing East Asian countries. Tables 3.4 and 3.5 show that investment rates (the ratio of GDI to GDP) in the large LAC economies are below 20 percent (except in Chile),

TABLE 3.4

Investment and Savings Rates in LAC, 1985-1995

(annual averages, percentages of GDP)

COUNTRY		1985–89	1990–95
Argentina	Investment	17.7%	18.9%*
	Savings	20.9%	18.9%*
Brazil	Investment	17.3%	15.6%
	Savings	22.3%	18.1%
Chile	Investment	21.9%	28.5%
	Savings	26.1%	30.3%
Colombia	Investment	17.5%	20.7%
	Savings	22.1%	20.6%
Mexico	Investment	17.0%	19.8%
	Savings	19.0%	17.0%
Peru	Investment	21.4%	24.1%
	Savings	21.9%	19.1%
Venezuela	Investment	17.7%	14.7%
	Savings	20.2%	18.3%

* 1990–1994
Investment = Gross Domestic Investment (local currency, constant prices)
Savings = Gross Domestic Savings (local currency, constant prices)
GDP = Gross Domestic Product (local currency, constant prices)

Source: International Economics Department Database, World Bank.

TABLE 3.5

Investment and Savings Rates in East Asia, 1985–1995

(annual averages, percentages of GDP)

COUNTRY		1985–89	1990–95
Korea, Rep.	Investment	30.3%	36.3%*
	Saving	34.5%	35.7%*
Hong Kong	Investment	26.8%	29.0%*
	Saving	35.1%	35.6%*
Indonesia	Investment	25.2%	32.6%
	Saving	26.8%	33.9%
Malaysia	Investment	26.3%	37.9%
	Savings	34.8%	36.5%
Singapore	Investment	37.5%	38.6%
	Saving	40.6%	54.8%*
Thailand	Investment	30.1%	41.7%
	Saving	29.3%	35.6%
Taiwan	Investment	20.4%	24.4%*
	Saving	31.9%	27.5%*

* 1990–94

Investment = Gross Domestic Investment (local currency, constant prices)

Savings = Gross Domestic Savings (local currency, constant prices)

GDP = Gross Domestic Product (local currency, constant prices)

Source: International Economics Department Database, World Bank.

while those of East Asia approach 35 percent. These tables also show that domestic-savings rates in LAC countries have declined since the late 1980s and remain relatively low, although Chile is an exception in this regard as well.[3]

Moreover, factors of production are, on average, less productive in LAC than in East Asia. Table 3.6 shows output-capital ratios for LAC and East Asian countries in the second half of the 1980s.[4] Only Chile and Colombia had ratios approximating those found in East Asia. Clearly the efficiency of LAC investments in human and physical capital needs to be greatly improved.

As discussed in Chapter 1, the first priority encompasses the need to consolidate stabilization gains, mainly through

TABLE 3.6

Output-Capital Ratios in LAC and East Asia, 1985-1990

LAC	AVG. Q/K	EAST ASIA	AVG. Q/K
Argentina	30.3%	Indonesia	46.0%
Brazil	33.9%	Korea, Republic of	46.4%
Chile	41.4%	Malaysia	35.5%
Colombia	43.2%	Taiwan, China	55.0%
Mexico	34.4%	Thailand	42.5%
Peru	30.1%		
Venezuela	25.5%		

Q = GDP (in local currency, constant prices)

K = Capital Stock (in local currency, constant prices)

AVG. = Annual Average

Source: STARS, World Bank Database.

fiscal strengthening and the safeguarding of sound financial systems. There are three main ways by which fiscal strengthening and financial stability promote economic growth. The first is by contributing to macroeconomic stability. This was discussed thoroughly in Chapter 1 and concerns the positive effects that stability has on both investment and the efficiency of resource allocation in the economy. As discussed there, the cornerstone for macroeconomic stability in today's world of high financial integration and capital mobility is a strong and flexible fiscal policy.

The second way that fiscal strengthening promotes economic growth is by affecting the level of national savings. In short, fiscal strengthening entails increasing the level of public savings, which in turn raises national savings. A rise in public savings directly raises national savings because the so-called Ricardian offset is less than proportional.[5] By assuring macroeconomic stability, fiscal strengthening also contributes indirectly to higher savings, because savings rates increase with higher growth rates. In the long run, a higher level of national savings will help maintain high levels of domestic investment. At the same time, it will reduce the LAC region's dependence on foreign savings and thus it will lower current-account deficits and external vulnerability to volatile capital flows.

The third way in which fiscal strengthening helps to accelerate economic growth is by permitting governments to provide adequate levels of investment in both human capital and infrastructure, which are critical for achieving high growth rates, as discussed below.

Education and health reform will be top priorities in LAC for years to come. Empirical studies have confirmed that indicators of educational inputs and outputs, such as access to education or the educational attainment of the labor force, are associated with subsequent growth.[6] There is little doubt today that human development is one of the most, if not *the* most, important determinant of long-term competitiveness and productivity growth. For example, healthy and well-educated workers lose fewer work days to illness, are more productive at work, have greater intersectoral mobility, and have longer working lives. A healthy and well-educated labor force is crucial for raising overall productivity.[7]

By international standards, some countries in LAC have high ratios of social expenditures to GDP, but most suffer from inefficient allocation of resources. For example, too many resources are devoted to subsidizing higher education and health services for the nonpoor at the expense of basic education and health services. These countries also suffer from poor incentive structures that do not promote improvements in performance by service providers, and from inefficient delivery practices. In general, efficiency and quality remain dismal in most of the region's education and health systems. Recent results of achievement tests taken by Latin American and Caribbean students are remarkably poor. Although there has been substantial improvement in life-expectancy, infant-mortality, and literacy rates, all these indices are still below those of East Asia and Eastern Europe, regions with which LAC will be competing in international markets.

Financial development is crucial both for consolidating macroeconomic stability (which, in turn, is a prerequisite for high growth rates) and for achieving more efficient physical and human capital investment.[8] The aftermath of the Mexican peso crisis of December 1994 brought a painful awareness of the weakness of financial sectors and institutions in LAC. Financial crises of different degrees and varieties affected countries as diverse as Argentina, Bolivia, Brazil, Ecuador, Jamaica, Mexico, and Venezuela, to name a few; these crises are proving to be very expensive in terms of both foregone output and fiscal costs.[9] These regrettable experiences have shown that in today's world of high financial integration, capital flows demand greater depth and strength from domestic financial sectors, which, in turn, require modern regulation and supervision. Many LAC countries today are well behind in such regulation, particularly in requiring loan loss reserves and adequate accounting standards for banks.[10]

The challenge for LAC countries is not only to safeguard the stability of banking sectors. There is also an urgent need to improve the efficiency of all financial markets and, particularly, to develop strong capital markets. Intermediation costs (and bank operating costs, as shown in Figure 3.2) are too high and credit is still not accessible to small enterprises, microenterprises, and the rural sector.[11] In many countries, state-owned banks still control a high proportion of the deposit and credit markets, and this fact alone accounts for high inefficiencies and risks.[12] Bond and equity markets are small, concentrated, and are not sufficiently deep or liquid. Such limitations dampen both the level and efficiency of investment in LAC. Furthermore, the development of bond and equity markets today is especially important because portfolio investments are likely to

be the most dynamic (and volatile) portion of international capital flows in the following decade.[13] Adequate access to the financial sector is also crucial for reducing poverty, since small entrepreneurs and rural producers have inadequate access to financial markets. (See Chapter 4.)

An effective *legal and regulatory environment for private-sector development* is indispensable for stimulating private investment and making it efficient. Recent theoretical work and empirical evidence show that property-rights protection, contract enforcement, and credible and stable regulatory systems significantly affect investment levels and investment efficiency.[14] Evidence presented in Chapter 2 showed that investors perceive that LAC is well behind OECD and East Asian countries in such matters.

Most LAC countries need to reduce uncertainties and transaction costs by improving the protection of property rights, the enforcement of contracts, and in general, regulatory frameworks. The latter is especially crucial for encouraging private participation in modernizing infrastructure, public utilities, and basic social services. For most LAC countries, promoting private investment in these areas is the only way to achieve the required level and quality of investment in human development and infrastructure, while still maintaining overall fiscal discipline. The alternative would require increasing tax revenues to levels above 40 percent of GDP, which is not only unlikely, given administrative and political constraints in the region, but would also be less efficient and less conducive to higher rates of economic growth.

Much has been accomplished in the LAC region, which has led the way in promoting private participation in these areas. Nevertheless, much remains to be done in all aspects of regulation, especially with respect to reducing and allocating risks associated with infrastructure projects, dealing with the contingent fiscal liabilities accumulated through the provision of government guarantees to private investors, and regulating private providers of social services.

Reducing the burden of inefficient regulation, especially in the labor markets, is also important. As discussed in Chapters 2 and 4, more flexible labor markets will improve overall efficiency, and thus lead to growth; economic growth will enhance employment opportunities, and thus help to reduce poverty.

Finally, there is the general issue of *public-sector modernization and governance*. In this instance as well, there is mounting evidence of the positive effect both of credible,

FIGURE 3.2

Banking Operating Costs

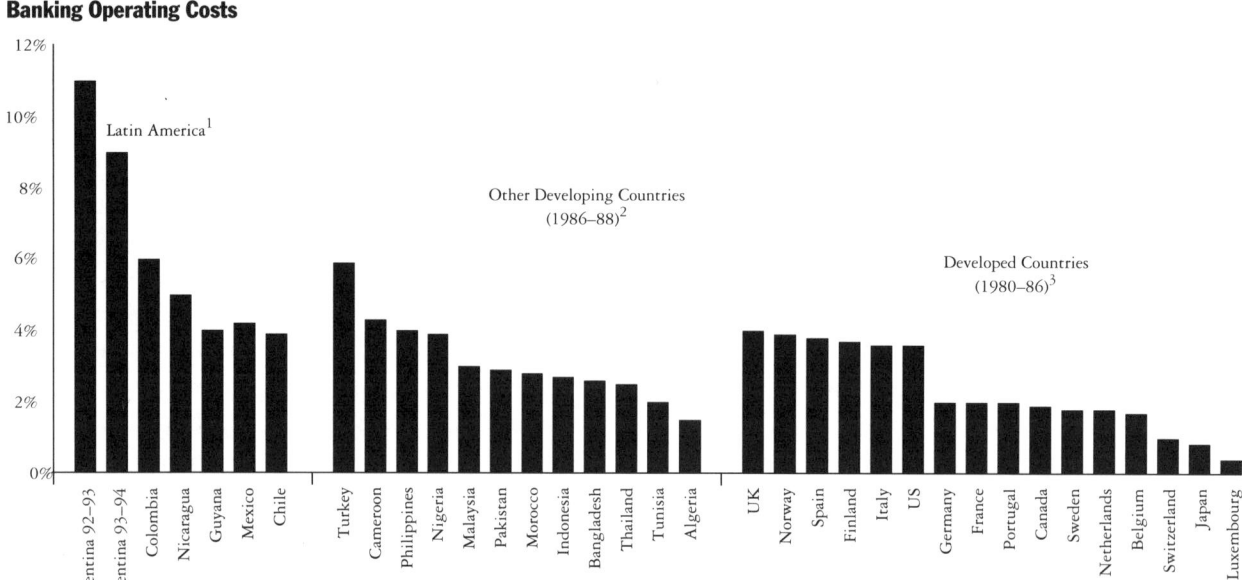

Notes:

[1] Superintendency of Banks (Colombia 1988–91; Nicaragua, Guyana 1991–93, Mexico 1990–92 Chile 1986–88).

[2] World Bank Report No. 8403-TH Thailand Financial Sector Study, May 1990.

[3] Dimitri Vittas, "Measuring Bank Efficiency," WPS 806, The World Bank. Washington, D.C., November 1991.

efficient governance and of the rule of law on growth.[15] Chapter 2 showed that investors perceive that LAC offers lower quality bureaucracies, higher corruption, and higher property insecurity than do the OECD and East Asian countries.

In most of the region, more result-oriented, transparent, and accountable governments are needed at both the national and subnational levels. Although progress has been made in modernizing some basic economic policy entities (for example, the central banks and the finance ministries), many government agencies, especially those providing social services, are still too often plagued by clientelistic practices and are often "captured" by specific political economic interests. In addition, the rule of law is weak in many countries, and so the problem is not just one of deficient laws and regulations, but also one of governance.[16] Furthermore, crime and violence are high and have been growing in LAC countries (see Table 3.7). All of these facts are imposing serious constraints to more rapid and equitable growth.[17] This priority area probably will prove to be the most difficult one in which to achieve reform, because it requires both political leadership and a deep understanding of LAC social structures and realities.

We are convinced that improvement and reform in the four areas that we have discussed (combined with the consolidation of macroeconomic stability) will permit LAC countries to achieve and maintain growth rates similar to those of Chile and the East Asian countries. As seen in Chapter 2, it is precisely the degree of progress in these

TABLE 3.7

Homicides per 100,000 Population

COUNTRY	LATE 70S/EARLY 80S	LATE 80S/EARLY 90S
Colombia	20.5	89.5
Kingston, Jamaica	n.a.	70.0
Brazil	11.5	19.7
Mexico	18.2	17.8
Venezuela	11.7	15.2
Trinidad and Tobago	2.1	12.6
Peru	2.4	11.5
Panama	2.1	10.9
Ecuador	6.4	10.3
United States	10.7	10.1
Argentina	3.9	4.8
Costa Rica	5.7	4.1
Uruguay	2.6	4.4
Paraguay	5.1	4.0
Chile	2.6	3.0

Source: World Bank (1997*b*)

areas that distinguishes most LAC countries from the Chilean and East Asian models. In what follows, we provide more detail about these priorities and illustrate their applicability throughout the LAC region.

C. Quality Investment in Human Development

As discussed above, reforms in the education and health sectors are indispensable to helping LAC raise the quality of its investments in human development. The following section addresses the challenges faced by the region in the areas of education and health. This section makes clear that the quality of services in both areas needs to be improved, and that some additional resources may be needed to achieve this improvement.

1. Education

While the LAC region has significantly improved access to the early years of basic schooling for almost all children,[18] three symptoms of poor educational performance have become evident: (1) average levels of *academic achievement* are very low, (2) average *educational attainment* of the labor force lags behind that of other regions, and (3) *inequalities in educational opportunities* contribute to high income inequality and slow growth.

Regarding LAC's low scholastic achievement, Figure 3.3 shows that the performances of Venezuela and of Trinidad and Tobago on international standardized tests were very low compared to those of OECD countries. A fol-

low-up study conducted by UNESCO showed that the performance of other LAC countries was similar to that of Venezuela.[19] The additional problem of *LAC's low educational attainment* is illustrated in Figure 3.4. Clearly, in LAC countries, there is a large gap between enrollment rates and educational attainment, which is measured in terms of number of grades passed. This is explained in part by primary school repetition rates, which are very high in LAC relative to other regions of the world.

In addition to low levels of educational achievement and attainment, LAC countries in general provide highly unequal educational opportunities. Most countries in the region now provide good access to primary education for poor and rich alike. However, in all but the very poor countries (such as Bolivia, Guatemala, Haiti, and Nicaragua), poor and nonpoor children have unequal access to preschool and lower secondary education. And in the countries with better developed educational systems (such as Argentina, Chile, and Uruguay), access to upper secondary education remains unequal for the poor and nonpoor. For all LAC countries, the other main source of inequality in human capital investments is the difference in the quality of schooling received by poor and nonpoor children. These issues are discussed more thoroughly in Chapter 4.

To deal with these three educational obstacles to economic growth, the LAC region needs to undertake reforms to achieve two general policy goals: (1) improve children's readiness for schooling, and (2) raise the quality of school-

FIGURE 3.3

Educational Achievement and Expenditures in a Sample of Countries

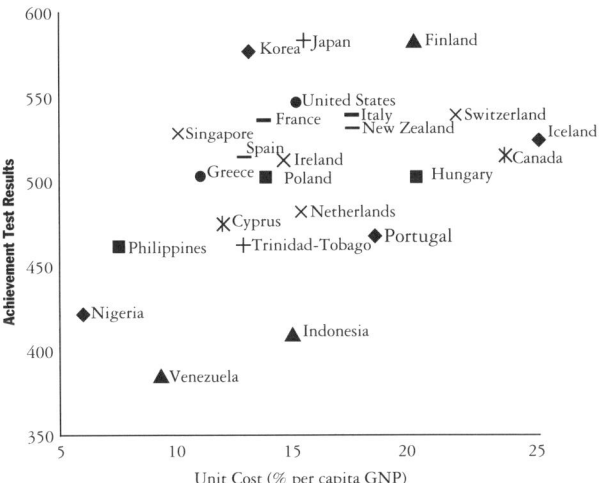

Source: World Bank (1995a)

FIGURE 3.4

Enrollment and Education Attainment in Developing Areas

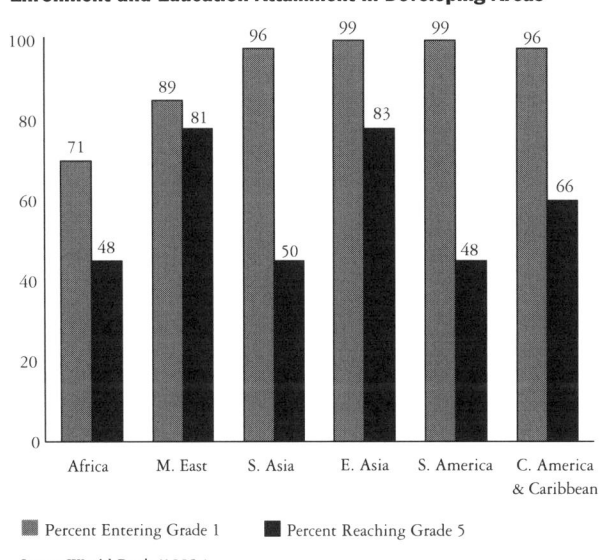

■ Percent Entering Grade 1   ■ Percent Reaching Grade 5

Source: World Bank (1995a).

ing, which includes improving the quality of teaching. Institutional reforms in the education sector are necessary to achieve these objectives.

Any serious effort to improve educational outcomes requires interventions to *raise children's readiness for schooling*. These can take the form of parental education, as in Mexico, community-based centers, as in Colombia and Bolivia, or school-based centers. Careful attention needs to be given to (1) stimulating the already important role of the private sector in daycare, (2) improving the educational programs of both private and public daycare, and (3) ensuring that the poor have equal access to daycare. In sum, educating parents, improving the instructional content of existing daycare facilities, and increasing public and private supply are the three key components for raising the quality of preschool learning by children in the LAC region.

Raising the quality (and quantity) of schooling requires three major efforts (listed here in order of priority): (1) improving the quality of teaching; (2) increasing student learning time by ensuring that both teachers and students participate in all intended days and hours of instruction, and by expanding the length of the school day and the number of days of instruction; and (3) enhancing the technology of teaching by supporting student-centered learning approaches through the use of workbooks and learning materials, and by integrating technology (radio, television, computers) into teaching.

The most technically difficult objective to achieve is *raising the quality of teaching*. While the precise strategy will vary by country, most strategies will entail

1. significantly restructuring and reforming teacher-training institutions (both preservice and in-service),
2. implementing reforms to give teachers and schools both increased responsibility and accompanying accountability,
3. revising pay scales to reward teachers for improving the skills that determine performance, and
4. increasing pay, especially for beginning teachers and for teachers of poor students.

Since learning depends on the quality as well as the quantity of schooling, *increasing student learning time*—by extending the school day and the school year—may turn out to be the simplest way of improving LAC's academic achievement in the short run. Furthermore, longer schooling time may have additional positive effects, such as

reducing demands on working mothers and reducing the likelihood that adolescents will get involved with drugs, crime, and violence. The current reform in Chile provides one model for the countries in the LAC region. There, the current government has increased the mandatory number of school weeks per year from 37 to 40. It has raised the weekly hours of schooling from 30 to 38 by consolidating morning and evening shifts into one longer school session. These reforms will raise total schooling time per year by approximately 25 percent.[20]

In most countries, *institutional reforms* should include a change in financing rules to provide incentives for quality and efficiency. There are numerous experiments in LAC ranging from providing vouchers in Chile, to contracting with nongovernmental organizations (NGOs) in El Salvador, to creating school councils with power to allocate resources in Minas Gerais, Brazil, to establishing competitive school grants in Uruguay and Chile, to creating charter schools in Nicaragua. While these experiments have not all been fully evaluated, they provide several lessons for reform. For example, Chile finances schools based on actual daily attendance, thereby providing an incentive for schools to develop programs to retain students. El Salvador's experience with reform shows that enhancing the responsibility of parent associations, for example, can improve substantially the coverage and quality of basic education, including teacher performance and attendance. Interestingly, El Salvador's education reform, despite involving a marked change in the employment regime of teachers, was accomplished without teacher strikes and has enjoyed full support across the political spectrum. A similar experiment is being tried in Guatemala, where the need to provide bilingual education for the large indigenous population creates an additional complication.

Nonetheless, education ministries need to be restructured to develop and carry out new functions (for example, testing, monitoring, regulating) and to eliminate old functions. Throughout Central America, for example, social funds have taken on most of the responsibility for the construction of primary schools, thus relieving the ministries of a burdensome task. Restructuring needs to take account of two new realities in LAC. The first is decentralization, which clearly translates into new ministerial responsibilities. The other is the very important role of the private sector in LAC education and the need for ministries to be converted from "public education ministries" to "education ministries." Without this change in orientation, LAC education policymakers will deprive themselves of a whole range of cost-effective policy options.

Finally, the largest gains in efficiency from institutional reforms are likely to come from the public universities and the payroll-tax-financed vocational-training institutions. Both of these types of institutions are typically poorly managed and have few incentives to improve either quality or efficiency. Both also have a great deal of autonomy, which means that the most productive reform policies are those that focus on providing the right incentives.

These policies will require increased public spending on education, at least in the short run. In principle, some LAC countries could finance these policies by (1) reallocating public spending from higher to basic education, (2) immediately addressing problems of ghost teachers and excessive administrative overhead, and (3) introducing market-based reforms. However, reallocating resources from tertiary to basic education is often politically difficult. Indeed, when overall resources were declining over the last decade, the share of public education spending that went to higher education actually increased.[21] Higher education's claim on public spending could be reduced in the long run by stimulating the supply and quality of private, postsecondary institutions and by developing capital markets to cover the costs of private and public tuition. Also, the evidence on market-based reforms, ranging from vouchers to financial incentives for performance, suggests that these reforms affect positively both quality and efficiency, but the magnitude of these effects is neither large nor immediate.[22] Hence, the public sectors in LAC will need to raise expenditures on primary education in the short run.

2. Health

In 1994 the LAC region's expenditures, both public and private, on health, totaled over 7 percent of its GDP, or approximately US$234 per person. The distribution of these expenditures varies greatly across the region, ranging from 10 percent of GDP (US$355 per person) in Argentina to less than 3 percent (US$12 per person) in Guatemala. Only the high-income OECD countries spend more on health as share of GDP (9.9 percent) and in per capita terms (US$2,329). The sources of those expenditures differ from those of the LAC region. Whereas in OECD countries, the vast majority of funds are public, in the LAC region, only about 44 percent of health are public, with the

remaining 56 percent coming from out-of-pocket expenditures and, increasingly, from private insurance.[23]

Most LAC countries have multi-tiered health systems. Social security systems usually serve the white-collar workers and their families, often with generous subsidies from general revenues and transfers from pension funds. Ministries of health provide coverage of varying degrees of quality to the poor. Furthermore, LAC's private health sector is itself multi-tiered, providing medical service of first-world quality to the upper classes and a lower level of services to lower income groups. Additionally, pharmacies often play an important role in medical advice and treatment.[24]

In this context we can identify two priority areas for improving the quality and cost-effectiveness of health services in LAC. The first priority is to address the fiscal implications of the rising costs of health care services, and the second is to improve the efficiency in the provision of both public and private health services. The latter will require actions to improve the incentive structure for public health institutions, to strengthen the regulation of the private sector involved in health services, and to raise the quality of medical education.

a. Fiscal implications of rising costs in health services
The fiscal implications of rising costs are evident. Over three-quarters of health budgets are devoted to health services (as opposed to preventive and public health services, such as providing vaccinations, health education, nutrition programs, and family planning), and these expenditures have been rising in much of the LAC region, particularly in middle-income countries. Underlying these rising costs are public pressures to meet health needs, which often lead to uncontrolled benefits (or the failure to limit the type or scope of services), and the wide availability of costly services, including technologically sophisticated treatments for the few. Efforts to control the volume of care either through ceilings on services or limits on the acquisition of expensive technology have not been effective in most of the region, and the rationing of services is usually implicit, unregulated, and random.

The surge of health reform agendas in the region reflects the realization within finance and health ministries and within social security institutes that restructuring is essential to improve the viability and affordability of health services. In Brazil in the mid-1980s, in Chile in the 1990s, and in Colombia in recent years, systemic reforms have been undertaken. Ongoing reforms in Costa Rica are equally broad, and Nicaragua has implemented a nation-wide restructuring of its hospital care. All of these countries have unlinked the health and pension systems within their social security systems as a move toward putting their fiscal houses in order. However, improvements in the efficiency of health services will be needed to slow the growth of health care costs.

b. Improving the quality and efficiency of health services

Public institutions associated with health services. Most ministries of health and social security systems finance and provide care through their own networks of service providers. These services face the same difficulties as do other public enterprises: they are not accountable, they have rigid staffing, and they are often highly inefficient. The trend in the OECD and in LAC countries undertaking reforms (such as Argentina, Brazil, Chile, and Colombia) is to separate financing and delivery into two different entities. This is a good first step towards putting the proper incentives in place. Within the public health sector, hospitals are of particular concern because of their leadership and training functions and their key role in treatment, especially for the poor. Providing incentives for performance and productivity, investing in strengthened management, improving training, and making institutions accountable are all part of the agenda for improving institutional capacity and performance.

Regulating the private sector in health services. Even though many ministries of health in LAC ignore the private sector, in the future they will undeniably need to pay greater attention to improving the regulation of the private sector that participates in the delivery of health services. Even in countries such as Brazil, where the government finances care through private providers and where over 70 percent of all care is private, there is tension and antagonism between the public and private sectors.

With the exceptions of Argentina, Brazil, Chile, Uruguay, and, increasingly, Colombia, the government typically does not finance private providers. Finding options for financing private providers at all levels of care should be a priority. This is particularly important with respect to basic care in rural areas where government programs have not been very effective, but programs run by NGOs can be. Because experience is limited, programs

deserve to be initiated as pilot programs that can be evaluated to determine the conditions for maximizing the gains from this type of public-private partnership.

Lapses in the quality of service delivery, lack of provider responsibility and accountability, and the absence of patient rights all stem from the lack of regulation of the health system. Furthermore, licensing of physicians is typically *pro forma* and medical schools do not adhere to any accreditation system, providers are completely unaccountable to payers or patients, and institutional providers (for example, hospitals) lack any accreditation arrangement. These problems affect the poor even more than the better-off since the latter are more likely to be able to reach and to afford the best health care, regardless of cost.

A common trend in the LAC region is the rapid growth of *private insurance* and the use of private providers through some combination of managed care, indemnity insurance, and out-of-pocket expenditures. Those purchasing insurance tend to be members of the upper and middle classes. In Brazil and Chile, only about 25 percent of their populations have access to these private insurance schemes. The obligations and performance of private health insurance companies are unregulated and this is leading to problems. For example, several factors have limited the access to the privately run health insurance schemes (ISAPRES) in Chile. One of the most significant factors is the complexity of the contracts that the purchasers must sign. There are a multitude of plans available, each with subtle differences regarding coverage and price. In addition, there are no standardized terminologies, definitions, or pricing methods among the contracts. As a result, prospective affiliates do not understand the numerous stipulations of the contracts. These problems are compounded by the fact that the ISAPRES impose various restrictions on access to care. These include exclusionary clauses that deny coverage for certain medical services (the treatment of some noncommunicable illnesses, for example), waiting periods after enrollment before services are provided, and the refusal to cover pre-existing conditions. Clearly the ISAPRES are catering to the healthy (low-risk) population. Indeed, coverage of the elderly, for whom the costs of care tend to be 4 or 5 times higher than for those of the young, has been insufficient. In fact, it has been estimated that more than 70 percent of ISAPRES affiliates are less than 40 years of age, and only 2 percent are 65 or older.[25] Public supervision and regulation may be needed to expand the coverage provided by private health insurance schemes, and to maintain high quality standards for insurance providers.

Medical education. Controlling the number of medical and nursing graduates and the quality of medical educational institutions is central to ensuring the quality and cost-effectiveness of health services. The OECD countries have discovered that the number of physicians and their specializations place a strong upward pressure on the demand for health services. In many LAC countries, the number of both physicians and private medical schools is growing. The oversupply of physicians in Argentina, the Dominican Republic, Mexico, and Uruguay, to name a few countries, is leading to unemployment among physicians and to increased pressures for public-sector hiring. Physicians in private practice generate demand for health services as well, because of the unique role physicians play in defining patient demand. Governments need to provide the necessary regulation to guarantee that medical school graduates can safely treat patients and that medical schools provide, at minimum, a basic curriculum to their students. These reforms, in addition to those already mentioned, with regards to education and health make clear how much needs to be done to raise the region's quality of human capital in the coming years.

D. Developing Efficient Financial Markets

The cost of capital in the LAC region remains very high while the efficiency of regional financial markets are low, even by the standards of developing countries. The region's commercial banks operate inefficiently (see Figure 3.2), and this creates high intermediation costs which affect the competitiveness of real-sector firms. Capital markets in the LAC region remain underdeveloped and fail to serve adequately the needs of small enterprises, microenterprises, and the rural sector. These deficiencies restrict investment and cause allocation inefficiencies. Accelerating financial development in the LAC region requires attention to two main areas: (1) competition and efficiency in the banking sector, and (2) the development of efficient bond and equity markets. The general issue of the regulatory "infrastructure" of capital markets, which affects both of these areas, is discussed at the end of this section.

1. Competition and efficiency in the banking sector

Chapter 1 already discussed issues related to the regulation and supervision of banks. However, we cannot overstate the importance of increasing competition, which will lead to greater efficiency in LAC banking sectors. Greater competition can be achieved mainly by (1) reducing public participation in the banking system, (2) liberalizing foreign participation in domestic financial markets, and (3) permitting nonbanking entities to compete in banking services.

a. Privatizing state-owned banks

Publicly owned banks still comprise large portions of LAC banking systems. This is the case in countries such as Argentina, Brazil, Costa Rica, Guyana, Honduras, and Nicaragua, where the public banks hold from 30 percent to 50 percent of total bank assets.[26] Since publicly owned banks compete for private deposits and yet are insulated from market forces, they operate less efficiently and engage in riskier credit activities than do private banks. In addition, publicly owned banks weaken the supervision, enforcement powers, and moral authority of bank regulators because, if they fail to meet regulatory requirements, they are often immune to closings or other consequences, unlike privately owned banks.

As discussed in Chapter 1, Argentina responded to the banking crisis of 1995 with a program to restructure its banking system, which included measures to deal with several public banks that had large nonperforming portfolios. In fact, nonperforming private bank loans amounted to about 9 percent of total lending in 1994, far less than the 25 percent of lending by public banks. To date, several provincial banks have been closed or privatized. Nonetheless, public financial institutions still accounted for over 33 percent of total credit in Argentina in early 1997, compared to 43 percent in September 1995.

Illustrative of the efficiency problems presented by the presence of public banks is the example of Brazil. The ratio of loans in arrears and in liquidation net of provisions to total loans (which provides a better indicator of soundness) for federal public banks was 23.3 percent in October 1996. This ratio was almost 9 percent for state public banks. In contrast, Brazilian private banks had a ratio of only 2.3 percent. Perhaps more revealing are the recently released (and incomplete) financial statements of Banespa (Bank of the State of Sao Paulo), Brazil's largest state-owned bank. Despite its efforts to expand private-sector lending in recent years, the bank made approximately 90 percent of its customer loans to the state of Sao Paulo and its operating subsidiaries. Moreover, Banespa's relatively small private-sector loan portfolio was of low quality. Overall, Brazil's federally owned and state-owned banks comprise almost 50 percent of total banking assets, despite a recent program to privatize and/or restructure the country's public banks.

In Central America, many countries continue to have relatively large public banks. In some cases, such as Honduras and Nicaragua, these banks perform a development function, whereas in Costa Rica, public banks are still involved in the more traditional aspects of commercial banking. Clearly, there is still substantial scope for privatization in the financial sector in several LAC countries.

b. Liberalizing foreign competition in banking services

Increasing foreign competition entails two distinct actions. First, by removing restrictions to capital flows, domestic borrowers can seek funds abroad at a lower cost, which increases competition with domestic banks. Second, liberalizing the FDI and foreign ownership regimes increases domestic competition in banking sectors.

As the capital account is liberalized, it is likely that the most credit-worthy borrowers will gain access to international capital markets, thus increasing competition for this segment of the domestic market. However, as pointed out in Chapter 1, liberalizing the capital account of the balance of payments can create boom-bust cycles which are associated with volatile capital flows. Therefore, the capital account should be liberalized gradually, so as not to exacerbate financial vulnerability to capital flows.

As mentioned in Chapter 1, liberalizing FDI and foreign-ownership regimes in banking sectors can help reduce the overall fragility of domestic banking sectors. In addition, a greater foreign presence can also promote efficiency because it will force domestic banks to compete with foreign banks. Some progress has been made recently in the liberalization of foreign competition, but there is still much room for improvement in many LAC countries.

In Mexico, for example, since the implementation of the North American Free Trade Agreement in 1994, 90 new foreign financial institutions, including 18 commercial banks and 10 financial groups, have been allowed to operate in the domestic market. The subsequent financial crisis in Mexico has led to further reforms in the regulation of foreign investment. For domestically owned banks, a single individual or company may now hold 10 percent of the share capital of a financial holding company or of a commercial bank, compared to 5 percent prior to the reforms. Also, under prior law, no more than 30 percent of the voting capital of domestic financial holding companies, commercial banks, or brokerage firms could be owned by non-Mexicans. This provision reflected Mexico's wariness of foreign ownership in the financial sector. Now, foreign individuals and companies as a group may have as much as 49 percent of the voting capital of a Mexican entity. In February 1995, an important change was made in Mexican law to allow the Ministry of Finance to waive the limits on market share that were set in the NAFTA (which limited market share to 15 percent by the year 2000 and to 30 percent by 2004). To encourage well-capitalized foreign institutions to merge with or take over existing Mexican banks, the legislation allows foreign banks to buy a controlling stake in Mexican banks, provided that the resulting foreign-controlled bank has no more than 6 percent market share. However, the holdings of foreign banks are still limited to no more than 25 percent of total assets in the banking system.[27]

In other LAC countries, foreign participation in domestic banking markets also remains quite low. A recent study published by the Institute for International Economics shows that foreign affiliates hold less than 10 percent of banking assets in Brazil, less than 5 percent in Colombia, and less than 2 percent in Venezuela.[28] In the future, LAC countries need to facilitate foreign competition in banking. Yet, even in countries such as Argentina, where the financial sector is open to FDI, the presence of public banks has tended to inhibit FDI in the banking sector, perhaps because of the perception that implicit public subsidies will constrain private profits. Evidence such as this supports the view that increasing domestic efficiency in domestic banking sectors entails moving ahead on several fronts.

c. Competition with nonbanking entities

Countries in the LAC region need to promote further competition in banking services by permitting nonbanking institutions to participate in deposit and lending activities. Bank for International Settlements data show that the percentage of the total assets of both banks and nonbank financial institutions held by the banking sector in 1994 was 98 percent for Argentina, 97 percent for Brazil, and 92 percent for Venezuela. Chile's banking sector, on the other hand, held only 62 percent of total financial assets, and

Korea, Malaysia, and Thailand had banking shares of 38 percent, 64 percent, and 75 percent, respectively. This dominance of deposit and lending activities by banks limits both the level and efficiency of investment in the LAC countries where financial sectors are still underdeveloped.[29]

2. Developing efficient bond and equity markets

Despite the importance of the banking sector and the crisis-induced attention paid to it, the capital markets already absorb the lion's share of financial savings. In February 1997, the market value of stocks in the seven largest Latin American countries was estimated at around US$543 billion, a figure well above the level of bank deposits. While bond market data are not readily available, the collective value of stocks and outstanding bonds is estimated to account for nearly two-thirds of the region's total annual income (or gross national product [GNP]), and for well over twice the amount of bank deposits in these countries. The capital markets are also expected to grow faster than the banks, because the securities markets and intermediaries (such as insurance companies, pension funds, mutual funds, investment banking, underwriting, and rating agencies) are all still generally less developed than the banking sector. Given their current size and expected growth, capital markets and intermediaries will create intermediation efficiencies that will be central to savings formation and investment.

Government debt-management policies often produce a fragmented bond market and lack of a yield curve benchmark for the private securities markets. There are several regulatory and taxation impediments to the issuing of asset-backed securities. While social security reforms are being implemented in many countries, significant efforts must be made to prevent the discouragement of both competition and efficiency in the management of sizable assets. Although significant progress is being made in the regulation of mutual funds and insurance providers, considerably more is needed before these two types of intermediaries will play a meaningful role in LAC financial sectors.

Direct transaction costs, such as brokerage fees, are only one factor affecting the intermediation efficiency of capital markets. More important aspects are the volatility of prices, the efficacy of settlement mechanisms, transparency, volume, liquidity, opportunities for diversification, professional investment advice, pricing benchmarks, and rating services. Improvements in these aspects increase security

prices and lower the cost of capital. The efforts of the LAC countries in this area will need to focus on the following agenda of problems and ways of resolving them.

a. Equity and bond markets

Latin American equity markets have long suffered from hyperinflation, and from excessive or discriminatory taxes and restrictions both on the issuing and trading of nonbank securities (such as stocks, bonds, commercial paper), and more generally, on the private placement of securities. These markets are typically shallow in terms of the number of listed companies (even large industrial companies belonging to conglomerates are frequently unlisted), of new equity issuance, of liquidity, and of concentration. For instance, Chapter 2 showed that, on average during the 1990s, the top ten stocks listed in the largest LAC stock markets comprised 50 percent of total market capitalization in contrast to a figure of approximately 34 percent for the East Asian NICs in 1995. There is a clear absence of an equity culture in Latin America, where excessive control and family-owned corporations are the norm. The development of strong bond and equity markets is especially important these days, because portfolio investments are likely to be the most dynamic portion of capital flows in the following decade.

Attention to four broad areas is needed to deepen equity markets and make them an important source of new corporate finance. First, certain taxes need to be lowered. Although direct stamp and transaction taxes largely have been removed in the major LAC countries, double taxation of equity from capital gains, as well as dividend taxation, should be reduced in most countries. Also, the direct "patrimony" taxes in certain countries, such as Uruguay, should be lowered. Second, market capitalization, liquidity, and a culture of equity can all be strengthened by further divestment of large state-owned assets, particularly in the extractive industries and utilities. Third, regulation of pension and mutual funds needs to be substantially liberalized to permit greater investment in equity. Finally, compelling evidence suggests serious deficiencies in both corporate governance and minority protection in many LAC countries, of which Mexico is the most glaring example.[30]

In terms of trading and market mechanisms, most regional markets are beginning to adopt modern trading and settlement mechanisms. But further improvements are needed in areas of dematerialized delivery, custodial provisions, and prudent regulation of securities markets (derivatives, insider trading, best-price execution, broker-capital adequacy, and self-regulation). Among the Caribbean and Central American countries, the development of subregional securities markets is needed.

b. Asset-backed securities

Development of the asset-backed securities (ABS) market promises considerable benefits for the region. Such development can significantly increase the supply of long-term funds, the competition in providing home loans, and infrastructure financing and other bank lending. It can also substantially reduce the high financial intermediation costs of mortgages and other banking products. Housing stocks are typically 1.5 to 3 times as large as the GNP of LAC countries. Housing is a very long-term capital investment. Thus the high cost of home financing (which has been 10 to 15 percent in real terms in some countries in recent years) results in massive welfare losses. However, the scope for reducing intermediation costs through mortgage-backed securities and other market-improving measures is enormous. By cutting financial intermediation spreads and by providing high-grade paper, asset-backed securities can substantially increase retail investment in long-term bond markets. Finally, such securities are well suited to the portfolios of pension funds, of life and retirement insurance companies, and of bond mutual funds; without these securities, the development of these institutional investors will be constrained.

Argentina and Chile have already implemented significant reforms in the legal structure for ABS. Other countries need to follow to improve currently inadequate legal frameworks, to reduce the high costs of restrictions and the transfer restrictions on the underlying assets, to eliminate collateral-related difficulties, and to rationalize the unequal or multiple taxation of ABS.

c. Government bonds

The aggregate issuance of government debt should always be governed by parameters set by responsible fiscal and monetary policies. However, within such parameters, programmatic and far-sighted management of public debt can generate important benefits for both the government and the financial markets. Such management would involve the maintenance of government yield curves within a certain maturity range, the regular issuance of debt at the highest maturity length to maintain liquid secondary trading, the selection of transparent public-security auctions or other issuance criteria, and the maintenance of a large and reasonably liquid market in treasury bills to permit the growth of other money market securities, such as commercial paper. In LAC, the management of public debt is largely governed by cash-flow needs and short-term cost considerations.

d. Municipal finance

It has already been mentioned that the LAC region has a substantial reform agenda which includes rationalizing the generation and expenditure of subnational revenue, improving revenue sharing mechanisms, and promoting fiscal responsibility and accountability at subnational levels. Subnational governments also have a large responsibility to provide infrastructure services. There is also a need to curb irresponsible subnational financing by provincial or municipal banks. Where fiscal responsibility and prudent control are well established, subnational investment objectives can be supported with access to private financial markets and without central government guarantees, and can be subjected to market-based discipline of ratings and due diligence.[31]

e. Pension funds

Major reforms of pension systems have already been carried out in Argentina, Bolivia, Chile, Colombia, Mexico, Peru, and Uruguay; they remain to be implemented in Brazil and the rest of the LAC countries. However, Chilean-style pension reforms do not necessarily maximize retirement wealth over the long run. Indeed, these reforms tend to foster similar portfolios across pension funds, high commercialization costs, a lack of competition between pension funds and other money managers, and disproportionately high commissions in the early years of their implementation.[32] Since pension funds manage large quantities of funds over a long time, even small losses in efficiency and returns can cause large losses of retirement wealth. Much of the pension-fund regulation thus needs to ensure that the system works for the long-term benefit of its affiliates.

f. Mutual funds

Mutual funds provide an important service by mobilizing savings, diversifying risks, providing professional money management, facilitating foreign investments, and possibly improving corporate governance. These services are especially valuable in the volatile and illiquid LAC markets that suffer from problems of insider trading, disclosure, and due diligence, that have poor trading mechanisms, and that are experiencing increased regional trading and cross-listing of securities. Mutual funds can also provide much-needed investment management services to the growing corporate and pension funds, to insurance companies, and to trusts that do not have investment management capacity. Through retail access to wholesale financial products, technological innovations, and direct competition for depositors, they increase competition and efficiency in the financial sector. In LAC, the growth of mutual funds is hampered by small national markets (especially in Central America), by the exclusion of mutual funds from the management of mandated savings (such as mandatory contributions to pension funds), by investment restrictions favoring banks, by restrictions on foreign investments and providers, and by the resulting high intermediation costs and the small size of the industry itself.

g. Insurance

The insurance industry throughout LAC is poised for significant growth. Aggregate premiums and assets are low by international standards. The life insurance industry in many LAC countries was destroyed by hyperinflation in the 1980s, and retirement insurance, a relatively new product, is becoming more important as pension funds are increasingly coming under private management. Endowment life and retirement insurance requires a significant accumulation of financial assets, and thus it has important consequences for securities markets. Insurance companies are typically major holders of long-term corporate and government bonds, asset-backed securities, commercial paper, and treasury bills. Thus their growth is vital to add depth and liquidity to LAC securities markets. Through variable annuities, the insurance industry can also raise savings and bring competition and efficiency to the management of retirement savings.

3. Financial market infrastructure

Weaknesses in the legal and institutional framework for secured lending are especially evident in LAC. Reform is needed to improve the mechanisms for granting secured

interests in both real and moveable property. Borrowers need the ability to create legally binding pledges of assets to securitize credit, while lenders need to be able to rely on timely and dependable procedures for repossessing the pledged assets in the event of default. A critical companion to this process is an efficient system for recording a creditor's interest in pledged assets. In LAC, the present process for securitizing credit is overly burdensome and, in many cases, prohibitively expensive. Also impeding the development of a proper legal and institutional framework are the poorly functioning credit bureaus and rating agencies. In sum, the legal and regulatory framework governing property rights and contract enforcement is less developed than those found in some industrialized countries, and this makes predictability and long-term orientation of investment behavior difficult.[33]

In more general terms, "infrastructure" is an important component of financial market development. Market infrastructure is made up of the systems and institutions that promote the security and efficiency of the means of payment, and that facilitate the trade and custody of securities. Overall, infrastructure efficiency is still very low even in the most developed capital markets in LAC.[34] In the industrialized countries, the average number of days taken to collect dividends ranges from two to less than one. The average number of days for Peru and Venezuela in 1995 was approximately 15. Furthermore, in most developed markets, the re-registration of securities is immediate. Although it takes only one to two days in Argentina, Brazil, Peru, or Mexico, it takes an average of more than 21 days in Venezuela. There is a need to gradually implement the 1989 recommendations presented in the Group of 30 (G-30) initiative and updated by the 1995 workshops of the International Society of Securities Administrators (ISSA) regarding delivery versus payment procedures, clearance and settlement mechanisms, and central depository systems.

Extension of credit is seriously hampered by the inadequate protection of creditors' rights throughout LAC, and particularly in Mexico.[35] There are several serious deficiencies in collateral laws and in registration requirements and processes throughout the LAC region. Notaries constitute a powerful lobby in many countries and charge high fees that are unrelated to the services performed and are not conducive to greater financial intermediation. There is also a need to develop both the legal framework and the incentives for greater use of credit bureaus while at the same time improving consumer protection and standards of fairness in credit reporting. In sum, the reform agenda for the development of sound financial systems is highly complex and specialized, and it will take a long time to develop in most LAC countries.

As the discussion in this section has made clear, property-rights protection, contract enforcement, and, in general, the legal and regulatory environment, are important for the development of financial markets. Both the development of financial markets and the availability of credit are inhibited or severely restricted when either the depositor or the lender is not legally protected. In many LAC countries, the judicial processes for seizing collaterals require considerable time and do not always produce reliable results. The development of long-term housing finance based either on mortgages or on securitization, to give just two examples, is often completely inhibited by the deficiencies of the legal and regulatory environment. In addition, adequate bankruptcy laws are critically important for the development of financial markets. The following section will revisit the issues more generally associated with the LAC region's legal and regulatory environment.

E. Improving the Legal and Regulatory Environment

The recent experience of transition economies in Eastern Europe has also made us aware of how important property rights are for the efficient functioning (and even the existence) of all markets, and more generally, for private-sector development.[36] At the same time, the rapidly growing work in institutional and information economics has provided us with the theoretical underpinnings needed to improve our understanding of, and ability to design, appropriate institutions and regulations.[37] In the following pages we discuss a few fundamental concepts that help us understand the requirements for designing efficient regulations. In addition, we cover issues related to

1. the protection and enforcement of property rights and contracts,
2. the elimination of "unnecessary" regulations,
3. the deregulation of LAC labor markets,
4. the enforcement of competition laws, and
5. the enhancement of regulation of private participation in infrastructure and social services.

1. Transaction costs and asymmetric information

Transaction costs and asymmetric information are two important concepts relevant to the design of proper regulatory and legal frameworks. The costs of conducting business transactions in an economy include the "costs of measuring the valuable attributes of what is being exchanged, and the costs of protecting rights and policing and enforcing agreements."[38] In other words, ascertaining the appropriate economic value of any transaction requires information regarding both the quality of the inputs needed to produce a given good or service, as well as the likelihood that the transaction will be honored at the time when payments need to be made. Moreover, when futures markets are incomplete or nonexistent, and when it is costly to gather all relevant information, as is usually the case in the "real" world, it becomes impossible to conduct cost-free transactions. In this context, different economic agents will have different types of information about the quality of products and inputs (including labor), and will have different perceptions about the viability of a business transaction.

The existence of incomplete markets and of asymmetric information is often offered to justify government intervention in the economy. However, Joseph Stiglitz has argued that "this pervasiveness of failures, while it reduces our confidence in the efficiency of market solutions, also reduces our confidence in the ability of the government to correct them."[39] Hence, the challenge of institutional design is to develop laws and regulations that reduce overall transaction costs, and thus expand the volume and diversity of the goods and services that are produced in a developing economy. Reducing transaction costs requires both a lessening of the burdens created by "unnecessary" regulation and the development of "efficient," or incentive-based, regulation to overcome the obstacles of asymmetric information and incomplete markets.

Both the reduction of transaction costs and the protection of property rights are issues related to the design *and* enforcement of legal and regulatory frameworks. Enforcement in turn depends on the design of institutions. In this report, we are somewhat arbitrarily separating issues of regulatory design and governance, the latter being covered in Section F.

2. Property rights and security of contracts

Investment, innovation, and economic transactions will be low if those who save, innovate, and engage in transactions lack reasonable certainty that they will indeed receive the fruits of their efforts. A few examples will suffice to highlight the crucial importance of protecting property rights. Good land titling and registry are essential for the smooth operation of land, housing, and credit markets, especially in developing countries where credit markets rely considerably on real estate as collateral. They are thus crucial to the development both of dynamic and efficient agricultural, housing, and financial sectors and of small business in general. Indeed, weak property titles are one of the most serious impediments to the access to financial sectors by large groups of microentrepreneurs and by small agricultural producers. Cumbersome legal and regulatory procedures, together with inadequate protection of property rights, have contributed to the widespread "informality" of business transactions in many LAC countries.

Appropriate design of *intellectual property rights* is essential to promote innovation and technology transfer. Some instruments of intellectual-property protection, such as patents, provide, in effect, monopolistic rights to acquired knowledge during the period of protection. Consequently, the long-term benefits of providing "high" protection of intellectual property in developing countries depend to a large extent on the country's capacity to innovate, which in turn depends on the quality of its human capital.[40] During the 1990s, some LAC countries have improved their intellectual property regimes. Mexico became a regional leader in this area since it joined NAFTA, which covers intellectual-property rights. After a comprehensive legislative debate, which acknowledged the benefits of effective intellectual-property protection, Brazil implemented a new intellectual-property protection law in 1996. The law protects pharmaceutical products for 20 years, and assures "pipeline protection" for medical products that are being tested. Similar protection was granted for food and chemical products. The requirements in Brazil's new law exceed those set forth in the agreement on Trade-Related Aspects of Intellectual Property Rights (TRIPs), which was part of the World Trade Organization Agreement, and the law puts them into effect ahead of schedule. Many LAC countries still have to adapt to TRIPs and the issue is in the agenda of the summit of the Americas.

3. Reducing the burden of unnecessary regulations

Many LAC countries still impose unnecessary economic, social, and process regulations. Economic regulations include restrictions on prices and quantities, and rules regarding entry into and exit from the market for specific industries. Social regulations are those regulations that affect a wide array of industries, and include environmental, public health, and safety regulations. Finally, the term "process regulations" refers to government management of the operation of the public and private sectors, which involves paperwork and administrative costs for both producers and consumers. In practice, the distinctions between these three terms is less clear. Throughout the LAC region, many anecdotal examples can be found of social, process, and economic regulations combining to produce inefficient economic outcomes.[41] Nonetheless, one key area deserving special attention is labor market regulation, which may be impeding faster growth and the reduction of poverty.[42]

4. Deregulating labor markets

A number of LAC countries have experienced lackluster employment creation despite the fact that they lowered inflation and accelerated growth in the mid-1990s.[43] While the destruction of jobs was an expected result of economic reform, job creation was also expected. Unfortunately, in some cases the creation of jobs has been slow and the pace lags considerably behind medium-term expectations. It is now clear that the disappointing pace of job creation in many economies undergoing reform can be attributed to the lack of reforms in factor markets, particularly the labor market. Argentina during 1991–94 provides the most striking example of this situation. During this period, the Argentine economy grew quite fast, experiencing an average growth rate of over 7 percent per year in real terms. Yet employment creation was quite disappointing, and the unemployment rate rose from 6.5 percent in 1991 to 11.5 percent in 1994. The rate subsequently rose to 17.5 percent during the economic recession of 1995.

In countries other than Argentina, the relationship between labor market distortions and employment creation in the economy is less clear. Indeed, the impact of both distortionary employment taxes and regulations depends on whether they are actually binding and/or effectively enforced. For instance, a recent study of Mexican labor markets found that very few workers actually earn the minimum wage, so clearly, the minimum wage is not binding in Mexico. In addition, the rate of both informal and formal employment in Mexico has tended to rise and fall with the ups and downs of the business cycle, so the informal sector is not absorbing workers during those times when the formal sector is shrinking.[44] The study of Mexican labor markets, which used data from urban employment surveys, also shows that the informal sector in Mexico is actually dominated by small entrepreneurs who sell nontradable goods and services. The informality of this sector is the result of regulations and taxes that affect the establishment of small businesses, rather than the result of distortions in the labor market. Nonetheless, it should also be recognized that informal employment itself may reduce the costs of labor market and other distortions (for the national economy) if the informal economy has resulted from the efforts of workers and small entrepreneurs to circumvent taxes and costly regulations.[45]

In the short run, the formal employment outlook in the LAC region may nonetheless improve if labor costs are reduced. A reduction in the costs of employment can result from two actions: the lowering of payroll taxes and other indirect labor costs, and the elimination of existing institutional rigidities that hinder wage flexibility.[46] Some lessons can be learned from the experience of a few LAC countries that have implemented labor reforms. Chile, Colombia, and Peru have made union representation contestable, have extended the freedom to organize unions, and have reduced the costs (or procedure-related uncertainties) of dismissals. All three countries reformed their labor codes to limit the costs of labor disputes to the parties directly involved. Peru also replaced the tradition of tripartite negotiations with "final-offer" arbitration and eliminated job-security legislation. In Colombia, labor reforms were enacted in 1990 that affected hiring conditions, severance payments, costs of dismissal, social security (which was reformed under different legislation from that which affected the other factors mentioned), minimum wages, and the rules regulating collective bargaining.

5. Competition laws and enforcement

Progress in the privatization of industries throughout LAC has brought to the forefront issues related to the structure of domestic markets.[47] It is well known that monopolies and other forms of uncompetitive market structures produce significant welfare losses. This is particularly true in smaller economies where one or a few firms can easily dominate a small market.[48]

Until recently, most LAC countries that had competition laws on their books tended to focus more on interna-

tional anti-competitive conduct (for example, price fixing and bid rigging), and much less on market structure (for instance, criteria for mergers and asset sales). In the absence of competition laws, LAC governments often made use of price controls and/or capacity licensing to "regulate" the private sector, which resulted in the imposition of unnecessary and costly distortions. The lack of private rights of action (that is, the right to bring private suits) has both legally and practically hindered effective enforcement. Moreover, the penalties and fines for misconduct have generally been too low to act as a deterrent.

However, since 1991 or so, a number of countries (including Brazil, Chile, Colombia, Costa Rica, Jamaica, Mexico, Panama, Peru, and Venezuela) have revised their competition laws and have begun to build an institutional framework. For the most part, the reforms have focused in considerable detail on both conduct and structural violations. These reforms have also been accompanied by consumer protection legislation. Venezuela's antitrust legislation has already worked significantly to break up both price agreements among competitors and officially sanctioned cartels and to prevent the formation of new ones. In Chile, the focus has been on successfully eliminating vertical restraints and collusive practices, whereas Mexico has focused mainly on merger policy. Most of Peru's attention and resources have been devoted to consumer protection issues. Only recently has that country begun to address antitrust cases, reaching decisions in two cases to break up the wheat-bread and chicken producers cartels.

Common issues in many reforming LAC countries are the scarcity of resources, and the lack of independence of the enforcing agencies, which are often staffed with inexperienced officers. For example, the Colombian and Peruvian agencies that deal with antitrust have fewer than six professionals, they have very thin budgets, and they depend for support largely on the executive branch of government rather than on independent allocations set by law.

Unfortunately, in some instances the benefits of these antitrust measures have been diluted by restrictive anti-dumping duties on imports or other forms of administered trade protection. With the exception of Peru, all LAC countries, following perhaps the examples of the U.S. and European Union, have separate agencies for dealing with antitrust and with anti-dumping cases. This practice is somewhat questionable since dumping is itself an anti-competitive behavior by a foreign firm, but there is no economic rationale for imposing different competitive requirements on foreign firms. In addition, recent advances in the reform of competition policy have raised the question of whether competition laws need to be harmonized across borders, especially among those countries that are undergoing formal economic integration, such as Argentina, Brazil, Paraguay, and Uruguay, all of which are members of the South American Common Market (MERCOSUR, in Spanish).[49]

6. Regulatory regimes for private investment in infrastructure and social services

Adequate regulation is especially important for private investment in infrastructure, in public utilities, and in social services. In fact, the most profound change in the role of the state in LAC is probably taking place in the provision of infrastructure services and public goods. Most of the region has come to the conclusion that just because the state must guarantee that the provision of infrastructure services and public goods is adequate and efficient does not mean that the state must provide these services and goods directly. On the contrary, involvement of the private sector, provided that it is adequately regulated and supervised, may be the only way to achieve an adequate supply of the high quality and low cost goods and services that are crucial to competitiveness and growth, and at the same time to maintain prudent fiscal policies (to avoid either excessive fiscal deficits or high tax rates that are distortionary and difficult to enforce). The regulations affecting private-sector participation in infrastructure, public utilities, and social services need to introduce market or quasi-market behavior into these three areas, which traditionally have been controlled by public monopolies and bureaucratic procedures, in order to ensure efficiency, equity, and environmental protection. This is especially true with respect to infrastructure (and particularly, telecommunications, energy, transportation, and water supply) and social services (social security, health, education, and nutrition).

The new role of the state in regulating the provision of infrastructure services and public goods is more demanding than was its previous role of exclusive or main supplier of these goods and services. Policy design, regulation, and supervision of privately financed infrastructure services and public goods are extremely complex tasks that require very specialized skills.

The complexity of both regulatory statutes and emerging private-public contracts in these sectors is overwhelming. Designing and enforcing efficient procedures that both guarantee as much competition as possible (which in many cases requires the construction of virtual markets where open markets cannot exist), and assure that private providers of infrastructure services and public goods do not leave out the poor, are huge challenges for regulators and supervisors. This is true of reforms affecting utilities, infrastructure, social security, and health. Strong, skilled, and credible regulatory agencies that are autonomous from the political process need to be established.

The question of which risks are shifted to the private sector and which remain with the government is critical to the efficiency of private investment and the avoidance of excessively high fiscal contingencies. Chile's new toll road contracts represent an important step in the right direction. The choice of instruments, the valuation of risks, the financial management of guarantees, and adequate budgetary provisions all require high expertise.[50] Few LAC countries are giving appropriate attention to these issues.

The goal is to increase private investment in infrastructure, in public utilities, and in social services. Doing so will improve both regulatory and risk-allocation systems so that overall risks are reduced, efficiency is guaranteed, and government contingencies are kept under control and are properly valued and budgeted. Although substantial progress in this area has been made in some LAC countries, notably Chile and in some sectors in Argentina and Colombia, most LAC countries still lack adequate and credible regulatory frameworks and agencies. As a consequence, private investment in infrastructure is still a costly and risky proposition in most of the region. Investors typically demand either high expected returns or high coverage, which in turn creates large unfunded and unbudgeted fiscal contingencies. Progress has been slower in the development of regulatory frameworks and agencies for private participation in the social services. Thus, regulatory reform and development of infrastructure and social services will be high on the LAC agenda for many years to come.

F. Public Administration and Governance

The fifth strategic priority is public-administration reform and governance. This is part of a broader agenda of state reform that permeates the four other strategic priorities.

Indeed, institutional reform is required to improve the efficiency and quality of educational and health services; fiscal strengthening requires more technocratic fiscal institutions (integrated government financial management, and improved budgetary institutions and tax administration); stable and efficient financial sectors require more competent regulatory and supervisory institutions; and improvement of the environment for private-sector development, especially in the infrastructure sectors, requires the establishment of new regulatory agencies.

Here we will focus on the interrelated challenges of reforming the civil service, decentralizing public service delivery, and reforming the judiciary.[51] A final section is devoted to the more general theme of governance.

1. Reforming the civil service

In most LAC countries, it is necessary to "right-size" public administrations. Generally, this involves downsizing in at least some areas, and raises difficult issues of redundancies, severance payments, and the like. For example, in 1992 the Mexican government merged the Ministry of Budget and Programming with the Ministry of Finance. This reform significantly reduced the number of bureaucratic personnel, but it also helped rationalize and strengthen the work of the Ministry of Finance that is aimed at enhancing the coordination of income and spending policies and at monitoring the federal budget.[52] Another country that has faced tough choices in reforming its civil service is Argentina, where reform began in December 1989. The reforms included deregulation, privatization, restructuring, and downsizing of the government. The tax administration offices—the *Dirección General de Impuestos* or DGI, for short, and the *Administración Nacional de Aduanas*—were excluded from the general reform, however, and, because of their key fiscal roles, were instead subjected to special reforms. More specifically, the reduction of jobs by DGI had to follow specific rules that were designed to minimize conflicts, and employees could not be fired unless they had participated in malfeasance. In addition, wages in DGI were raised in 1992, and training programs for its employees were instituted to improve the quality of its work force.[53]

It is essential to improve the incentive structures of civil service agencies. This includes improving the financial remuneration and other reward systems of public-sector workers and using "performance contracts," through which public-sector workers (or units) and agencies can be held accountable for the realization of goals. In some cases, new structures may be needed to mitigate "principal-agent" problems. For example, it is important to ensure some congruence in the incentives and behaviors of bureaucrats and politicians. Reforms may include the creation of institutional checks and balances and the introduction of mechanisms to increase contestability.

Several LAC countries, such as Argentina, Mexico, Nicaragua, Trinidad and Tobago, and a number of individual states, such as some in Brazil, have already downsized their public-service sector. Often, however, this downsizing has been carried out without the benefit of either a clear vision of the overall role to be played by the state or a functional audit of government entities to determine their proper place in a reoriented public sector.

The downsizing of public sectors presents many challenges and many countries need to devise mechanisms to

1. rationalize the organizational and functional structure of the public sector,
2. avoid losing the most capable people during restructuring,
3. minimize the social and political costs of releasing large numbers of public servants into the economy,
4. encourage participation in organizational assessments to ensure "ownership" by public servants and, at the same time, to minimize resistance to change,
5. strengthen the institutional capacity and management of essential functions such as education, health, and public security, and
6. involve the private and nonprofit sectors in state reform through alternative ways of providing public services.

Finally, an important aspect of civil service reform relates to the legal and regulatory reforms required to accelerate growth in the region that were discussed above. These reforms have a vital institutional dimension. In the post-privatization regulatory environment, considerable attention must be paid to the precise nature of the new institutions likely to be required, including institutions that regulate capital markets, utilities, competition, and institutions that provide consumer and environmental protection. Determining how to structure such regulatory institutions vis-à-vis the line agencies of government and how to ensure that the interests of the broader public are represented will be challenging.

2. Decentralization and service delivery

One of the most significant organizational changes in LAC over the past decade, roughly, has been the administrative and fiscal decentralization of government responsibilities. The state and municipal share of public-sector expenditure in Brazil increased from 31 percent in 1980 to 47 percent in 1991. The regional and municipal share of public-sector expenditure increased from about 5 percent in Chile in 1980 to almost 20 percent in 1992. The departmental and municipal share of centrally collected revenue in Colombia increased from 38 percent in 1991 to 55 percent in 1997. And the municipal share of centrally collected revenue in Bolivia increased from 10 percent in 1993 to 20 percent in 1995.[54]

Decentralized governments are expected to be more efficient in responding to demands for the delivery of services, to be more flexible in adapting to changing local circumstances, and to be more accountable to the local population than are centralized governments. Because local governments are better than national governments at recognizing the needs and preferences of local residents, and because local governments are at least as efficient as national governments at delivering public goods that benefit only local residents, it will be more efficient to have local governments provide the optimal level of public goods in each local jurisdiction. Local governments can be expected to be more efficient than national governments because local residents may find it easier to hold accountable local, as opposed to national, officials. Moreover, decentralization can increase efficiency by forcing local governments to "compete" for residents, because whenever residents have to pay fees for public services, they are free to change jurisdictions to find better and cheaper services.[55] Long-term efficiency considerations, therefore, suggest that the recent drive to decentralize in LAC is a welcome development.

Since the popular election of mayors in many cities in the region, a number of examples of "best practice" may be found at the local level in LAC. Such examples of best practice include an increase in the professionalism of municipal management; more effective mobilization and management of local and regional resources; innovations in the delivery of public services; enhanced public-private partnerships, including both a dramatic increase in the involvement of nongovernmental organizations as partners in service delivery and a greater role for the private sector; and increased local participation in public decision-making. Despite this anecdotal evidence, however, we still need to enhance our understanding of how widespread these improvements are, and whether they have actually had concrete positive effects. It is likely that, in practice, a variety of factors in addition to decentralization will affect the quality of the social services that are delivered by local governments. Chief among these factors are the quality of the local institutions and other aspects that are associated with the effectiveness of local governance, including the extent of corruption.

In fact, while decentralization offers great potential benefits, it also poses macroeconomic and microeconomic challenges. As discussed in Chapter 1, the macroeconomic challenges arise from the risk that subnational governments will use their growing autonomy to expand public-sector deficits. This has occurred in Brazil, where states have financed growing operational deficits by defaulting on debt service that they owed to the federal government. The national, or federal, fiscal deficit can expand if central governments are unable to cut their own expenditures to compensate for increasing transfers to subnational governments. The expansion of deficits in both these ways has occurred in Colombia. In contrast, intergovernmental transfers in Chile have increased, but they have been linked explicitly to spending on education and health under a tightly regulated regime. The microeconomic challenges arise from the increasing role that subnational governments have played in the delivery of public services, particularly education and health, and the risk that the quality of services may decline as the subnational role increases in the transition period.

Clearly, the LAC region faces major challenges as it makes decentralization a prime component of public-sector modernization. As already discussed, an important obstacle to successful decentralization is the still-commonplace mismatch between the responsibilities assigned to local governments and the revenues which they are assigned or must raise on their own and that are necessary to carry out these responsibilities. While there is a clear need to ensure that local governments have the resources needed to fulfill their new responsibilities, care must be taken so that the fiscal difficulties of state or local governments do not undermine the fiscal discipline of the central government.[56] This is a problem in Argentina, Brazil, and Colombia, where significant reforms at the state or provincial level that involve many aspects of public-sector management are only recently underway.

Efficient taxation and revenue sharing are essential both to the decentralization process and to overall fiscal balance. When decentralization depends almost exclusively on increased transfers of revenues that are collected by the central, or federal, government with no relation to local tax effort (as has been the case in Colombia), then there are few incentives to use resources efficiently or to accept local, or community, control. In fact, the tenets of public-choice theory that presume that local governments are more efficient and responsive than central ones break down if the link between local expenditures and local tax effort is severed.

In such a case, the burden on the finances of the central government may easily become unsustainable. This problem is compounded when revenue-transfer mechanisms are poorly designed. "Co-participation," or the automatic sharing of a few efficient tax revenues between national and local governments, induces central authorities to rely on unshared but inefficient taxes to solve overall fiscal imbalances. This creates costly distortions in the economy. A prime example of this is the Argentine tax on employment that distorts the domestic labor market but cannot simply be replaced by income taxes because the revenues from income taxes are shared with provincial governments. Colombia's experience since 1993 provides a different example. There, a fixed proportion of the central government's revenues is shared with local governments. This implies a heavy loss of fiscal flexibility because any attempt by the central government to increase revenues to offset fiscal deficits will lead automatically to increased expenditures by subnational governments.

Such problems are aggravated, in turn, by insufficient regulation of the indebtedness of subnational governments. In extreme cases, the states or provinces that own banks can easily finance huge deficits, at least on a temporary basis, and may eventually require bailouts by the central bank or central government. Recent reforms of state and provincial governments in Argentina and Brazil have focused on making this impossible. Yet even when subnational governments do not own financial institutions, there remain serious moral hazards that may easily lead commercial banks to overlend to entities that require national government transfers as collaterals.

Among the challenges posed by decentralization is how to prevent this process from increasing intraregional inequalities. One answer is to require targeted national transfers to subnational governments with smaller fiscal

bases. As the previous discussion suggested, creating adequate incentives for improving both the efficiency of expenditures and community control remains difficult. The most serious challenge posed by decentralization, however, is to prevent the "capture" of benefits by local elites. Addressing these challenges, as well as those related to the political economy of local governance, such as how to frame the issues of public choice and how to improve both the local electoral process and the relations of local governments to local community organizations and/or NGOs, will be important to the success of decentralization in LAC well into the next decade.

3. Judicial reform

Any discussion of modernizing the public sector in LAC must address judicial reform. The judicial systems of the region's countries do not presently satisfy the increasing demands of the private sector for contract enforcement. Furthermore, they do not enable the public sector to carry out its new responsibilities in an efficient, effective, and credible manner and they do not provide sufficient access to the wider citizenry, especially the poor.

In general, court systems in most LAC countries have suffered from major inefficiencies and delays. The result has been high costs, a process lacking in transparency, widespread corruption in many countries, a lack of predictability in the outcomes of cases, and, in some instances, political interference in judicial decisions by the executive branch. To reduce the high transaction costs associated with the absence and/or belated enforcement of laws and regulations, entrepreneurs often choose to deal only with well-known suppliers and to rely on personal relations and multiple collaterals to conduct business. This produces heavy efficiency losses and aggravates market concentration and segmentation. Micro-, small-, and medium-sized enterprises are especially hurt, because they are placed at a comparative disadvantage and, particularly, because their access to the financial sector is severely restricted. Not surprisingly, surveys of general public opinion in many LAC countries reveal a general distrust of LAC judicial systems, and particularly, of the criminal justice systems.[57]

A number of the region's countries are making considerable progress in judicial reform, some with the support of multilateral institutions. But the judicial reform agenda is large, varied, and for the most part, still unrealized. This agenda includes strengthening legal education, improving court administration, promoting judicial training, developing alternative dispute resolution systems, and improving access to the justice system. In these, as in other areas of public-sector modernization, there are formidable political constraints to reform. For example, in some of the region's countries, the executive branch is not fully committed to judicial reform and does not fully support the creation of a fully independent judiciary.

4. Governance

Governance means the enforcement of law and order by accountable and transparent government entities. In the LAC region today, we can observe two concurrent problems. First, although most countries in the region are now ruled by democratic regimes, corruption remains a source of concern. Second, many countries are suffering from a surge in crime and violence. Even though the issue of governance is broader than just the problems of corruption and violence, LAC countries are currently under great public pressure to deal with these two important and complex issues, which we discuss below.

a. Accountability, transparency, and corruption

The welcome phenomenon of democratization in the LAC region has heightened demands for greater accountability and transparency of public-sector institutions. Charges and countercharges of corruption in the region's political systems and electoral processes have played a key role. Mechanisms for enhancing accountability and transparency include various kinds of "democracy initiatives," such as electoral reform, the strengthening of electoral institutions, support for political parties, and direct human rights advocacy.

Enhanced accountability and transparency are closely related to the three themes (public administration reform, decentralization, and judicial reform) discussed above, and in particular to

1. the development of systems to help ensure that norms and regulations (for example, accounting standards for financial institutions) are consistently applied;
2. the strengthening of oversight institutions (especially those in charge of auditing financial entities);
3. the reduction of rent-taking by simplifying rules and procedures, and the replacement of administration with market mechanisms (for example, through reforms of tax and trade regimes);

4. the strengthening of institutions to improve financial controls, the elimination of licensing requirements, and the development of competitive pay scales for public servants; and
5. the improvement of government procurement through better bidding documentation, enhanced training, and more transparent procedures.

b. Crime and violence

While inadequate or nonexistent data make it extremely difficult to ascertain the magnitude of the problem, the overall regional homicide rate (which we use here as an indicator of crime and violence in general) is about 20 murders per 100,000 inhabitants. This is about twice the homicide rate in the United States and makes LAC the most violent region in the world. Colombia has the dubious distinction of placing first in homicide rates among the countries of the world, with a rate that has continued to accelerate since 1990 and now stands in excess of 80 homicides per 100,000 inhabitants (see Table 3.7).

In theory, crime and violence have a negative effect on economic development for at least four reasons. First, crime and violence adversely affect the stock of physical capital in several ways, the most obvious of which is the outright destruction of physical infrastructure. Additionally, crime and violence have a negative impact on the overall investment climate (affecting, for example, the tourist industry in some of the Caribbean countries, and the agriculture and mining sectors in Peru).

Second, crime and violence erode the development of human capital. A violent climate, for example, may prevent some children, especially girls, from attending school. Also, domestic violence negatively affects women's health. More generally, crime and violence are costly, requiring larger police forces, for example, and thus forcing governments to expend funds that might otherwise go to education and health.

Third, crime and violence destroy social capital. They destroy the trust, the norms, and the social networks that research has shown correlate positively with economic growth and the reduction of poverty.[58] Community-based organizations and other social networks suffer when crime and violence are high: access to their facilities may be reduced and they may thus lose members, vandals may destroy their property, and alternative organizations, such as gangs of delinquents, may draw away some of their members.

Fourth, crime and violence erode governmental capacity. They directly and indirectly contribute to corruption within agencies of the public sector. Public security is being privatized, and the state is increasingly seen as ineffective in providing basic services, and thus, as irrelevant or illegitimate.

Not surprisingly, the most thorough empirical work on this subject has focused on Colombia. One analyst recently estimated that gross capital formation is about 38 percent lower in Colombia today than it would be if homicide rates had remained at the level they were at in 1970. The cumulative "lost growth" as a result of crime and violence in Colombia between 1970 and 1993 is significant. Colombia's per capita income would be approximately 32 percent higher than it is today had homicide rates remained at their 1970 level.[59] Some estimates suggest that the costs of protection, the associated indirect costs of crime and violence, and the direct costs resulting from criminal activity together make up somewhere between 5 and 13 percent of Colombia's GDP.[60]

A recent World Bank paper suggests at least five key "policy domains" for dealing with crime and violence in cases where the potential for more—and more effective—public action seems large.[61] These policy domains address one or more of the central elements of the framework discussed briefly above. That is, they aim to reduce and/or reverse the corrosive effects of crime and violence on physical capital, human capital, social capital, and governmental capacity.

The policy domains are

1. programs to combat urban poverty, especially to provide basic urban infrastructure and social services;
2. programs in urban areas that target at-risk youth (especially male adolescents), women, and the victims of alcohol and substance abuse;
3. programs designed to build or strengthen social capital, especially in poor urban neighborhoods;
4. programs to improve the capacity of governments, especially at the municipal level, to monitor, understand, and reduce crime and violence (with a focus on involving local communities); and
5. programs to reform the criminal justice system.

Each of these areas, however, raises formidable analytical and operational issues as well as numerous (and difficult) problems for the international community.

The foregoing topics by no means exhausts the list of what is required for public-sector modernization and the enhancement of governance in the LAC region. However, it is clear that LAC's economic and social development goals cannot be met in a sustainable way when the region suffers from bloated and inefficient public bureaucracies, improper stewardship of public finances, central governments that have little regard for localities in the hinterlands, and a judicial system that is either reserved for the rich or barely functions.

Public-sector modernization and enhanced governance are thus central to attaining accelerated and sustained growth. However, we clearly still have much to learn about how to design and implement the policies and programs that effectively will bring the Latin American and Caribbean region into the twenty-first century.

Notes to Chaper III

1. On the impact of external shocks on economic growth, see Easterly et al. (1993).

2. For a recent survey of the empirical growth literature, see Lederman (1996).

3. GDI and Gross National Savings (GNS) data for the majority of LAC countries are discussed in Chapter 1.

4. The output-capital ratio is a measure of the productivity of labor and capital, since the average output of each unit of capital depends on the quality and quantity of the labor using this capital.

5. "Ricardian offset" is a technical term used to describe how public savings behavior affects private savings behavior. Namely, when the public sector reduces current expenditures, the private sector may expect that future taxes will be lower, and hence, private individuals will tend to reduce their current savings (thus expanding current consumption) because they expect to need less savings to cover future tax payments. See Schmidt-Hebbel and Servén (1997), Edwards (1997), and Gavin, Hausmann, and Talvi (1997). Edwards (1997) estimates that for each dollar saved by the public sector, national savings (public plus private savings) increase by approximately 50 cents.

6. See, for example, Barro (1991), Mankiew, Romer, and Weil (1992), and Barro and Lee (1993). On the role of human capital development in the growth of East Asian countries see, for example, Young (1995) and Lau (1996). For a critical view, see Pritchett (1996b), which argues that education may not promote growth if the "institutional environment is sufficiently bad" (42). This argument strengthens the importance of improving the quality and priorities of education.

7. See also World Bank (1993c) on the role of health, and World Bank (1995e) on the role of education.

8. On the relationship between financial development and growth, see Roubini and Sala-i-Martin (1992), King and Levine (1993), Berthelemy and Varoudakis (1996), and Levine (1996). On the role of stock markets, see Levine and Zervos (1996).

9. Estimates of the "costs" associated with recent banking crises in several LAC countries range from 5 percent to 20 percent of GDP. See Caprio and Klingebiel (1996), and Rojas-Suarez and Weisbrod (1996).

10. See Rojas-Suarez and Weisbrod (1996).

11. Figure 2 also shows that by the late 1980s, Chile had a relatively efficient banking sector.

12. Calvo (1997), for example, credits the existence of state-owned banks with the low efficiency of Argentina's banking system. The ratios of bad loans to total loans, for example, are much higher in Argentine and Brazilian banks that are owned by the federal government, the states or provinces, than in those that are privately owned. See the subsection on privatizing state-owned banks within the section, "Developing Efficient Financial Markets."

13. For an historical perspective on capital flows, see Eichengreen and Fishlow (1995).

14. On the empirical relationship between institutions and growth, see Knack and Keefer (1995), and Brunetti, Kisunko, and Weder (1997).

15. World Bank (1997i).

16. World Bank (1997i, Figure 2.3) shows that private investors believe that the "credibility" of the LAC state is low due to lack of "security of property" and "unreliable judiciaries."

17. World Bank (1997i, Figure 2.4) shows that a composite index of "state credibility" is associated with higher levels of investment and growth rates.

18. However, four LAC countries have primary enrollment rates under 90 percent: Bolivia, El Salvador, Guatemala, and Haiti. See World Bank (1995e, p. 39).

19. The results from the Third International Math and Science Study (TIMSS) show that Colombia, the only LAC country that participated in the study, was the second worst performer out of 41 countries. See *The Economist*, March 29, 1997, p. 21.

20. José Pablo Arellano, "El sentido de la reforma educacional," *El Mercurio,* January 5, 1997, p. E7.

21. See Cominetti (1996, p. 50-52), and Wolff, Schiefelbein, and Valenzuela (1994, p. 94).

22. See West (1997) and Carnoy (1997) for a lively debate over the theory of, and experience with, education vouchers across the globe.

23. These are GDP-weighted averages. Using purchasing power parity measures, the region spent approximately US$412 per person. The country that spends the least in per capita terms is Haiti (US$3 per person). See World Bank (1997g) and Chapter 4 for further discussion of health expenditures in LAC.

24. Chapter 4 examines in more detail the relationship between health services and expenditures and poverty in LAC.

25. World Bank (1995a, p. 8).

26. In contrast, the participation of state-owned banks in total bank assets is zero in the U.S., Japan, and Singapore; 13 percent in Korea and Malaysia; and 7 percent in Thailand. See Goldstein (1997, Table 2.5).

27. This paragraph is based on Aiyer (1996, p. 10).

28. Goldstein (1997, Table 2.4).

29. See Bank for International Settlements, *66th Annual Report,*

1996 (Basle: Switzerland).

30. See La Porta et al. (1996).

31. A more in-depth discussion of decentralization appears in the section of this chapter titled "Public Administration and Governance."

32. See Shah (1997).

33. La Porta et al. (1996).

34. World Bank (1997f, p. 332-7).

35. See La Porta et al. (1996).

36. See World Bank (1996b).

37. For accessible theoretical expositions, see North (1991) and Stiglitz (1994). For empirical evidence of the relationship between institutional development and economic growth, see Knack and Keefer (1995).

38. See North (1991, p. 27).

39. Stiglitz (1994, p. 44).

40. Recent theoretical work has shown that if developing (or southern) countries are the imitators of technology, and the industrialized countries are the innovators, then offering intellectual property rights may result in net welfare losses to the developing countries. This result holds even when considering the benefits of higher domestic innovation and foreign direct investment. See Helpman (1993). However, recent empirical work suggests that intellectual property protection is a significant determinant of economic growth, especially for more open economies. See Gould and Gruben (1996).

41. For example, in Peruvian municipalities, companies are required by law to fumigate their factories once every year; this is an example of a social regulation. Yet some municipalities have licensed only one firm to be the official fumigator and this company imposes a process regulation demanding firms to obtain a certificate of compliance. The problem is that, while the accredited fumigator charges double what the other fumigation companies charge, and its service is very poor, it is the only fumigator than can issue a certificate of compliance with the regulations. The regulations affecting the taxi-cab market in Montevideo, Uruguay provide another example. Licensing requirements (an example of a process regulation) imposed a cost of entry of approximately US$60,000 for entrepreneurs seeking to offer taxicab services. These entry costs have produced a scarcity of taxicabs in the downtown area as well as higher costs for consumers. See Guasch and Spiller (1997).

42. However, research regarding the impact of labor market flexibility on growth and on poverty reduction has just begun, and the evidence is mixed. See Rama (1995), and Squire and Suthiwart-Narueput (1997).

43. This section is based on Guasch (1996).

44. See Maloney (1997). This study defined the "informal" sector as "owners and workers in firms under 16 employees who do not have social security or medical benefits and are therefore not protected" (5).

45. Maloney (1997, Appendix 1, pp. 8-9) argues that wage differentials between formal and informal employment *may* reflect the costs associated with formal employment; hence informal workers and entrepreneurs may actually earn higher net wages and profits than they would in the formal sector.

46. A more detailed analysis of LAC labor regulations is pre-

THE LONG MARCH: A REFORM AGENDA FOR LATIN AMERICA AND THE CARIBBEAN IN THE NEXT DECADE

sented in Chapter 2.

47. This section is based on Rowat (1996, p. 19) and Guasch and Rajapatirana (1997, pp. 17-18).

48. However, it should be pointed out that the number of firms is less important than market structure, because a single firm can indeed behave as if it operates in a perfectly competitive market as long as there are threats of entry into the market. The basic textbook explanation can be found in Stiglitz (1986, p. 84).

49. For a detailed comparison of competition policies in MERCOSUR countries, see World Bank (1997b).

50. See World Bank (1997c).

51. These and other issues are discussed in Rowat (1996).

52. Camps and Noriega Curtis (1994).

53. Tiboni (1994).

54. Peterson (1997).

55. See Tanzi (1996).

56. Recent research on decentralization in Latin America has correctly emphasized this potential pitfall. See, for example, Garman, Haggard, and Willis (1996), and Peterson (1997).

57. Survey data show that between 55 percent and 75 percent of the public has a very low opinion of the judicial sector. See Buscaglia, Dakolias, and Ratliff (1995, p. 5).

58. The term "social capital" originated in Coleman (1990), and was popularized by Putnam (1993). For recent empirical work assessing the relationship between social capital and growth, see Helliwell (1996).

59. Rubio (1996).

60. Moser (1996).

61. World Bank (1997a).

IV
The Challenge of Poverty Reduction

THE BIGGEST CHALLENGE CONFRONTING DEVELOPMENT IN THE COUNTRIES OF LATIN America and the Caribbean is the persistence of poverty. Widespread poverty is a moral outrage, a profound obstacle to sustainable growth, a threat to the consolidation of democracy, and arguably the single greatest impediment to long-term political and social stability. In recent years, poverty has been a prime factor in the deterioration in the quality of life in many of the region's countries, a deterioration which is marked by the decline in the ability of families and schools to socialize children and adolescents, the increase in crime and violence, the rise in alcohol and drug addiction, and the erosion of social capital. For this reason, reducing poverty must be at the top of the regional development agenda, and the strategic priorities for reducing poverty require urgent and systematic attention.

A. The Incidence of Poverty

The appropriate way of measuring poverty and the numbers of people living in poverty has been the subject of considerable debate in both the policy and scholarly literature. Estimates of the number of people in Latin America and the Caribbean living in poverty—or the "headcount index" of poverty—vary substantially, depending on the methodology used, including the value assigned to the poverty line (below which people are considered poor), and the critical assumptions employed in formulating the estimates.[1] The World Bank's most recent publication on poverty estimates that about 24 percent of the region's population was living in poverty in 1993, based on a poverty line of US$1 per day (in 1985 prices) that was converted into local currencies using the latest estimates for purchasing power parity (PPP) exchange rates.[2] Employing a somewhat different methodology and a higher poverty line, the Economic Commission for Latin America and the Caribbean (ECLAC) recently estimated poverty in the region in 1994 at 39 percent (and "extreme poverty" at 17 percent).[3] Even those who are slightly above the poverty line—however

that line is defined—generally lead lives of drudgery and squalor that would shock a first-time visitor from any of the advanced industrial countries.

In comparison to other regions of the world, the Latin American and Caribbean countries occupy an intermediate position in the headcount indices of poverty, as they do with respect to many other economic and social indicators. Obviously, poverty by any measure is much higher both in South Asia (where 43 percent of the population was poor in 1993, according to World Bank estimates) and in Sub-Saharan Africa (where the figure was 39 percent). On the other hand, the incidence of poverty in Latin America and the Caribbean is considerably higher than it is in East Asia, excluding China (14 percent), in Eastern Europe and Central Asia (4 percent), and in the Middle East and North Africa (4 percent).[4]

1. The Poverty Profile in the Region

The poverty profile for the Latin American and Caribbean region has a number of distinguishing characteristics, the most apparent of which is the urbanization of poverty. Urban poverty has increased dramatically over the past two decades, a consequence of high rates of rural-to-urban migration, of the effects of the deep recession during much of the 1980s on the urban population, and of the inability of the emerging cities to supply the poor with basic urban services because these cities lack both financial resources and administrative capacity. It is now estimated that between two-thirds and three-fourths of all poor people in Latin America and the Caribbean live in urban areas.

Péronism as ex.

However, the fact that the region's poor are increasingly concentrated in cities should not obscure the extent of the poverty that still characterizes rural areas. In virtually all countries of the region, the majority of those falling in the poorest deciles (that is, the extremely poor) live in rural areas. In at least twelve countries in the region, the majority of the poor are rural. Rural areas generally show poorer results on social indicators. For example, the percentage of illiteracy in rural areas is about 2 to 6 times higher than in urban areas. A comparison of the average years of schooling in rural and urban areas indicates that, in all countries of the region, the rural averages are approximately three years lower than the averages for urban areas. Similarly, in most countries, infant mortality rates are considerably higher in rural than in urban areas.[5]

The World Bank has completed "poverty assessments" for virtually all the countries in Latin America and the Caribbean during the 1990s. These assessments have portrayed the demographic and socioeconomic characteristics of the region's poor. In addition to urban-rural distinctions, the assessments have highlighted the poverty conditions of a number of particularly vulnerable groups. These include women, especially single women who are heads of households; children and adolescents; the disabled and the elderly; and indigenous people, who comprise a substantial proportion of national populations in a number of countries. The World Bank's poverty assessment found in Guatemala, for example, that fully 90 percent of the indigenous population was living in poverty.[6] One somewhat surprising finding of the poverty assessments is that, in many countries of the region, considerable poverty exists among the employed; the "working poor" frequently are not paid well enough to raise them above the poverty line.

2. Trends in poverty

However it is measured, poverty in Latin America and the Caribbean increased in the years following the debt crisis of the early 1980s. It has been estimated by ECLAC that the headcount index of poverty increased from 35 percent in 1980 to 41 percent in 1990.[7] The most recent study by ECLAC estimates that the incidence of poverty declined only slightly in the early part of the 1990s, shrinking from 41 percent in 1990 to 39 percent in 1994.[8] According to World Bank estimates for 1993, the extent of poverty in the region remained virtually unchanged from what it was a decade ago. However, because the total population grew, the absolute number of poor people in the region (using the World Bank's somewhat restrictive definition) also rose—from about 91 million in 1987 to approximately 110 million in 1993.[9] More recent figures that reflect the experience of stabilization in high inflation economies such as Argentina and Brazil indicate a more positive trend in poverty reduction in the 1990s.[10]

B. Growth and Poverty

As argued in the World Bank's 1990 *World Development Report* on poverty, and confirmed by many subsequent analyses, robust and sustained rates of economic growth are fundamental to reducing poverty in Latin America and the Caribbean—or anywhere else, for that matter. Klaus Deininger and Lyn Squire discovered a strong, systematic relationship between aggregate growth and growth in the income of the poorest fifth of the population, finding that this group's income rose in 85 percent of the 88 "growth episodes" they studied.[11]

The positive correlation between growth and poverty reduction in Latin America and the Caribbean is apparent from several assessments carried out for this study. The relationship holds for different data bases, time periods, and poverty definitions. There have been differing estimates, however, of the region's growth-poverty reduction elasticity. Samuel Morley found a two-percentage point reduction in poverty for every one-percentage point increase in growth.[12] Others have found a lower elasticity, however; for example, George Psacharopoulos et al. found an elasticity of −1.60 for 1980 and −1.42 for 1989.[13] Estimates formulated by the Inter-American Development Bank yield lower elasticities: −1.08 for 1980, −0.91 for 1989, and −0.84 when pooling 59 observations over the period 1980–95.[14] The lower estimates suggest that the growth-poverty reduction elasticity may be lower in Latin America and the Caribbean than in other regions of the developing world, although other studies have indicated no significant differences between regions in this respect.[15]

FIGURE 4.1

International Comparisons of Land Inequality

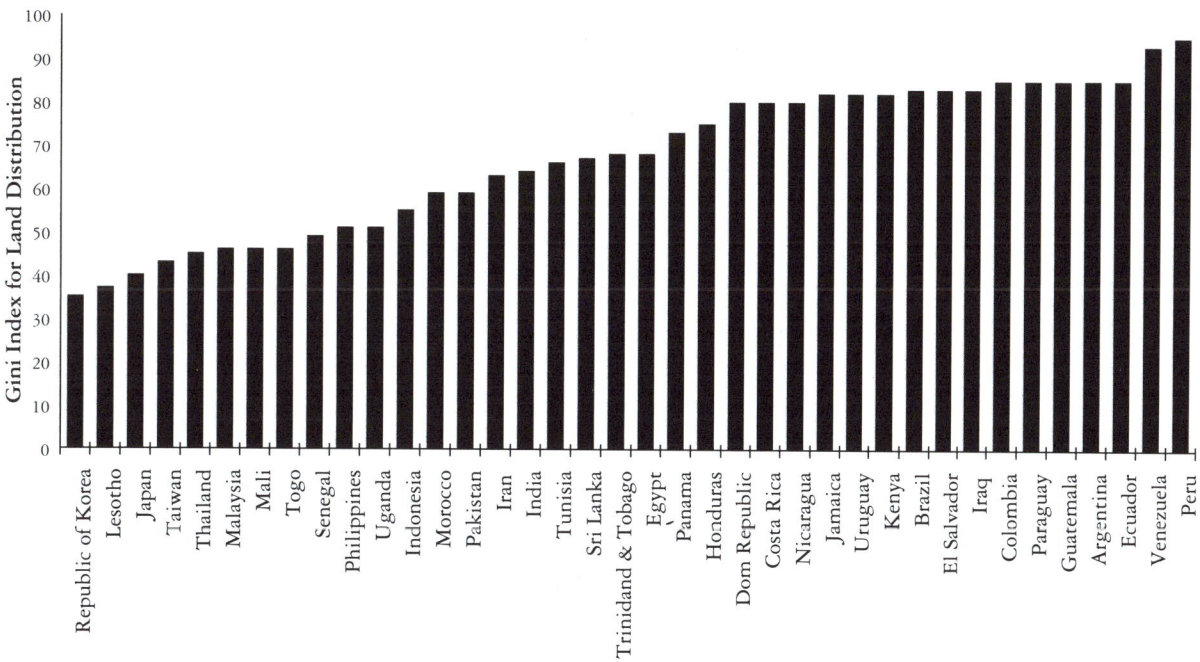

Source: Based on data supplied by K. Deininger and L. Squire, 1996.

The failure of poverty to decline faster in most countries, and more evenly within countries, in Latin America and the Caribbean during the 1990s suggests—but in the absence of more detailed analysis, does not definitively confirm—that a number of factors are attenuating the relationship between economic growth and poverty reduction in the region. One likely factor, discussed increasingly in recent years, is inequality. Simply put, the LAC region is notoriously inegalitarian.

The data in this regard are quite striking. The most comprehensive data set ever assembled on worldwide income distribution reveals the inequality that characterizes

Latin America and the Caribbean. In the 1990s, only 4.5 percent of regional income accrued to the lowest quintile of income earners; in contrast, 52.9 percent of regional

TABLE 4.1

Income Shares of Lowest and Highest Quintiles, 1960s–1990s (percent)

REGION OR GROUP	1960S	1970S	1980S	1990S
Lowest Quintile				
East Asia and the Pacific	6.4	6.0	6.3	6.9
Europe and Central Asia	9.7	9.8	9.8	8.8
Latin America and the Caribbean	3.4	3.7	3.7	4.5
Middle East and North Africa	5.7		6.6	6.9
South Asia	7.4	7.8	7.9	8.8
Sub-Saharan Africa	2.8	5.1	5.7	5.2
Industrial and High-Income Developing Economies	6.4	6.3	6.7	6.3
Highest Quintile				
East Asia and the Pacific	45.9	46.5	45.5	44.3
Europe and Central Asia	36.3	34.5	34.6	37.8
Latin America and the Caribbean	61.6	54.2	54.9	52.9
Middle East and North Africa	49.0		46.7	45.4
South Asia	44.1	42.2	42.6	39.9
Sub-Saharan Africa	62.0	55.8	48.9	52.4
Industrial and High-Income Developing Economies	31.2	41.1	39.9	39.8

Source: The World Bank, World Development Indicators, 1997, p. 57. Based on data in Deininger and Squire, 1996, op. cit.

income accrued to the highest quintile of income earners.[16] These income distribution figures are the lowest and highest, respectively, for any region of the world. Deininger and Squire argue that the concentration of assets may have an even greater effect on growth than does income concentration. Here, too, the LAC region offers a dismal profile. According to recently calculated Gini coefficients for the distribution of land, the seven countries in the world with the most severe concentration of land are all in the LAC region.[17]

These facts about inequality in Latin America and the Caribbean are important because the extent to which growth reduces poverty depends, among other things, on the extent of inequality. Generally speaking, the higher the inequality in a country—especially inequality in the distribution of assets, such as land—the greater the rate of growth that is required to reduce poverty by a given amount. Deininger and Squire found that only two of the fifteen developing countries with a Gini coefficient for land distribution above 70 managed to grow by more than 2.5 percent a year during 1960-92.[18]

The Latin American and Caribbean region has experienced a regional average growth of about 3.2 percent a year since 1990. As indicated above, this resumption of growth has not resulted in an appreciable diminution of poverty, however. Some observers have argued that the region needs

to grow by almost twice that amount—that is, by about 6 percent a year—to reduce the number of people living in absolute poverty. It is unclear whether or not this is a herculean goal. In any case, only two countries in the region have managed to exceed this target growth rate per year between 1991–96: Chile, with an average yearly growth rate of 7.1 percent, and Guyana, with a rate of 8.1 percent.

C. The Pattern and Quality of Growth

While there is now virtually universal agreement on the crucial importance of growth for achieving poverty reduction, the preceding discussion indicates that the effect of growth on poverty is mediated by a number of factors. The varying effect of growth on poverty has led scholars and policy analysts to focus on the pattern or quality of growth. Some patterns of growth appear more likely to reduce poverty than others. The World Bank's 1990 *World Development Report* recognized this and emphasized that some patterns of growth are "broad-based" and "inclusive" whereas others are not.[19] Generally speaking, the growth process in Latin America and the Caribbean has been narrowly based and exclusive. While some patterns of growth have made productive use of the most abundant asset of the poor—their labor—this has not been typical of the growth process in the region.

Insufficient attention has been paid to what precisely is

FIGURE 4.2
Growth and Poverty in LAC, 1979-1994

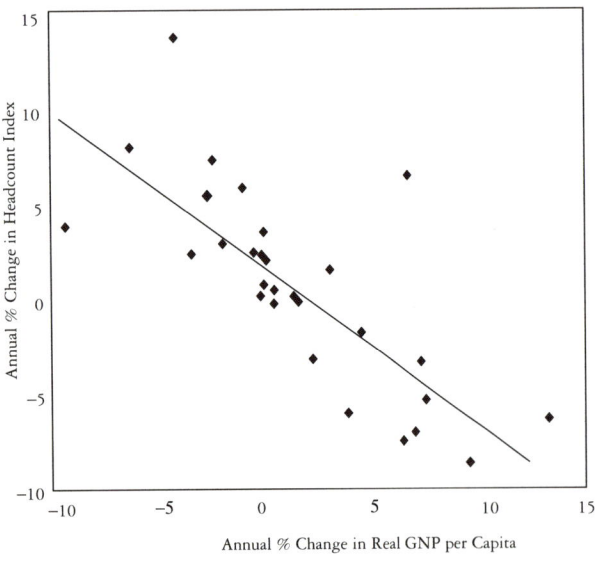

Source: UNECLAC, 1996.

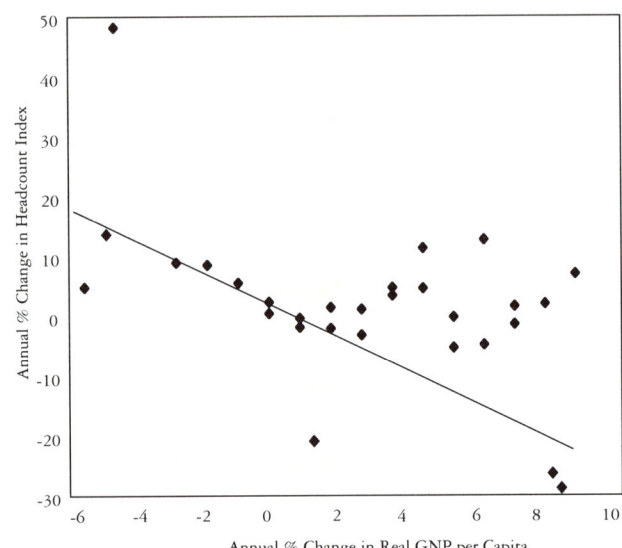

Source: World Bank Poverty Assessments.

implied by the notion of a "broad-based," or qualitatively superior, growth process.[20] A distinguishing feature of such a process may be found in the nature of factor markets, that is, markets for labor, capital, and land.

Over the past decade, most countries in Latin America and the Caribbean have taken the important step of liberalizing the markets for goods and services; these policy reforms have been responsible, to a large extent, for the resumption of the regional growth that has occurred. However, these countries have paid considerably less attention to removing distortions in factor markets (with a few obvious exceptions, such as Chile). The result, according to this hypothesis, is that the growth that has occurred has tended to benefit disproportionately the better-off members of the population and has been insufficiently inclusive of the poor. And the conclusion is that, if the prevalent distortions in factor markets were corrected, then the growth process in the region would be more broad-based and the reduction of poverty would be greatly facilitated. Phrased differently, a given increase in regional growth would yield greater poverty reduction than would the same increase in growth unaccompanied by factor market reforms. What follows is a brief discussion of the characteristics of factor markets in the region and an assessment of the nature and scope of the required reforms.

1. Labor markets

Recent assessments of labor markets in Latin America and the Caribbean have emphasized developments in urban areas and the discussion here will concentrate on these areas. However, many of the issues discussed are also relevant to rural areas.

The growth process in the region has been qualitatively deficient in one key respect: it has generally failed to make productive use of labor. The average annual growth rate of the LAC region's labor force since 1990 has exceeded the average annual growth rate of employment. Open unemployment persists and has actually been increasing in a number of countries since 1990. Unemployment rates are highest for women, youth, and the uneducated. For those between 15 and 24 years of age, the unemployment rate is twice the average rate. Underemployment has also increased sharply, with numerous workers employed in casual, temporary, and home-based jobs.[21]

A key distinction within regional labor markets is that between the formal and the informal sectors, which results in labor market segmentation. The informal sector is variously characterized but is usually defined by the number of workers in the workplace (with fewer than five or ten being commonly used cut-off points). The formal sector tends to be characterized by relatively higher productivity and wages than the informal sector. Workers in the formal sector are more likely to be unionized, have access to a wide range of benefits including social security, and have greater job stability. However, employment in the formal sector has been virtually stagnant in recent years; it has been growing at only 1 percent a year.[22] This situation is explained to a considerable extent by the impact of the structural economic reforms carried out by many countries over the past decade. These reforms caused significant aggregate and sectoral labor displacement, particularly in the manufacturing sector and in parastatal companies.

The informal sector, on the other hand, has been growing rapidly. The International Labor Office (ILO) estimated that, in 1995, no less than 57 percent of the region's workers were employed in the informal sector, an increase from approximately 52 percent in 1990. According to ILO estimates, 84 of every 100 new jobs created in the region between 1990–95 were in the informal sector.[23] The informal sector has thus been a crucial absorber of labor in recent years. Whether this is good or bad is a subject of considerable debate. Some who view the challenge of development as moving workers from the informal to the formal sector point to low productivity, low wages, job instability, lack of benefits, and often poor and unhealthy working conditions as evidence of the informal sector's shortcomings. Others, however, believe that excessive governmental regulation and a lack of financial and technical assistance are choking off the entrepreneurial dynamism of the informal sector.

One response to the perceived problems with regional labor markets is that such problems will be solved for the most part by higher levels of investment and by sustained and vigorous growth. It is undoubtedly true that sustained high growth is essential for the creation of more productive employment opportunities over the long term. However, a strong case can be made that a number of structural distortions and rigidities in the LAC region's labor markets are preventing the growth that is occurring from producing higher levels of employment, particularly employment that pays well enough to raise people out of poverty.

Such distortions include the following: various restrictions on the use of temporary contracts; high job protection for workers in the formal sector which entails substantial costs for firms seeking to adjust their labor forces; high labor taxes that raise employers' costs of doing business; noncompetitive wage determination mechanisms that frequently ignore productivity considerations; direct government intervention in some wage determination decisions; and inefficient labor conflict resolution schemes. The consequence of these various rigidities in the labor market appears to be substantial inflexibility, and in the new global competitive environment, flexibility is fundamental to success. The consequence of inflexibility, according to an argument increasingly heard in the region, is a weaker labor demand and expansion of the informal sector.

The policy agenda arising from an emphasis upon labor market segmentation includes a number of proposed measures to increase the demand for labor by reducing both wage and nonwage labor costs. They include a reduction in mandated payroll taxes, reform of the severance payment system, reduction or elimination of the government's role in setting wages, and decentralization of the collective-bargaining process. The limited evidence from international experience, including the very limited experience in Latin America and the Caribbean, indicates that such reforms have a positive effect on labor demand. One estimate is that the wage elasticity of labor demand is between 0.5 and 0.8, which suggests that a reduction of labor costs by 10 percent will increase employment by 5 to 8 percent.[24]

While the arguments for labor market reforms in the region are persuasive, it is important that such reforms not be seen as a panacea or as a new "theology" that imposes its own set of rigidities. The relative absence of solid empirical studies of the effects of the various proposed labor market reforms on job creation argues for caution, particularly when attempting to assess whether one aspect of labor market reform is more likely than another to affect employment. Also important and remarkably unstudied is the political economy of labor market reforms, including the role of labor unions in the region's new productive structure. Finally, even if labor market reforms can overcome political economy constraints and be enacted successfully, they are unlikely to be sufficient (even if they are necessary) to create a more labor-absorbing growth process. Other initiatives also seem to be required, and attention might usefully be directed to the three following areas.

a. Understanding the diversity of the informal sector

At present, the informal sector has not been adequately "mapped." Identifying the informal sector by referring simply to the number of workers employed in its workplaces is insufficient. A much better awareness of the varieties of informal sector employment is required for the design of well-articulated interventions in support of the sector. Recent research on this sector in Mexico found substantial heterogeneity in many aspects of small- and medium-scale enterprises, including firm characteristics, entrepreneurial dynamics, and the extent of participation in formal market and legal institutions.[25] The behavior of the informal sector in Mexico does not appear to correspond in all respects to the behavior predicted by the model of labor market segmentation.[26] This finding may reflect some particularities of the Mexican case and may not be generalizable. It does, however, illustrate the need for additional investigation into the nature and functioning of this important part of the labor markets in the LAC region. While the development of small- and medium-scale enterprises seems to be a key factor in alleviating the region's employment problem, more analysis is needed of the effectiveness of various policies for supporting such enterprises in all their considerable diversity.

b. Educating and training workers

The new competitive environment of production in the region puts a great emphasis on the acquisition of skills and knowledge. The wage gap between skilled and unskilled workers is increasing sharply and, in the absence of efforts to increase the capacity of the currently uneducated and unskilled, this gap could create a permanent wage-earning underclass. At present, worker-training initiatives are meager or nonexistent in most countries of the region. Government fiscal constraints make it difficult to implement substantial training programs, and private-sector firms frequently lack the incentives to create them. Nevertheless, the policies required for creating worker-training initiatives by the private sector require more systematic attention. This issue is clearly related to the issue of the general educational system (discussed below), because the private training of workers is likely to be more successful and profitable when the workers have already received a good basic education.

c. Focusing on women in the labor force

Increased attention needs to be devoted to the many implications of the increased participation of women in the labor markets of the region. This would include looking at ways to further increase the participation of women in the formal sector, such as greatly expanding child care for working women and ending discrimination against women in the workplace. Imaginative approaches are also required to assist the vast majority of women who work in the informal sector, and to expand credit to women who wish to open their own businesses.

In sum, the obstacles to a more employment-creating growth process in Latin America and the Caribbean are many and formidable. They are not all economic or technical in nature; indeed, various political and social constraints may be the biggest hurdles to overcome. Broad-based growth in the region is unlikely to occur, however, until the LAC countries address seriously the barriers to productive employment that arise from a rigid and outdated system of labor relations and until they examine fully the issues and policy implications of how the evolving productive structure affects workers in the informal sector, workers with little or no education, and women.

2. Credit markets

The poor in Latin America and the Caribbean lack productive employment opportunities. They also lack access to credit in both rural and urban areas. Credit markets function in ways that discriminate against the poor, which is another prominent characteristic of the region's narrowly based and exclusive growth process.

Small business borrowers in the region, including small-scale farmers and employers in small- and medium-scale businesses, generally find it difficult if not impossible to obtain credit from the formal commercial banking sector. One study of northeast Brazil found that 90 percent of small agricultural producers had no access to credit at all.[27] A study of rural financial markets in Mexico in 1990-94 found that fewer than one-fourth of rural entrepreneurs received cash loans from any source, that only about 8 percent received credit from the formal sector, and that the probability of receiving credit was lowest for small farms with no credit history.[28] A World Bank assessment of the credit markets in Argentina found that the commercial banks were unlikely to meet the financing needs of small- and medium-scale enterprises, which faced both a significant credit shortage and real interest rates on the order of 35 to 45 percent.[29] Similar examples of the lack of credit

available to small business may be found in many other countries throughout the region.

There are many different reasons why small borrowers, many of whom are poor, find it so difficult to obtain credit. Among these reasons are small borrowers' inability to provide the collateral required, their lack of formal credit histories, and, in rural areas, their geographical dispersion. Lending to small-business borrowers may create particular problems for commercial banks. For example, the costs of establishing credits and making disbursements are large, and the costs of collecting and enforcing debts are similarly high, especially relative to the size of credits. Rural areas, particularly those with large concentrations of the poor, have generally been seen by banks as excessively risky, and banks have thus been reluctant to establish branches or to make new loans there. Banks will usually place lower limits on farmers' leverage, will charge higher interest rates, will generally be more reluctant to invest in gathering information about the individuals who are seeking loans, and will hesitate to enter rural markets with little accumulated wealth.[30] In urban and industrial areas, a key constraint has been that credit risks and the costs of lending to small- and medium-scale producers are "front-loaded," whereas the profit from the undertakings that are financed are often substantially "back-loaded."[31]

In Latin America and the Caribbean, as in the developing world in general, a fairly typical set of policies has evolved to deal with this situation. They include providing "directed" credits, setting ceilings on interest rates, creating specialized agricultural or small-enterprise banks and programs that are funded or assisted by either the government or multilateral agencies, and, increasingly, establishing lending programs that involve volunteer effort, social or community participation, and the assumption of group liabilities.[32]

The record of directed-credit initiatives in the region, and in the developing world generally, is decidedly mixed and, on balance, is probably negative. The problems are numerous. The poor have received little of the financial assistance that has been extended under subsidized rural-credit programs in the LAC region, in part because eligibility criteria are too broad. Much of the credit intended for small- and medium-scale producers has been misdirected and has wound up in the pockets of large-scale producers and of those who are already well off. Many of the specialized institutions created to dispense directed credits to the poor have been mismanaged and unbusinesslike.

Bad loans and poor repayment histories have characterized other initiatives. Some official credit programs have led to excessive and perpetual dependence on government or external funding. In general, it has proven difficult to replicate successful programs because they seem to place a very high demand on the commitment of beneficiaries to make good use of the credit and to repay loans in a timely fashion.[33]

The considerable experience in the region with directed-credit programs has made it possible to compile a set of lessons which, if properly applied, could improve the performance of such programs on behalf of the poor. A recent World Bank assessment of its own experience concluded that credit services to small-business borrowers must be understood as business, and not as welfare, services to a far greater extent than is currently the case. A strong effective demand for credit services must be ascertained before the services are provided. A strong commitment from participating institutions is vital. Monitoring mechanisms must be enhanced. Careful assessment, selection, and where necessary, training, of financial intermediaries is necessary. A blend of innovative incentives and sanctions needs to be used to achieve high repayment rates.[34]

One particularly fruitful approach to improving the performance of directed-credit programs involves various kinds of group-lending and mutual insurance arrangements. While the most famous example is that of the Grameen Bank in Bangladesh, there are some promising initiatives along this line in Latin America and the Caribbean. For these initiatives to be successful, they must provide incentives to individuals to monitor and report cheating, give enforcement powers to the members of the group, require regular repayment of principal, and exclude defaulting groups from future loan programs.[35] If these and other requirements are met, such initiatives can provide a system of distribution that can reach producers who have relatively small financial requirements but for whom transaction costs are too high to be attractive to commercial financiers. Nongovernmental intermediaries are increasingly prepared to absorb such transaction costs, and where circumstances warrant it, a case can be made for subsidizing these costs.

Beyond the necessity of substantially improving directed-credit programs, a number of recent World Bank assessments suggest that there may be considerable merit to a quite different approach to the problem of providing credit to the poor. This alternative approach locates the problem within the larger context of all types of credit available to the poor, including both consumer and business credit as well as credit from both the banking and nonbanking sectors.[36]

There appear to be a number of opportunities for extending the financial system to the poor. For example, developing a broader home-mortgage market in the LAC region might be an indirect but very important way to reduce constraints on credit to small enterprises and farmers. It would liberate the personal equity of a large fraction of the region's population since a very large part of home investments are currently equity-financed. In Peru, for example, mortgage loans are currently being made successfully for units worth between US$3,000 and US$5,000.[37]

Suppliers' credits are another attractive option. Substantial credit might be channeled through equipment suppliers who may have natural business relationships with farmers, small entrepreneurs, or other relevant target groups. Such suppliers generally have extensive information about their clients, strong incentives to extend credit, and the ability to possess and resell collateral.

Removing the common legal restrictions on the goods that can be offered as collateral constitutes another important innovation that might be highly likely to benefit the poor, since current restrictions severely limit the ability of the poor to collateralize debts.

Developing the leasing industry, which is considerably underdeveloped in many countries of the region, is another promising avenue. Leasing is a particularly attractive source of financing for small- and medium-scale enterprises, farmers, or small rural industrialists. It can provide "point-of-purchase" financing, up to 100 percent financing, and greater assurance against technical obsolescence. Unlike straight debt-financing, it can reduce debt-equity ratios.

Finally, there is vast untapped potential for expanding the use of credit cards which facilitate lending to very small borrowers. A number of adaptations are required in the provision of credit cards to poorer and small-scale borrowers but these adaptations are, in principle, feasible and manageable. Credit card technology can, for example, mitigate the constraints on lending to dispersed, small-scale rural producers, for whom branch-banking is currently the only option.

In sum, a wide gamut of underutilized financial products, markets, and technologies may help mobilize additional credit for the poor and for other small borrowers, and thus reduce the cost to them of the credit they receive. These products and technologies can complement—and need not necessarily replace—the credit that is provided through traditional institutional mechanisms. Experience suggests that the traditional mechanisms require improvements. Such improvements, together with new programs and technologies to extend the region's financial systems to the poor, can help to overcome the segmentation that currently characterizes credit markets. Greater integration of these markets, as in the case of labor markets, will provide economy-wide benefits while also improving the economic situation of the poor.

3. Land markets and rural poverty

There are important issues regarding land markets in urban areas. For example, the lack of secure title to land on which the residents of many squatter settlements live is a major obstacle to residents' access to credit and thus to their ability to improve their dwellings. However, much attention continues to focus on land issues in rural settings.

The extreme concentration of land ownership in Latin America and the Caribbean has already been noted. In an earlier era in the region's development, the policy response of a number of countries, including Bolivia, Chile, and Colombia, was the "expropriation model" of agrarian reform (although each country's reform measures differed somewhat from the others). Debates over the desirability and viability of the various agrarian reform schemes adopted under this rubric were vigorous and intense. In a sense, these debates were resolved by the course of events, which included severe political conflicts over the reforms; increased fiscal pressures on governments that made difficult the public provision of the complementary inputs required for successful reform; and apparent declines in productivity and output of many of the expropriated properties. Over time, the expropriation model came to be seen by many as excessively costly, as demanding too much in the way of complementary technical assistance, and not least, as simply not viable politically given the constellation of political forces in most of the countries of the region during the late 1970s and throughout the 1980s.

More recently, an alternative approach to land reform has attracted considerable attention. Known as "market-assisted" land reform, its essential aim is to assist small farmers to enter the land market as purchasers of land.[38]

Programs of market-assisted land reform have been launched in Brazil and Colombia, and a program is under consideration in Guatemala.

One rationale for such land reform is similar to that concerning imperfections in credit markets. If small operators (who are generally poor) have greater difficulty obtaining credit than do larger operators (who are generally better off), and if this prevents them from breaking into owner-operated farming, then land reform is justified.

But that is only one justification for market-assisted land reform. The other is that there must be substantial tracts of potentially arable land that are not being fully exploited. Where there is little unused land, or where land is unsuitable for farming, land reform is unlikely to prove an appropriate approach for the reduction of rural poverty. A crucial justification for market-assisted land reform thus hinges on the nature of the land market; where land markets are sluggish or highly segmented, there may be a case for land reform.

These prerequisites for market-assisted land reform have policy implications for both supply and demand. On the one hand, it is necessary to remove policies that provide incentives for people to retain farm land for reasons other than farming (for example, for speculative gain), and to introduce an incentive regime, which includes an appropriate mix of taxes and subsidies that will enhance efficiency. On the other hand, it is necessary to provide subsidies to the poor to buy land, to offer the training that is essential to the design of sound farm projects, and to invest in the economic and social infrastructure that makes farms likely to be viable.

The key difference between market-assisted land reform and the expropriation model is that the former is not coercive. Instead, it involves negotiations between willing sellers and willing buyers. In market-assisted land reform, the state has a key role to play even if it is not the confiscatory role of the past. The state needs to delimit the areas deemed environmentally appropriate for farming, to implement the policy reforms needed to increase the supply of farm land available on the market, to draw up the criteria for selecting the beneficiaries of the reform, to subsidize the purchase of land and the training of beneficiaries, to fund the supporting infrastructure, and to monitor and evaluate the land reform process to make certain that it is equitable and efficient. This is a substantial agenda for public policy that, in most countries, will require administrative and managerial reforms of the relevant government agencies.

The Colombian approach illustrates both the potentials and pitfalls of the market-assisted land reform approach. The sale price for the family farm units into which property is divided has exceeded initial estimates. The mean size of family farm units appears to have been unnecessarily large. Insufficient attention was originally given to the financing of the required on-farm investments. As a result, the number of farms that have been distributed so far have fallen considerably short of what was initially anticipated, as has the number of beneficiary families. A series of modifications to the original approach show considerable promise, however, and pilot efforts in five Colombian municipalities are encouraging.

Even if efforts at market-assisted land reform prove replicable throughout the region, it will be difficult for these reforms to reduce landlessness significantly, and thus to contribute decisively to reducing rural poverty. The sheer magnitude of the inequality of landholding in rural areas of the LAC region, as well as the political economy constraints to redressing this inequality, obliges consideration of alternative reforms as well.

The regularization of land titles is seen as another promising approach, and considerable headway has been made in a number of countries, in many cases with World Bank support. Programs of individual land titling are relevant in cases in which family farms are the predominant form of tenure and the community does not control sales to outsiders. There are several benefits from titling. Titled lands generally have higher value than untitled lands of the same quality and location. Evidence from diverse countries in the region, including Bolivia, Chile, Costa Rica, Honduras, Jamaica, and Paraguay, shows that titled farmers generally have readier access to institutional credit than do farmers without title.[39] Land titling, however, is a time-consuming, technically complex, and politically charged process that requires considerable bureaucratic effort. Still, it is undeniably important and merits continued support, particularly in the context of other initiatives (including reforms of laws and institutions that affect the rural poor, and reform of land taxation).

Previous efforts to supply the rural poor, many of whom are landless, with various support services have been largely susceptible to the "benefit capture" so characteristic of the region. Agricultural extension efforts, for example, failed to reach most smallholders, mainly because only credit recipients were eligible for extension assistance, and as previously discussed, credit was largely conditioned on the ownership of land. Much the same can be said for government-sponsored irrigation works in the region, which for the most part were not targeted at the poor and which largely succeeded in promoting intensive production by a few who used modern technology at an extremely high cost per hectare or per beneficiary. Technical packages for rainfed agriculture, which is relevant to the crops grown by, and the farming practices of, the smallholders, were largely neglected.[40]

Some recent initiatives appear to be making headway in tilting the distribution of benefits in the direction of the smaller and poorer farmers. These have been called "demand-driven rural investment funds."[41] They emphasize participation by the beneficiaries, often with the assistance of nongovernmental organizations, in identifying, financing, and implementing small, grant-financed subprojects that usually involve providing basic economic and social infrastructure. These rural investment funds appear to do a reasonably good job of targeting the poor, increasing beneficiary ownership over project interventions, minimizing bureaucratic costs, and responding flexibly to varying conditions in different communities. Their apparent shortcomings stem from their inability both to confront fundamental issues of land tenure and to provide the technical packages appropriate to smallholder conditions.[42]

Analysts of the rural scene in Latin America and the Caribbean are increasingly of the view that it is necessary, when designing policy interventions, to distinguish among several different types of the rural poor and among their different sources of income.[43] At least three groups have been identified. One includes those who appear to have a realistic chance of increasing their agricultural productivity and output. A second is composed of those whose realistic opportunities for increasing their income appear to lie either in the off-farm labor market or in nonfarm self-employment. Those in the third group have few realistic prospects of escaping abject poverty for any of the following reasons: because they have no land, because they lack education and are illiterate, because they have too many dependents, because they lack labor power, or because they are aged and infirm and unable to migrate out of resource-starved areas that have little or no agricultural potential. (Some, and perhaps many, in this group possess all of the characteristics listed here.)

While these classifications are highly suggestive, the percentage of people in each of these categories in each of the countries in the LAC region have yet to be estimated. The nature and scope of policy interventions will clearly have to vary according to the relative incidence of these three groups. Since ownership of land and secure tenure are likely to be essential for the first group, market-assisted land reforms, cadastral and titling programs, and relevant technology and other support services might usefully be targeted at them. This assumes that it is possible to determine with reasonable accuracy who falls or might potentially fall within this category, an assumption that may be incorrect.

It is the second group—that segment of the rural poor for whom the future appears to lie not in agriculture but in activities off the farm—that deserves special attention. The proportion of the total income of small farmers in Chile that is derived from off-farm activities was recently estimated at 59 percent. Although the figure is lower in other countries, it is still surprisingly high in many (for example, the figure is 23 percent for Honduras).[44] The scope of opportunities for expanding off-farm income for the rural poor in Latin America and the Caribbean appears substantial. However, these off-farm opportunities must piggyback on the dynamic growth of the agricultural sector itself. Additional analysis is needed of the policies that might facilitate the generation of more income from off-farm employment. Education and training appear to be at the center of the requisite initiatives, which suggests that the relatively low levels of secondary education in the rural areas of the LAC region need to be raised substantially.

Finally, there is the difficult issue of the "rural underclass." For this group, migration to the cities may be the only answer. But the people in this group are precisely those who are least able to move, often for reasons of sheer physical incapacity. Indigenous peoples, the aged, and many women are represented disproportionately in this group. This is not to argue that nothing can be done for this group, but it does suggest that any investment in areas of extreme poverty is likely to be relatively small, to be focused on such activities as small-scale processing, marketing, and handicraft work, and is unlikely to be repaid. In assisting this group, it is desirable to rely upon the poor themselves to identify their own needs and priorities. One useful technique for gathering this information is through the use of "participatory poverty assessments," which are intended to extract open-ended responses from the poor

about how they see their problems and about how they might be solved. One finding that has emerged from participatory poverty assessments conducted in the region is that the poor do not see land reform or other "radical" solutions to the problem of rural poverty as either feasible or even necessarily in their own interest. They tend to give priority to achieving relatively modest and incremental improvements in their daily lives.

In conclusion, the extremely high concentration of landholdings in rural areas of the region, and the seeming inability, given the current political context, to tackle this problem head-on, calls for consideration of a range of initiatives. Market-assisted land reform is only one possible initiative. Others may hold equal, if not more, promise. Whatever approach is chosen, reducing rural poverty, which has been perceived as less urgent since the days when confiscatory land reform and rural-based guerrilla movements brought great attention to the countryside, again needs to be placed high on the agenda of what is required to make the growth process in the region more inclusive.

D. Human Capital Development

In order for people to take advantage of the opportunities provided by growth, they must be educated and they must be healthy. If human capital is unequally distributed, however, then the maldistribution of physical assets and income, which was previously discussed, will be exacerbated, resulting in cumulative inequalities. Unfortunately, this situation prevails in much of Latin America and the Caribbean.

1. Education

Education is crucial to reducing poverty, most directly because education affects the earning power of the poor. Investing heavily in the education of poor children ensures that they will earn more in their productive years than if they had received little or no education. A recent study showed that in six countries (Brazil, Colombia, Costa Rica, Panama, Uruguay, and Venezuela), the average incomes of the urban employed population between the ages of 15 and 24 increased linearly with the increase in the number of years of education completed. In Brazil in 1990, the average income of those with more than ten years of education was 3.4 times higher than the poverty line, whereas the average income of those with five or fewer years of education was only 1.2 times higher than the poverty line. The multiples for Costa Rica were 4.4 and 2.1, respectively. The figures for the other countries studied were similar.[45] This linear relationship between educational attainment and income level may be explained by the fact that those with less education tend to be concentrated either in the informal sector or in the lowest rungs of the formal sector, where productivity and wage levels are lower. The widening income differentials within the occupational structure, particularly the increasing gap between the wages of skilled and unskilled workers, reflect in large measure the disparities in educational attainment between the poor and the nonpoor.

There are also numerous positive correlations between education and various nonincome dimensions of poverty, including health and nutritional status. In addition, better-educated people tend to participate in societal institutions and political life to a greater extent than the less educated; they are also less prone to engage in antisocial behavior, such as crime and violence. Because of these direct and indirect consequences, education must be the cornerstone of poverty reduction.

Some educational attainments in Latin America and the Caribbean appear impressive. For example, virtually universal coverage has been attained in primary education in most countries in the region. Substantial strides have been made since 1980 in expanding access to preschool education, which is increasingly seen as critical to subsequent educational success. For the most part, gender disparities have been eliminated at the primary level, and differences between male and female literacy rates, although still apparent in some LAC countries, are smaller than those in other regions of the developing world.

TABLE 4.2

School Enrollment, Primary (% gross)

	1993
Argentina	107
Chile	98
Colombia	119
Costa Rica	105
Cuba	104
Dominican Republic	97
El Salvador	79
Guatemala	84
Honduras	112
Mexico	112
Nicaragua	103
Paraguay	112
Peru	119
Trinidad and Tobago	94
Uruguay	109

Source: The World Bank, World Development Indicators Database, 1997.

However, enormous problems remain.[46] Dropping out of school is commonplace in the region; only about half of the students who start primary education ever complete it. Repeating grades is also common. Of the 9 million children who enter primary school every year, approximately 4 million fail in the first year. Overall, 29 percent of all primary students each year repeat their grade. Enrollment at the secondary level lags far behind primary enrollment. Educational quality, especially in the public schools of the region, is generally agreed to be extremely poor. The limited evidence available indicates that students in Latin America and the Caribbean perform significantly worse on standardized achievement tests than do students from other regions.

Latin American and Caribbean countries spend a substantial 4.3 percent of GDP, or approximately US$50 billion per year, on education.[47] The result, especially in terms of quality, is far from commensurate with the expenditure. Poorly managed and highly inefficient educational systems, antiquated teaching methods, and a resistance to change (until recently in some countries) have together yielded poor educational outcomes which do not position the region to contend successfully in today's demanding and competitive world.

As might be expected, the poor bear the brunt of the system's inadequacies. The physical conditions in many schools in poor areas are appalling. In poor areas of Peru, for example, it has been estimated that only 2.4 percent of the schools have water, drains, and electricity. In three of the poorest provinces in Northern Argentina, over 50 percent of the school buildings do not have indoor plumbing and over 30 percent have no electricity.[48] Poor rural populations are particularly disadvantaged. Significant differences in the distribution of educational spending between the urban and rural areas of many countries accentuate the disparities between the poor and the nonpoor. Poor students in rural areas are less prepared for school than are urban children because, in comparison to those children, the rural poor lack access to preschool education. Also, the quality of the schools attended by the rural poor is low and marked by frequent teacher absences. In general, the educational attainment of the rural poor is lower than that of urban children. Additionally, the poor in rural areas also have very little access to secondary education.

Ethnic and linguistic minorities are also noteworthy for their relative lack of participation in the educational systems of the LAC region. In Guatemala, for example, the average number of years of education for indigenous boys is only 1.8 and that for indigenous girls, only 0.9.[49] In rural Peru, where the majority of the population is indigenous, 70 percent of Quechua-speaking people over the age of five have never been to school, compared to 40 percent of nonindigenous Peruvians.[50] Although, on average, the gender gap in education in the region is narrow, enrollment rates for girls, especially indigenous girls, in rural areas are lower than for men.

While the poor lack access to education in comparison to the nonpoor, they also receive a lower quality of education. In Chile, for example, results of a national standardized test of educational performance reveal a clear socioeconomic split, with students who attend private schools scoring, on average, about 30 percent higher than do students in the public municipal schools.[51] A UNESCO study conducted in eight countries of the region found that only about 2 percent of students from the lowest socioeconomic stratum who took standardized tests scored in the top quartile, whereas 28 percent of students from the highest socioeconomic stratum scored in the top quartile.[52] The reasons for the lower performance of the poor are complex and undoubtedly include the fact that poor children tend to come from homes that do not prepare them well for school and do not nurture them well during the early school years. The lack of preparation and nurturance, when combined with the generally poor quality of education offered in the schools themselves, dramatically lowers test performance.

Not unexpectedly, the poor drop out of school at considerably higher rates than the nonpoor. For young people in the bottom quartile of the regional income distribution, the percentage who leave school before completing the primary cycle is substantially higher (on the order of 40 to 80 percent in the countries of the region) than it is for those better off.[53]

The reasons for the markedly higher dropout rates among the poor are several. First, the poor often cannot afford to pay even the relatively modest amounts of money (for books and supplies, uniforms, transportation, and the enrollment fees levied by some public school systems) that are required to keep their children in the public schools. A study in Peru based on household survey data showed that a moderate increase in fees for secondary education discouraged enrollments among the lowest income groups.[54] Second, the lack of commitment to education is transmit-

ted from one generation to the next. There is a positive correlation between parents' years of schooling and those of their children. A third reason for high dropout rates among the poor, and one that is integral to the perpetuation of poverty, is that the opportunity cost to the poor of having a child in school who could instead be earning an income is high, and often very high. Dropping out of school is closely linked to prematurely entering the labor force. In Colombia, for example, 41 percent of working males between the ages of 12 and 14 attend school; in contrast, 91 percent of those who do not work attend school.[55] One recent study found that minors in Paraguay contribute almost one-fourth of total family income.[56] A key reason that the demand by parents for education for their daughters is low in much of the region is because the direct and opportunity costs of educating them are high; for example, daughters play a crucial role in child care and carry out many other household tasks.

Very few of the poor ever attend institutions of higher education. Although precise data are skimpy, it has been estimated that 77 percent of higher education students in Venezuela come from the top 20 percent of households in terms of income; the figure for Colombia is 67 percent, and for Chile, 63 percent.[57] Yet in most countries of the region, higher education is the most heavily subsidized level of education. World Bank studies have consistently shown that the private and social rates of return are highest for primary education, and yet public subsidies for higher education tend to be much greater than those for the primary level. This just exacerbates the educational inequalities confronted by the poor.

There is now considerable agreement on the regional agenda for educational reform. In general, there is a perceived need to improve dramatically the efficiency of educational systems, to upgrade significantly the quality of the education offered in the public schools, and to correct the manifest inequities in the provision of educational services.

The goal of greater equity in education is being pursued in a number of ways. In a number of cases, access is being improved through programs and projects that target poor regions, girls, and minority groups (through bilingual education programs, for example). In Chile, for example, the Ministry of Education has used the results from a national assessment system in four subjects and other social indicators to assist it in targeting additional support to the poorest schools. Guatemala has established a scholarship program for girls, which provides free tuition and pays stipends to parents to compensate them for other direct costs, such as books, and for the loss of their daughters' time. Greater involvement of local community groups in the management of schools seems to pay off in improvements in the quality of education for the poor, as it has in the rural areas of El Salvador, for example. There is renewed interest in providing some types of specialized vocational education, which, as the example of Chile suggests, may produce higher returns than does general secondary education. Various programs in the LAC region are aimed at assisting "at-risk" youth, particularly male adolescents, to remain in school. The increase in preschool programs in the region may prove particularly beneficial to the poor. Evidence from Brazil, Peru, and elsewhere shows that such early childhood interventions can enhance school readiness and reduce the dropout rate as well as the repeating of grades.[58]

Considerably more is likely to be required in addition to the enhanced targeting of educational resources at the poor, however. Indeed, it is highly likely that more vigorous efforts to introduce system-wide reforms will produce an even greater payoff for the poor since the poor bear a disproportionate burden of the educational systems' current deficiencies. Thus, experiments with decentralization and autonomous local decision-making, the introduction of market mechanisms and competition among schools, curriculum reform, teacher training, and the employment of more systematic methods for measuring educational quality, all hold considerable promise for redressing the most prominent educational problems in Latin America and the Caribbean. The challenge, however, is to watch closely how the various systemic reforms that are adopted and implemented affect the poor. With proper monitoring, and with appropriate public interventions to tilt the distribution of benefits from systemic reforms in the direction of the previously disadvantaged groups, educational reform may result in a more equitable endowment of regional human capital. It may thus equip the poor to take better advantage of the opportunities provided by growth than has thus far been possible.

In the area of systemic reforms, as in other areas, political economy considerations loom large. The prevalent structure of educational systems in the region and the consequences of this structure for educational decision-making have provided little or no incentive to the major actors (including strong teachers' unions in many countries and the entrenched educational bureaucracy at the national level) to change their behavior. Reforming the educational system, including improving educational access by and quality for the poor, requires coming to grips with often severe political constraints. Failure to recognize and deal with these constraints may frustrate the attainment of a reform agenda that, from a purely technical standpoint, appears clearly desirable.

2. Health

In recent decades, there have been substantial improvements in many commonly cited health indicators for the LAC region. For example, infant mortality (per 1,000 live births) has declined sharply in every country of the region, including the poorest country, Haiti, over the 1970–95 period. Life expectancy has increased substantially in every country as well over the same period. As a consequence, most people in Latin America and the Caribbean—regardless of their per capita income—enjoy much better health today than previously. For example, Chile in 1990 had a real per capita income similar to that of the United States in 1900; yet average life expectancy in Chile in 1990 was 71 years whereas that of the United States in 1900 was only in the high 40s.[59]

TABLE 4.3

Mortality Rate, Infant (per 1,000 live births)

	1970	1995
Argentina	51.6	22.0
Bolivia	153.4	69.0
Brazil	94.6	44.0
Chile	77.0	11.8
Colombia	73.6	25.6
Costa Rica	61.5	12.7
Cuba	38.7	9.1
Dominican Republic	98.4	37.2
Ecuador	99.8	35.9
El Salvador	103.4	35.6
Guatemala	100.2	43.8
Haiti	141.0	72.3
Honduras	110.2	45.4
Jamaica	43.2	12.6
Mexico	72.4	32.6
Nicaragua	106.0	45.8
Panama	46.6	22.6
Paraguay	55.4	40.6
Peru	108.0	46.7
Trinidad and Tobago	52.0	13.2
Uruguay	46.4	18.3
Venezuela	53.4	22.7

Source: The World Bank, World Development Indicators Database, 1997.

The reasons for these improvements in health remain a source of debate. In part, they result from gains in income, increases in educational achievements, and the accompanying improvements in nutrition, hygiene, housing conditions, water supply, and sanitation. In part, they result from the spread of knowledge about diseases (for example, about the role of microbes), the development of effective interventions (for example, vaccines for childhood diseases and antibiotics to control infections), and the introduction of policies that make such interventions readily accessible to the population.

Despite the impressive gains, a number of severe problems remain. There are still some significant disparities in some key health indicators among the countries of the region. For example, the mortality rate (per 1,000 live births) for children under the age of five is only 15 in Chile and 16 in Costa Rica, but it is 96 in Bolivia and 101 in Haiti.[60] Another example is the percentage of births attended by health staff. Whereas virtually 100 percent of all births are attended by health staff in Uruguay, and 98 percent of births are so attended in the Dominican Republic, the percentage for Ecuador is only 27 and for Guatemala, it is only 22.[61] In general, Central American countries (with the exception of Costa Rica), Haiti, the Andean countries, and Paraguay do less well—in many cases considerably less well—than do the countries of the Southern Cone, Colombia, Venezuela, Mexico, and the English-speaking Caribbean countries.

The problem does not appear to be that insufficient resources are devoted to health care expenditures. Almost all countries in Latin America and the Caribbean spend "enough" on health. In fact, as discussed in an earlier chapter, total health expenditures (both public and private) as a percentage of GDP are higher in the LAC region than in any other region of the developing world. The same can be said for per capita total health expenditures, which in 1994 were US$234 for the region, compared, for example, to only US$21 in the East Asia and Pacific region (including China).[62]

Again, there are significant disparities within the LAC region. Health expenditures per capita range from a low of US$3 in Haiti in 1995 to a high of US$355 in Argentina in the same year. Intermediate countries show considerable variation; for example, per capita health expenditures were US$12 in Guatemala, US$17 in Honduras, US$20 in Bolivia, and US$95 in Brazil.[63] In general, however, the

region's health problems are not due to the lack of expenditure on health per se, but rather to the misallocation of financial resources and to the internal inefficiency of the health care system. There is considerable scope for reallocating resources (from tertiary to primary care, for example, from curative care to preventive care, or from the nonpoor to the poor), and there is considerable scope, as previously noted, for improving the internal efficiency of the health care system.

In terms of a concern with poverty reduction, there are a number of key issues in the health sector. One is access of the poor to services (which is basically analogous to the situation in education). Simply put, the poor have less access to health care—especially quality health care—than do the nonpoor. It has recently been estimated that more than 100 million people in the region do not have regular access to a formal health care system.[64] Coverage is particularly low in eight countries (Bolivia, Ecuador, El Salvador, Guatemala, Haiti, Honduras, Paraguay, and Peru), where more than 40 percent of the population is estimated to have no access to basic health services.[65] Even in Brazil, which is a significantly wealthier country, about one-third of the population is unable to obtain basic care. Lack of access is especially pronounced for the indigenous poor, the poor in isolated rural areas, and the less educated among the poor. The denial of access to the poor reflects fundamentally the deficiencies in the functioning of the health care system, in which different social groups are segregated into diverse institutions that operate with very different levels of resources—governmental institutions, social security institutions (covering formal-sector workers), and private-sector institutions, which vary considerably with respect to both access and quality.

As a result, the incidence of disease is generally higher among the poor than among the nonpoor, although precise, systematic data are lacking to validate this assertion. It has been estimated that the poorest 40 percent of the region's population has a disease burden (as measured by "disability-adjusted life years") that is 4 times greater than that of the richest 20 percent.[66] Clearly, public health issues and the incidence of communicable diseases are more salient for the poor than for the nonpoor. A key reason for this is that the poor lack access to proper sanitation. The percentage of people with access to sanitation varies greatly among the countries of the region, and is very low in several—44 percent in Bolivia, 54 percent in Ecuador, 24 percent in Haiti,

30 percent in Paraguay, 45 percent in Peru, and 55 percent in Venezuela.[67] The poor are the main victims of the diseases caused by unsanitary living conditions that prevail in much of the region.

Access to services is thus a key issue for the poor. The quality of these services is another issue (again, as in the case of education). There are significant differences between the quality of health care received by the poor and by the nonpoor, although these differences, as in the case of access to health care, are difficult to quantify with precision. One key reason, previously noted, is that the poor rely preponderantly on the public sector—that is, the Ministry of Health and its various dependencies—for the health care services they receive, whereas the nonpoor can afford private physicians and services that are often of better quality than those provided by the public sector. It should be noted, however, that the poor quality provided by public facilities has driven many of the poor to spend a large proportion of household income on private health care services. Indeed, the poorest quintile of the population in the LAC region is estimated to spend approximately twice what the poor, on average, spend in comparable developing countries for private medical services and medications. Health services, in short, are fragmented and segmented among different social groups in different countries. It is now widely recognized that the roles of the public sector and of social service providers, and the rules under which they both operate, lead to significant differences in the quality and effectiveness of the services provided to different groups of the population.

In addition to access and quality, two other issues—the internal efficiency of the health care system and the fiscal management of the system—are related to poverty. There are numerous public-sector management issues in the health field, and the ways in which these are addressed can be expected to have different effects on the poor. There is, for example, a widely recognized need to reform the delivery of health care services, with the tendency being to introduce greater competition among providers of services. In moving toward greater competition, however, care must be exercised to protect the interests of the poor. Private provision, or joint public-private provision, of health care must not price the poor out of the system.

There are also many questions relating to fiscal sustainability and the need to rationalize public expenditures on health to obtain a better value for the money spent. A more

rigorous pursuit of cost-effective approaches is required, although these approaches may well encounter severe political economy constraints, such as the vested interests of doctors and nurses in the public health bureaucracy.

The foregoing analysis suggests a number of future policy priorities.[68] First, it is necessary to focus on helping countries to finance adequate access to affordable and effective health care that will address the major problems of the poor, including communicable diseases, childhood malnutrition, unwanted fertility, and epidemics of AIDS, tuberculosis, and malaria. Additionally, it is necessary to pay increased attention to programs and projects that address the large and rapidly increasing prominence of noncommunicable diseases (heart disease, stroke, psychiatric disease, and injuries, among others) in the epidemiological profiles of poor countries. These noncommunicable diseases are becoming a greater concern for the poor as well as for the nonpoor.[69]

Second, it is necessary to focus on a systemic approach to health care reform that seeks to strengthen the overall capacity of this sector, to improve performance, and to secure sustainable financing. System-wide reform that secures better value for money in the public sector and more effective use of the resources available in the private sector is a necessary complement to extending services to the poor.

In short, the provision of health care services in the countries of Latin America and the Caribbean is marked by various disparities that thwart the development of an equitable pattern of human capital in the health sector. As a result, the poor, or at least large numbers of them, are not healthy enough, or strong enough, or do not live long enough, to take advantage of the opportunities that may be opened to them by economic growth. Stated differently, the systemic deficiencies in the health sector of the LAC region, together with the consequences of these deficiencies for the poor, tend to exacerbate rather than to ameliorate the distribution of physical assets and income discussed earlier.

E. Poverty and Targeted Programs

Although the policies previously discussed may be expected to reduce poverty in the LAC region because they affect growth, remove the distortions in factor markets, and contribute to human resource development, all of the poor will not benefit from them. Some poor people simply may not be able to participate fully in the growth process, even if the growth is reasonably broad-based; these people are the chronically poor, who suffer from physical or mental disability, long-term illness, or old age. Some may be particularly vulnerable because of temporary events or shocks that produce a decline in their capacity to work or earn; they are the transient poor.[70] The chronically poor are best helped through a system of social insurance. The transient poor require targeted programs, which may take different forms according to event-specific and country-specific circumstances, to help them through short-term stress and calamities.[71]

The distinction between those suffering from acute deprivation and those experiencing inadvertent declines in income cannot always be drawn sharply. Generally, however, efforts to assist the elderly and the disabled are closely related to the development of formal social security systems in Latin America and the Caribbean, and social security reform is increasingly a policy priority in many of the region's countries. Efforts to assist the transient poor are more closely identified with various short- or medium-term transfer and employment-generation initiatives. The discussion here focuses mainly on the latter initiatives, because such policy responses to the social costs of adjustment since the mid-1980s have been at the center of both national and international debate.

Providing programs for the poor is commonly identified with the emergence of social investment funds (SIFs) throughout Latin America and the Caribbean over the past decade.[72] It should be noted, however, that numerous programs existed in the region before SIFs. Also, some significant safety net programs, particularly various in-kind transfer programs, continue to exist apart from the operations of the social investment funds. The SIFs are delivery mechanisms with innovative processes for delivering development programs to the poor; thus, their emphasis on providing education and health services or employment-generation schemes is not necessarily a substantive departure.

1. Transfer programs

Many transfer programs intended to benefit the poor have a long history in Latin America and the Caribbean. There are few cash transfer schemes in the region and they account for a negligible proportion of regional GDP. They occur mainly in the form of family assistance programs tied to social security. Various in-kind transfer programs are considerably more common. These generally lend themselves more easily to self-selection, enable targeting at the poor, and maintain their real value during inflationary periods. They are also often preferred on political economy grounds; targeting in-kind transfers at particularly vulnerable groups, for example, may evoke greater political support from the nonpoor than might the provision of cash transfers.

Three in-kind transfer programs have historically been employed in Latin America and the Caribbean. They are food subsidies, housing subsidies, and energy subsidies. At least ten countries in the region have had some kind of food transfer scheme since the 1970s. The experience with such schemes in reaching the poor in a cost-effective way has been mixed. In descending order of preference (in terms of targeting benefits and cost-effectiveness) are programs addressing nutritional deficiencies of specific groups, food-for-work programs, food stamps, general price subsidies, and quantity rationing. Untargeted programs, not surprisingly, have experienced a high proportion of leakage of benefits to the nonpoor. Programs that are targeted—whether by geography; by type of food consumed by the poor; or by a link to work, to attendance at school, or to visits to a health clinic by the poor—have generally been more successful in concentrating benefits. Food programs have varied widely in their costs per beneficiary; in this regard, again, targeted programs have performed better than universal ones. In Honduras, a food stamp program administered through health centers provided 1,000 calories per day to each poor person at an estimated cost of only US$0.13; the cost was US$0.20 when the program was administered through the schools.[73]

The experience with housing subsidies is decidedly less sanguine. Housing subsidies have been common in the LAC region, although historically they have claimed a small share of the national budget. Looking at the experience with housing subsidies worldwide, a World Bank study concluded that they are markedly regressive.[74] This conclusion applies to Latin America and the Caribbean. For example, housing subsidies have benefited only 6 percent of the households with income below the median in Ecuador, 20 percent in Jamaica, and 16 percent in Venezuela.[75] The experience in Chile has been somewhat better, but even there an effort to target the housing subsidies did not prevent half of them from accruing to house-holds with income in the top 50 percent of the income distribution.[76]

Finally, a number of countries in the region have adopted energy subsidy programs. Assessments of energy subsidies have reached conclusions similar to those reached for housing subsidies. The distribution of energy subsidies in Latin America and the Caribbean has not favored the poor. In Ecuador, for example, energy subsidies disproportionately benefited those in the top quintile of the income distribution. The petroleum and electricity subsidies adopted in Venezuela in the late 1980s and early 1990s clearly benefited the nonpoor more than the poor.[77]

In sum, the studies of housing and energy subsidies appear to be quite definitive in concluding that these subsidies generally have not helped the poor very much. The experience with various kinds of food transfer programs has been more diverse, and there are some promising initiatives that have helped the poor weather adversity. While no particular targeting mechanism has proven superior to another, those programs that appear most successful are those that select beneficiaries not through income-based means tests but according to their participation in work, schools, or clinics.

2. Employment schemes

A number of public-employment schemes in the region also antedated the advent of social investment funds. These schemes were mainly intended to provide temporary employment to those suffering from economic shocks and were not conceived as a long-term solution to poverty. Temporary employment programs face a number of the issues that were discussed with regard to transfer programs. For example, they must meet the challenge of targeting their benefits at the poor and supplying these benefits in a cost-effective way. In addition, they must determine how to ensure an equitable distribution of the secondary benefits from the assets that are created by the programs. Without careful monitoring, the secondary benefits can easily accrue disproportionately to the nonpoor.

Prominent examples of public-employment schemes in the region are those that were undertaken in Chile and Peru in the 1980s. The Chilean program was particularly notable; at its peak in 1983, it provided employment to 13 percent of the labor force.[78] Its targeting record was good. In 1986-87, two-thirds of the workers in the program were from the poorest 20 percent of the population. Another distinguishing feature of the Chilean program was its ability to attract female workers; about 25 percent of the workers under the program were women.[79]

A key to targeting the poor through such public-employment programs is to keep the wage level low enough to discourage the participation of the nonpoor. This was demonstrated in the Chilean case, where the wage rate was set at 70 percent of the minimum wage. According to a recent study, the total cost for each job that was created under the Chilean program was the lowest among a dozen employment-generation programs throughout the world.[80]

Peru's public employment program was also notable for its relatively broad coverage. It too paid low wages, and thus encouraged self-selection, which helped ensure that the program targeted the poor. It also attracted large numbers of female workers; indeed, one estimate is that three-fourths of the workers who benefited from the program in the 1980s were women.[81]

The major lessons from the LAC region's experience with public-employment schemes are being incorporated into an employment support project (known as Trabajar) that is currently being implemented in Argentina and for which World Bank assistance is contemplated. In planning the Bank's support, it was explicitly emphasized that the program wage should be set at the prevailing market wage for unskilled labor, that efforts should be made to strengthen the secondary benefits to the poor of the assets created by the program, and that the involvement of non-governmental and other grassroots organizations should be emphasized in determining the specific interventions to be financed by the program.[82]

3. Social investment funds

Increasingly, targeted development assistance has been provided in Latin America and the Caribbean through the vehicle of social investment funds, which are in use in most countries of the region. The first such fund, the Emergency Social Fund (ESF) in Bolivia, was established in 1986.

While social investment funds differ in some respects from country to country, they share certain distinguishing characteristics. All are financial intermediaries for providing small-scale, multi-sectoral investments aimed at reducing poverty among targeted groups of the poor. The funds invest mainly in programs to improve education, health, nutrition, water supply, and sanitation. Most of the funds' operations are demand-driven; that is, the subprojects they finance are chosen in large measure by the participation and involvement of local community groups. All SIFs employ some form of targeting mechanism to try to ensure that the projects they finance help their intended beneficiaries.

The SIFs have also had an unusual degree of autonomy within the bureaucratic structures of the countries where they have been implemented. They have usually been exempt from control by the line ministries, they have generally paid salaries that are competitive with those paid in the private sector, they have been free from the normal budgetary cycle of the central government, and thus they have been quite flexible in their operations.[83]

The SIFs in Latin America and the Caribbean have been evaluated recently in several studies.[84] These evaluations have assessed the targeting record of the funds, the impact of the funds on employment and on the generation of income, their ability to stimulate and maintain the participation of the intended beneficiaries, and the relationship of the funds to the line ministries of government (such as those in education, health, and public works).

Successfully targeting benefits at the poor is generally considered one of the achievements of the SIFs. The funds in Latin America and the Caribbean support a wide variety of targeting mechanisms. These mechanisms include geographic "poverty maps," which are based on a basic-needs index and are used to assign resources to geographic units; self-targeting or built-in incentives to encourage the poor to participate and deter the nonpoor; and social worker evaluations or on-site visits to ensure that the poor within the designated areas are indeed reached.[85] Targeting has improved over time, especially with the refinement of the poverty maps. A number of issues remain, however. Although the targeting systems appear to have worked well in reaching the poor, they have performed less well in reaching the very poor. Also, the poorest geographical districts are often at a disadvantage in the competition for funds because they lack "effective demand" for projects.[86] In response, many funds now sponsor promotional activities to stimulate or "prime" the demand within the poorest areas and groups.

The overall impact of the SIFs on the employment, income, and living conditions of the poor is difficult to gauge given the inadequacy of data and the brevity of experience with the funds. A World Bank assessment concluded that the employment that was generated by the

investments that were financed by the various SIFs was modest in relation to the size of the labor force and the amount of unemployment and underemployment, but was still significant.[87] In no country for which data exist, however, has fund-generated employment exceeded 0.8 percent of the labor force.[88] The income generated as a result of the SIFs appears to have been relatively modest.[89] The impact of the SIFs on the daily living conditions of the poor—the creation of schools and health clinics where there were none before, and the provision of safe water and other simple amenities crucial to leading a better life—has been considerably more substantial. This claim is borne out by the recent surveys of beneficiaries. An assessment of the Social Development and Compensation Fund (FONCODES) beneficiaries in Peru found that 75 percent of those interviewed rated the fund's impact as positive.[90] In general, school projects have received especially favorable evaluations from beneficiaries. The health posts created under the auspices of the SIFs are also viewed favorably.[91] Water and sanitation projects have received somewhat lower marks, although FONCODES beneficiaries cited improvements to infrastructure as those having the most direct impact on their incomes.[92]

The increased participation of the beneficiaries in the projects funded by SIFs appears to be borne out by the limited evidence available. There seems to be an emerging discrepancy, however, between participation in the choice and execution of the projects that are carried out with the SIFs' resources and participation in the subsequent maintenance of the projects. Again, FONCODES may serve as an example. According to a recent assessment, 90 percent of beneficiaries reported participating in the selection of projects and 67 percent reported participating in project execution. However, only 33 percent were involved in project maintenance and only 28 percent were paying for the use of services in order to cover operating costs.[93] Findings about the lack of project maintenance in a number of other countries have given rise to increasing concerns about the sustainability of the investments being financed by the SIFs.

The relationship between the SIFs and the line ministries of the LAC region's governments is an important issue for the future. If the SIFs are to become permanent fixtures in the social policy frameworks of the region's countries, their priorities will need to be coordinated more effectively than at present with other agencies that are also pursuing agendas related to poverty reduction. A recent assessment of this issue concluded, however, that presently there is no model or program in the region to indicate how the SIFs should adapt to changing conditions, what role they should play in the government if they become permanent, and what their future objectives should be.[94] Another important question is to what extent SIFs should shift their focus from supporting small-scale social and economic infrastructure to financing more directly productive activities. Regardless of the answer, it is clear that although social investment funds have been a significant innovation for reducing poverty in the region, their role is inevitably limited. They can complement, but cannot substitute for, the fundamental reforms—many of them discussed previously—that are needed to expand the scope and improve the effectiveness of the services delivered to the poor.

4. Social security reform

Finally, the current status of formal social security systems in the LAC region and the evolving agenda of social security reform will be mentioned briefly. Social security reform is necessary to ensure that the issue of chronic poverty in the region is addressed effectively.

Given the concerns raised in this chapter, it is important to address the issue of the failure of the region's obligatory social security systems to provide adequate coverage. These systems on average cover only 38 percent of the economically active population and provide pensions to only about 31 percent of the population over the age of 60. While protection levels are high among public-sector workers and among workers in the private formal sector, including many high-wage workers, they are very low in rural areas and for those in the informal sector.[95]

Since the poverty rate is disproportionately high in rural areas, in the informal sector, and among the elderly, formal social security systems, at least in their unreformed state, are clearly contributing little if anything to reducing poverty in the region. Indeed, they may even be exacerbating disparities between the poor and nonpoor. The low level of coverage and the large disparities in coverage between workers, sectors, and regions—as well as the growing financial imbalances of most systems owing to demographic and other factors—have stimulated the consideration of an array of reforms.

Chile led the way in 1981 with a reform that established a fully funded private-pension management system based on individual capitalization accounts. The new

Chilean system has attracted considerable attention throughout the world and has led to varying assessments of its replicability. In the 1990s, five more countries—Peru in 1993, Colombia in 1994, Argentina in 1994, Uruguay in 1996, and Mexico in 1997—adopted some kind of social security reform that incorporated some but by no means all of the features of the Chilean model. Bolivia is on the verge of adopting social security reform and eight additional countries—Brazil, Ecuador, El Salvador, Guatemala, Nicaragua, Panama, Paraguay, and Venezuela—are in various stages of discussion about the possibility of reforming the structure of their pension systems.[96]

The regional debate about social security reform has included widespread discussion of alternative contribution requirements, of alternative ways of investing the funds that are contributed, and of administrative complexities. Less discussed have been the benefits that the poor can expect from expanded coverage and other reforms. Restoring financial balance to the region's social security systems must go hand in hand with turning these systems into effective mechanisms for assisting the chronically poor. This will obviously entail difficult choices for policymakers in a policy domain that, in developed and developing countries alike, is the subject of intense political debate.

• • •

The preceding discussion underlines the fact that there is no "quick fix" for reducing poverty in Latin America and the Caribbean. The profound inequality in the region makes reducing poverty substantially and rapidly a formidable challenge. Although robust rates of economic growth sustained over many years are clearly fundamental for poverty reduction, it is somewhat less clear how that growth, if it can even be attained, can be spread widely enough to lift up the poor as well as enrich those who are already better off. While the agenda for reforming the social sector in order to reduce poverty is reasonably clear, the implementation of this agenda faces constraints, not the least of which are political in nature. The experience with social safety nets, and particularly with the use of social investment funds to support them, demonstrates that, given appropriate policies, short-term poverty alleviation is feasible. But the contribution of social safety nets to long-term poverty reduction remains debatable. In sum, the obstacles to the widespread and sustained reduction of poverty in the LAC region appear rather daunting.

Nevertheless, this chapter also points the way toward

the reforms—in factor markets, in human resource development, and in compensatory policies targeted at the poor—that are likely to produce broad-based growth and thus to create a "bias for hope" that poverty will at long last be tackled and reduced in the region.[97] With real political commitment, with reformed political institutions and processes to effectively implement this commitment, and with an arsenal of policies in favor of the poor that are derived from a systematic assessment of best practice in the region, the countries of Latin America and the Caribbean may yet ensure that the "long march" includes a vast contingent of the poor.

Notes to Chapter IV

1. See Mejia and Vos (1997).

2. See World Bank (1996d, p. 4).

3. See ECLAC (1997, p. 28).

4. See World Bank (1996d, p. 4).

5. These data are from Valdes and Wiens (1996).

6. World Bank (1995b, p. 4).

7. ECLAC (1997, p. 28).

8. ECLAC (1997, p. 28).

9. World Bank (1996d, p. 4).

10. Recent estimates based on data collected by the National Household Survey Program in Brazil (PNAD) reveal a drop in the incidence of poverty between 1993 and 1995, from 30.4 percent to 20.6 percent. These data are based on a poverty line defined by the cost of a basket of goods across 23 areas within Brazil, ranging from R$86.28 per month in metropolitan Sao Paulo to R$22.79 in a rural area in the Northeast. See Rocha (1997). This sharp fall in poverty would imply an unusually high elasticity of poverty to changes in income, thus reflecting the key role played by the reduction of inflation on poverty, since the purchasing power of the poor rises tremendously when inflation declines. Likewise, data collected by the National Statistics and Census Institute (INDEC) of Argentina show a fall in the headcount index from 35 percent in 1990 to 20 percent in 1996. See Oxford Analytica (1997). We are grateful to Samuel Morley of the IDB for his comments regarding the impact of inflation stabilization on poverty in countries suffering from hyperinflation.

11. Deininger and Squire (1997, p. 3).

12. Morley (1994, p. 27).

13. Psacharopoulos et al. (1993).

14. Mejia and Vos (1997, p. 47).

15. Ravallion and Chen (1996, p. 21).

16. See World Bank (1997h, p. 57).

17. This information is based on data provided to the author by Deininger and Squire.

18. Deininger and Squire (1997, p. 3).

19. World Bank (1990). See especially Chapter 3.

20. See, however, Ravallion (forthcoming).

21. These data are from Guasch (1996).

22. Guasch (1996).

23. Guasch (1996).

24. Guasch (1996).

25. Maloney and Cunningham (1997).

26. Maloney (1997).

27. Howe and Goodman (1992).

28. World Bank (1995d).

29. Shah (1995, p. 2).

30. Binswanger and Rosenzweig (1986).

31. Calomiris and Himmelberg (1993, p. 14).

32. For a discussion of these various approaches, see Shah (1994).

33. The experience with directed-credit programs is reviewed in Shah (1994).

34. For a thorough discussion of these and related issues, see World Bank (1993b).

35. Calomiris and Himmelberg (1993, p. 13).

36. For a more complete discussion of this approach, see Shah (1994).

37. Shah (1996, p. 6).

38. Much of the ensuing discussion of market-assisted land reform is taken from Heath (1997a).

39. Heath (1997b).

40. For further discussion of the arguments in this paragraph, see Valdes and Wiens (1996).

41. Valdes and Wiens (1996, p. 20).

42. Valdes and Wiens (1996, p. 20).

43. Valdes and Wiens (1996, pp. 23–5).

44. Valdes and Wiens (1996, p. 9).

45. See Sainz and Leon (1996, p. 46), which is based on data from ECLAC.

46. Both the data and this discussion are drawn from Waiser (1997).

47. Inter-American Development Bank (1996, p. 276).

48. Inter-American Development Bank (1996, p. 278).

49. Inter-American Development Bank (1996, p. 279).

50. Psacharopoulos and Patrinos (1994).

51. Waiser (1997, p. 2).

52. UNESCO (1994).

53. World Bank (1996e, p. 9).

54. Gertler and Glewwe (1989).

55. World Bank (1996e, p. 9).

56. Patrinos and Psacharopoulos (1995).

57. Data are cited in World Bank (1995e, p. 45).

58. These and other examples are cited in World Bank (1995e).

59. Coll (1997, p. 2).

60. World Bank (1997h, p. 86).

61. World Bank (1997h, pp. 78–80).

62. World Bank (1997g, p. 59).

63. World Bank (1997g, p. 59).

64. Coll (1997, p. 4).

65. Inter-American Development Bank (1996, p. 301).

66. Inter-American Development Bank (1996, p. 303).

67. World Bank (1997h, pp. 78–80).

68. The discussion in this and the following paragraph draws on Coll (1997).

69. For an extensive discussion of the policy issues regarding the increasing incidence of noncommunicable diseases in Chile, see World Bank (1995a).

70. For this distinction, see Subbarao et al. (1997, p. 2).

71. See the arguments in World Bank (1990, p. 90).

72. For a discussion of the social investment funds in the region, see Glaessner et al. (1994).

73. Subbarao et al. (1997, pp. 50–1).

74. World Bank (1993a).

75. Persaud (1992).

76. Subbarao et al. (1997, p. 56).

77. Subbarao et al. (1997, p. 62).

78. World Bank (1990, p. 119).

79. Subbarao et al. (1997, p. 75).

80. Subbarao et al. (1997, pp. 74–5).

81. World Bank (1990, p. 119).

82. For a discussion of these and related considerations regarding the effectiveness of Trabajar in reducing poverty, see Ravallion (1996).

83. For a more complete discussion of the characteristics of the social investment funds in the region, see Glaessner et al. (1994, pp. 4–7).

84. See, for example, Inter-American Development Bank (1997), Glaessner et al. (1994), and Subbarao et al. (1997, chapter 6).

85. World Bank (1997e, p. 17).

86. Inter-American Development Bank (1997, pp. 15–6).

87. Glaessner et al. (1994, p. 9).

88. Inter-American Development Bank (1997, p. 21).

89. Inter-American Development Bank (1997, p. 23).

90. World Bank (1997d, p. 7).

91. Inter-American Development Bank (1997, pp. 27–8).

92. World Bank (1997d, p. 7).

93. World Bank (1997d, pp. 6–7).

94. Inter-American Development Bank (1997, p. 64).

95. Inter-American Development Bank (1996, p. 207).

96. Inter-American Development Bank (1996, p. 209).

97. The phrase is from Hirschman (1971).

References

Aiyer, Sri-Ram. 1996. *Anatomy of Mexico's Banking System Following the Peso Crisis.* Latin America and the Caribbean (LAC) Technical Department, Regional Studies Program Report No. 45 (revised). World Bank, Washington, D.C., December.

Aizenman, Joshua, and Nancy P. Marion. 1993. "Policy Uncertainty, Persistence, and Growth." *Review of International Economics* 1(2):145–63.

Arellano, José Pablo. 1983. "De la liberalización a la intervención: El mercado de capitales en Chile, 1974–1983."*Colección Estudios CIEPLAN* 11(December):5–49.

Argy, Victor. 1990. "The Choice of Exchange Rate Regime for a Smaller Economy: A Survey of Some Key Issues." In *Choosing an Exchange Rate Regime,* edited by Victor Argy and Paul De Grauwe. Washington, D.C.: International Monetary Fund.

Arrau, Patricio, and Stijn Claessens. 1992. "Commodity Stabilization Funds." World Bank Policy Research Working Paper No. 835. World Bank, Washington, D.C.

Atje, R., and B. Jovanovic. 1993. "Stock Markets and Development." *European Economic Review,* April.

Balassa, B. 1985. "Exports, Policy Choices and Economic Growth in Developing Countries After the 1973 Oil Shock." *Journal of Development Economics,* May/June.

Baldwin, R. 1989. "Measuring Nontariff Trade Policies." National Bureau of Economic Research (NBER) Working Paper No. 2978. National Bureau of Economic Research, Cambridge, Massachusetts.

Barro, Robert J. 1991. "Economic Growth in a Cross-Section of Countries."*Quarterly Journal of Economics* 106(2):407–43.

_____. 1995. "Inflation and Economic Growth." *Bank of England Quarterly Bulletin* 35(2):166–76.

_____. 1996. "Determinants of Economic Growth: A Cross-Country Empirical Study." NBER Working Paper No. 5698. National Bureau of Economic Research, Cambridge, Massachusetts.

Barro, Robert J., and Jong-Wha Lee. 1993. "International Comparisons of Educational Attainment." *Journal of Monetary Economics* 32(3):363–94.

_____. 1994. "Sources of Economic Growth." *Carnegie-Rochester Conference Series on Public Policy* 40:1–57.

Barro, R., and X. Sala-i-Martin. 1995. *Economic Growth.* New York: McGraw-Hill, Inc.

Bartolini, Leonardo, and Allan Drazen. 1996. "Capital Account Liberalization as a Signal." NBER Working Paper No. 5726. National Bureau of Economic Research, Cambridge, Massachusetts.

Berthelemy, J.C., and A. Varoudakis. 1996. "Economic Growth, Convergence Clubs, and the Role of Financial Development." *Oxford Economics Papers* 48:300–28.

Binswanger, Hans, and Mark Rosenzweig. 1986. "Behavioral and Material Determinants of Production Relations in Agriculture." *Journal of Development Studies* 22(April):503–39.

Brunetti, Aymo, Gregory Kisunko, and Beatrice Weder. 1997. "Credibility of Rules and Economic Growth." World Bank Policy Research Working Paper No. 1760. World Bank, Washington, D.C.

Bruno, Michael, and William Easterly. 1995. "Inflation Crises and Long-Term Growth." NBER Working Paper No. 5209. National Bureau of Economic Research, Cambridge, Massachusetts.

_____. 1996. "Inflation's Children: Tales of Crises that Beget Reforms." *AEA Papers and Proceedings,* May.

Burki, Shahid J., and Sebastian Edwards. 1996. *Dismantling the Populist State: The Unfinished Revolution in Latin America and the Caribbean.* Latin American and Caribbean Studies Viewpoints, World Bank, Washington, D.C.

Buscaglia, Edgardo Jr., Maria Dakolias, and William Ratliff. 1995. *Judicial Reform in Latin America: A Framework for National Development.* Stanford, Calif.: The Hoover Institution Press.

Calomiris, Charles W., and Charles P. Himmelberg. 1993. "Directed Credit Programs for Agriculture and Industry: Arguments from Theory and Fact." Paper prepared for Annual World Bank Conference on Development Economics, Washington, D.C., May 3–4.

Calvo, Guillermo A. 1997. "Argentina's Experience After the Mexican Crisis." In *Currency Boards and External Shocks, How Much Pain, How Much Gain?* edited by Guillermo Perry. Washington, D.C.: World Bank.

Calvo, Guillermo A., Leonardo Leiderman, and Carmen M. Reinhart. 1996. "Inflows of Capital to Developing Countries in the 1990s." *Journal of Economic Perspectives* 10(2):123–139.

Camps, Mauricio, and Carlos Noriega Curtis. 1994. "Civil Service in

Mexico." In *Civil Service Reform in Latin America and the Caribbean: Proceedings of a Conference,* edited by S.A. Chaudry, G.J. Reid, and W.H. Malik. World Bank Technical Paper No. 259. World Bank, Washington, D.C.

Caprio, Gerard, and Daniela Klingebiel. 1996. "Bank Insolvencies: Cross-Country Experiences." World Bank Policy Research Working Paper No. 1620. World Bank, Washington, D.C.

Cardenas, Mauricio. 1991. *Coffee Exports, Endogenous State Policies, and the Business Cycle.* Ph.D. diss., University of California, Berkeley.

Carnoy, Martin. 1997. "Is Privatization through Education Vouchers Really the Answer?: A Comment on West." *The World Bank Research Observer* 12(1):105–16.

Caselli, F., G. Esquivel, and F. Lefort. 1996. "Reopening the Convergence Debate: A New Look at Cross-Country Growth Empirics." *Journal of Economic Growth,* September.

Chenery, H., and M. Syrquin. 1975. *Patterns of Development.* New York: Oxford University Press.

_____. 1989. "Three Decades of Industrialization." *World Bank Economic Review,* May.

Coleman, James. 1990. *Foundations of Social Theory.* Cambridge: Harvard University Press.

Coll, Xavier. 1997. "Poverty-Related Issues in Health in Latin America and the Caribbean." Background Note. World Bank, Washington, D.C.

Cominetti, Rossella. 1996. "Social Expenditure in Latin America: An Update." Mimeo. United Nations and Economic Commission for Latin America and the Caribbean, Santiago, Chile.

de Gregorio, Jose. 1996. "Inflation, Growth and Central Banks." World Bank Policy Research Working Paper 1575. World Bank, Washington, D.C.

Deininger, Klaus and Lyn Squire. 1997. "New Ways of Looking at Inequality and Growth." *DEC Notes* 28 (February).

de Juan, Aristobulo. 1996. "The Roots of Banking Crises: Microeconomic Issues and Supervision and Regulation." In *Banking Crises in Latin America,* edited by Ricardo Hausmann and Liliana Rojas-Suarez. Washington, D.C.: Inter-American Development Bank and Johns Hopkins University Press.

Demetriades, P., and K. Luintel. 1996. "Financial Development, Economic Growth and Banking Sector Controls: Evidence from India." *The Economic Journal,* March.

Demirguc-Kunt, A., and R. Levine. 1996. "Stock Market Development and Financial Intermediaries: Stylized Facts." *World Bank Economic Review,* May.

Diaz-Alejandro, Carlos. 1985. "Good-bye Financial Repression, Hello Financial Crash." *Journal of Development Economics* 19:1–24.

Dollar, D. 1992. "Outward-Oriented Developing Countries Do Grow More Rapidly: Evidence from 95 LDCs, 1976-85." *Economic Development and Cultural Change,* April.

Dooley, Michael P. 1996. "A Survey of Literature on Controls over International Capital Transactions." *International Monetary Fund Staff Papers* 43(4):639–87.

Easterly, William, Michael Kremer, Lant Pritchett, and Lawrence H. Summers. 1993. "Good Policy or Good Luck? Country Growth Performance and Temporary Shocks." *Journal of Monetary Economics* 32(3):459–83.

Easterly, William, and Ross Levine. 1996. "Africa's Growth Tragedy: Policies and Ethnic Divisions." Mimeograph. World Bank Policy Research Department, Washington, D.C.

Easterly, William, Norman Loayza, and Peter Montiel. 1997. "Has Latin America's Post-Reform Growth Been Disappointing?" *Journal of International Economics* (forthcoming). Also published as World Bank Policy Research Working Paper No. 1708. World Bank, Washington, D.C., January.

Easterly, William, and Sergio Rebelo. 1993. "Fiscal Policy and Economic Growth: An Empirical Perspective." *Journal of Monetary Economics* 32(3):417–58.

Easterly, William, and Klaus Schmidt-Hebbel. 1994. "Fiscal Adjustment and Macroeconomic Performance: A Synthesis." In *Public Sector Deficits and Macroeconomic Performance,* edited by William Easterly, Carlos A. Rodriguez, and Klaus Schmidt-Hebbel. New York: World Bank and Oxford University Press.

Echavarria, J. J. 1997. "Liberalization, Integration, and Trade in the Western Hemisphere." Mimeograph. Organization of American States Trade Unit, Washington, D.C.

Economic Commission for Latin America and the Caribbean (ECLAC). 1997. *The Equity Gap.* Santiago, Chile: ECLAC.

Edwards, Sebastian. 1992. "Trade Orientation, Distortions and Growth in Developing Countries." *Journal of Development Economics* 39:31–57.

_____. 1995. *Crisis and Reform in Latin America.* New York: Oxford University Press.

_____. 1997. "Why Are Latin America's Savings Rates So Low? An International Comparative Analysis." In *Annual Bank Conference on Development in Latin America,1995,* edited by S.J. Burki, S. Edwards, and S. Aiyer. Washington, D.C.: World Bank.

Eichengreen, Barry, and Albert Fishlow. 1995. *Contending with Capital Flows: What Is Different about the 1990's?* New York: Council on Foreign Relations.

Fernandez-Arias, Eduardo. 1996. "The New Wave of Private Capital Inflows: Push or Pull?" *Journal of Development Economics* 48(2):389–418.

Fernandez-Arias, Eduardo, and Peter J. Montiel. 1996. "The Surge in Capital Inflows to Developing Countries: An Analytical Overview." *The World Bank Economic Review* 10(1):51–77.

_____. 1997. "Reform and Growth in Latin America: All Pain, No Gain?" Mimeograph. Office of the Chief Economist, Inter-American Development Bank, Washington, D.C.

Fields, G.S. 1990. "Labour Market Modelling and the Urban Informal Sector: Theory and Evidence." In *The Informal Sector Revisited,* edited by D. Turnham, B. Salome, and A. Schwarz. Development Centre Seminars, Organization for Economic Cooperation and Development, Paris.

Fischer, Stanley. 1993. "The Role of Macroeconomic Factors in Growth." *Journal of Monetary Economics* 32(3):485–512.

Garman, Christopher, Stephan Haggard, and Eliza Willis. 1996. "Decentralization in Latin America." Paper presented at the Annual Meeting of the American Political Science Association, San Francisco, California, August 29–September 1.

Gavin, Michael. 1997. "A Decade of Reform in Latin America: Has it Delivered Lower Volatility?" Mimeograph. Inter-American Development Bank, Washington, D.C.

Gavin, Michael, and Ricardo Hausmann. 1996. "The Roots of Banking Crises: The Macroeconomic Context." In *Banking Crises in Latin America,* edited by Ricardo Hausmann and Liliana Rojas-Suarez. Washington, D.C.: Inter-American Development Bank and Johns Hopkins University Press.

Gavin, Michael, Ricardo Hausmann, and Ernesto Talvi. 1997. "Saving Behaviour in Latin America: Overview and Policy Issues." In *Promoting Savings in Latin America,* edited by R. Hausmann and H. Reisen. Paris: Inter-American Development Bank and The Organization for Economic Cooperation and Development.

Gertler, Paul, and Paul Glewwe. 1989. "The Willingness to Pay for Education in Developing Countries: Evidence from Rural Peru." World Bank Living Standards Measurement Study Working Paper No. 54. World Bank, Washington, D.C.

Glaessner, Philip J. et al. 1994. "Poverty Alleviation and Social Investment Funds: The Latin American Experience." World Bank Discussion Paper No. 261. World Bank, Washington, D.C.

Goldstein, Morris. 1997. *The Case for an International Banking Standard.* Institute for International Economics, Washington, D.C.

Goldstein, Morris, and Philip Turner. 1996. "Banking Crises in Emerging Economies: Origins and Policy Options." Bank for International Settlements (BIS) Economic Paper No. 46. Bank for International Settlements, Basle, Switzerland.

Gosh, Atish, Anne-Marie Gulde, Jonathan Ostry, and Holger Wolf. "Does the Nominal Exchange Rate Regime Matter?" International Monetary Fund (IMF) Working Paper WP/95/121. International Monetary Fund, Washington, D.C.

Gould, David M., and William C. Gruben. 1996. "The Role of Intellectual Property Rights in Economic Growth." *Journal of Development Economics* 48:323–50.

Gramlich, Edward M. 1994. "Infrastructure Investment: A Review Essay." *Journal of Economic Literature* 32(3):1176–196.

Guasch, J. Luis. 1996. "Labor Reform and Job Creation: The Unfinished Agenda in Latin American and Caribbean Countries." Paper prepared for the Second Annual World Bank Conference on Development in Latin America and the Caribbean, Bogota, Colombia, July.

Guasch, J. Luis, and Robert W. Hahn. 1997. "The Costs and Benefits of Regulation: Some Implications for Developing Countries." Background paper prepared for *World Development Report, 1997.* LAC Regional Office, World Bank, Washington, D.C..

Guasch, J. Luis, and Sarath Rajapatirana. 1997. "Antidumping and Competition Policies in Latin America and the Caribbean: Total Strangers, Rival Siblings or Soul Mates?" Paper prepared for the Institute of the Americas Hemispheric Policy Forum: Outlook for Free Trade in the Americas, Washington, D.C., March 10–11.

Guasch, J. Luis, and Pablo Spiller. 1997. *Managing the Regulatory Process: Design, Concepts, Issues and the Latin America and the Caribbean Story.* Washington, D.C.: World Bank.

Harris J., and M. Todaro. 1970. "Migration, Unemployment and Development: A Two-Sector Analysis." *American Economic Review,* March.

Harrison, A. 1996. "Openness and Growth: A Time-Series, Cross-Country Analysis for Developing Countries." *Journal of Development Economics,* March.

Heath, John. 1997a. "Market-Assisted Land Reform: Theory and Practice." Background Note. World Bank, Washington, D.C., March 27.

Heath, John. 1997b. "Land Titling Initiatives in Latin America." Background Note. World Bank, Washington, D.C., May 7.

Helliwell, John F. 1996. "Economic Growth and Social Capital in Asia." NBER Working Paper No. 5470. National Bureau of Economic Research, Cambridge, Massachusetts.

Helpman, Elhanan. 1993. "Innovation, Imitation, and Intellectual Property Rights." *Econometrica* 61(6):1247–280.

Helpman, Elhanan, Leonardo Leiderman, and Gil Bufman. 1994. "A New Breed of Exchange Rate Bands: Chile, Israel, and Mexico." *Economic Policy* 19(October):259–306.

Hirschman, Albert O. 1971. *A Bias for Hope: Essays on Development and Latin America.* New Haven, Conn.: Yale University Press.

Howe, Gary, and David Goodman. 1992. *Smallholders and Structural Change in the Brazilian Economy.* Rome: International Fund for Agricultural Development.

Hubbard, G.R., A. Kashyap, and T.M. Whited. 1995. "International Finance and Firm Investment." *Journal of Money Credit and Banking.* 27(3).

Inter-American Development Bank. 1995. *Economic and Social Progress in Latin America,. 1995: Towards a Less Volatile Economy.* Washington, D.C.: Inter-American Development Bank.

Inter-American Development Bank. 1996. *Economic and Social Progress in Latin America, 1996: Making Social Services Work.* Washington, D.C.: Inter-American Development Bank.

_____. 1997. "Social Investment Funds in Latin America: Past Performance and Future Role." Washington, D.C.: Inter-American Development Bank.

International Finance Corporation. *Emerging Stock Markets Factbook.* Various editions. Washington, D.C.: International Finance Corporation.

International Labour Office. *1996 Labour Overview.* Lima, Peru: International Labour Office.

Kaminsky, Graciela, Saul Lizondo, and Carmen Reinhart. 1997. "Leading Indicators of Currency Crises." Board of Governors of the Federal Reserve System, World Bank and the University of Maryland, Washington D.C. and College Park.

Kaminsky, Graciela, and Carmen Reinhart. 1996. "The Twin Crises: The Causes of Banking and Balance-of-Payments Problems." Board of Governors of the Federal Reserve System and the University of Maryland, Washington D.C. and College Park.

King, R. 1993. "Finance and Growth: Schumpeter Might Be Right." *Quarterly Journal of Economics,* August.

King, Robert G., and Ross Levine. 1992. "Financial Indicators and Growth in a Cross-Section of Countries." PRD Working Paper No. 819. World Bank, Washington, D.C.

_____. 1993. "Finance, Entrepreneurship, and Growth: Theory and Evidence." *Journal of Monetary Economics* 32(3):513–42.

Knack, S. 1997. "Stagnation and Stability in Latin America and the World: The Economic Role of Institutions Revisited." In *The Political Dimension of Economic Growth*, edited by S. Borner and M. Paldam. Indianapolis, Ind.: Macmillan.

Knack, Stephen, and Philip Keefer. 1995. "Institutions and Economic Performance: Cross-Country Tests Using Alternative Institutional Measures." *Economics and Politics* 7(3): 207–28.

Knight, Malcolm, Norman Loayza, and Delano Villanueva. 1996. "The Peace Dividend: Military Spending Cuts and Economic Growth." *International Monetary Fund (IMF) Staff Papers* 43(1):1–37.

Laban, Raul, and Felipe Larrain. 1993. "Can a Liberalization of Capital Outflows Increase Capital Inflows?" Instituto de Economia Working Paper No. 155. Pontificia Universidad Catolica de Chile, Santiago, Chile.

Lane, Philip, and Aaron Tornell. 1996. "Adjustment of Savings and the Current Account to Windfalls." Columbia University and Harvard University, New York and Cambridge, Massachusetts.

La Porta, Rafael, F. Lopez-de-Silanes, A. Shleifer, and R. Vishny. 1996. "Law and Finance." NBER Working Paper No. 5661. National Bureau of Economic Research, Cambridge, Massachusetts.

Lau, Lawrence J. 1996. "The Sources of Long-Term Economic Growth: Observations from the Experience of Developed and Developing Countries." In *The Mosaic of Economic Growth,* edited by R. Landau, T. Taylor, and G. Wright. Stanford, Calif.: Stanford University Press.

Lederman, Daniel. 1996. "The Sources of Economic Growth: A Survey from a Latin American Perspective." Mimeograph. Office of the Chief Economist for LAC, World Bank, Washington, D.C.

Levine, Ross. 1996. "Financial Development and Economic Growth: Views and Agenda." Mimeograph. World Bank, Washington, D.C.

_____. 1997. "Financial Development and Economic Growth." *Journal of Economic Literature* (forthcoming).

Levine, Ross, and Sara J. Zervos. 1996. "Stock Market Development and Long-Run Growth." *The World Bank Economic Review* 10(2):323–40.

Lindgren, Carl-Johan, Gillian Garcia, and Matthew I. Saal. 1996. *Bank Soundness and Macroeconomic Policy.* Washington, D.C.: International Monetary Fund.

Loayza, Norman. 1994. "Labor Regulations and the Informal Economy." World Bank Policy Research Working Paper No.1335, World Bank, Washington, D.C.

_____. 1996. "The Economics of the Informal Sector: A Simple Model and Some Empirical Evidence From Latin America." *Carnegie-Rochester Conference Series on Public Policy* 45:129–162.

Lora, Eduardo, and Felipe Barrera. 1997. "Una década de reformas estructurales en América Latina: El crecimiento, la productividad y la inversión ya no son como antes." Office of the Chief Economist, Inter-American Development Bank, Washington, D.C..

Lora, Eduardo, and C. Pages. 1996. "La legislacion laboral en el proceso de reformas estructurales de America Latina y el Caribe."

Mimeograph. Inter-American Development Bank, Washington, D.C., December.

Mackenzie, G. A., and Peter Stella. 1996. *Quasi-Fiscal Operations of Public Financial Institutions.* IMF Occasional Paper 142, International Monetary Fund, Washington, D.C.

Maloney, William F. 1997. "Labor Market Structure in Mexico: Time Series Evidence on Competing Views." Mimeograph. Economics Department, University of Illinois at Urbana-Champaign, and Draft, World Bank, Washington, D.C.

Maloney, William F., and Wendy V. Cunningham. 1997. "Heterogeneity in Small-Scale LDC Enterprises: The Mexican Case." Draft. World Bank, Washington, D.C., April.

Mankiew, N. Gregory, David Romer, and David N. Weil. 1992. "A Contribution to the Empirics of Economic Growth." *Quarterly Journal of Economics* 107(2):407–37.

Marshall, Jorge, and Klaus Schmidt-Hebbel. 1994. "Chile: Fiscal Adjustment and Successful Performance." In *Public Sector Deficits and Macroeconomic Performance,* edited by William Easterly, Carlos A. Rodriguez, and Klaus Schmidt-Hebbel. New York: World Bank and Oxford University Press.

Mauro, P. 1995. "Corruption and Growth." *Quarterly Journal of Economics* 100:681–712.

McKinnon, R. 1973. *Money and Capital in Economic Development.* Washington, D.C.: Brookings Institution.

Mejia, Jose Antonio, and Rob Vos. 1997. *Poverty in Latin America and the Caribbean: An Inventory, 1980–95.* Washington, D.C.: Inter-American Development Bank.

Montiel, Peter J.. 1996. "Policy Responses to Surges in Capital Inflows: Issues and Lessons." In *Private Capital Flows to Emerging Markets After the Mexican Crisis,* edited by Guillermo A. Calvo, Morris Goldstein, and Eduard Hochreiter. Washington, D.C. and Vienna, Austria: Institute for International Economics and the Austrian National Bank.

Morley, Samuel A. 1994. *Poverty and Inequality in Latin America: Past Evidence, Future Prospects.* Washington, D.C.: Overseas Development Council.

Moser, Caroline. 1996. "Urban Poverty and Violence: Consolidation or Erosion of Social Capital?" Paper presented at the Second Annual World Bank Conference on Development in Latin America and the Caribbean. Bogota, Colombia, July.

North, Douglass C. 1991. *Institutions, Institutional Change and Economic Performance.* New York: Cambridge University Press.

Oxford Analytica Latin America Daily Brief. 1997. "Argentina: Poverty Polemic." *May 30.*

Patrinos, Harry A., and George Psacharopoulos. 1995. "Educational Performance and Child Labor in Paraguay." *International Journal of Educational Development* 15(1):47–60.

Perry, Guillermo E., and Ana Maria Herrera. 1994. *Public Finances, Stabilization, and Structural Reforms in Latin America.* Washington D.C.: Inter-American Development Bank and Johns Hopkins University Press.

Perry, Guillermo E., and Ana María Huerta. 1997. "La Historia de una crisis anunciada: Regulando el Endeudamiento de las Municipalidades y los Departamentos en Colombia" To be published by

ECLAC.

Psacharopoulos, George, Samuel A. Morley, Ariel Fiszbein, Haeduck Lee and Bill Wood. 1993. *Poverty and Income Distribution in Latin America: History of the Decade of the 1980s.* LAC Technical Department Report No. 27. World Bank, Washington, D.C.

Psacharopoulos, George, and Harry A. Patrinos. 1994. "Indigenous People and Poverty in Latin America." World Bank, Washington, D.C.

Putnam, Robert D. 1993. *Making Democracy Work: Civic Traditions in Modern Italy.* Princeton, N.J.: Princeton University Press.

Rama, Matín. 1995. "Do Labor Market Policies and Institutions Matter? The Adjustment Experience in Latin America and the Caribbean." Mimeograph. World Bank Policy Research Department, Washington, D.C., May (forthcoming in *Labour*, edited by Basil Blackwell.[NL: need to give publisher and city here as well])

_____. 1996. "A Labor Market Cross-Country Database." Mimeograph. World Bank, Washington, D.C.

_____. 1997. "Efficient Public Sector Downsizing." Mimeograph. World Bank, Washington, D.C.

Ravallion, Martin. 1996. "Argentina's Trabajar Program." Background Note. World Bank, Washington, D.C., December 12.

_____. 1997. "Good and Bad Growth: The Human Development Reports." *World Development.* Forthcoming.

Ravallion, Martin, and Shaohua Chen. 1996. "What Can New Survey Data Tell Us about Recent Changes in Distribution and Poverty?" World Bank Policy Research Working Paper No. 1694. World Bank, Washington, D.C.

Rocha, Sonia. 1997. "Crise, Estabilizacao e Pobreza 1990-95." *Conjuntura Economica* 51 (1): 22-26.

Rodriguez, Carlos A. 1994. "Argentina: Fiscal Disequilibria Leading to Hyperinflation." In *Public Sector Deficits and Macroeconomic Performance*, edited by William Easterly, Carlos A. Rodriguez, and Klaus Schmidt-Hebbel. New York: World Bank and Oxford University Press.

Rojas-Suarez, Liliana, and Steven R. Weisbrod. 1996. "Banking Crises in Latin America: Experiences and Issues." In *Banking Crises in Latin America*, edited by Ricardo Hausmann and Liliana Rojas-Suarez. Washington, D.C.: Inter-American Development Bank and Johns Hopkins University Press.

Roubini, Nouriel, and Xavier Sala-i-Martin. 1992. "Financial Repression and Economic Growth." *Journal of Development Economics* 39:5–30.

Rowat, Malcolm D. 1996. "The Emerging Role of the State in Latin America and the Caribbean." Mimeograph. LAC Technical Department, Public Sector Modernization Unit, World Bank, Washington D.C.

Rubio, Mauricio. 1996. "Crimen y crecimiento en Colombia." In *Hacia un enfoque integrado del desarrollo: Etica, violencia, y seguridad ciudadana. Encuentro de reflexión.* Washington, D.C.: Inter-American Development Bank.

Sainz, Pedro, and Arturo Leon. 1996. "Educacion y movilidad social en America Latina." *Estadistica y Economia.* Primer Semestre.

Schadler, Susan, Maria Carkovic, Adam Bennet, and Robert Kahn.

1993. *Recent Experiences with Surges in Capital Inflows.* IMF Occasional Paper 108. International Monetary Fund, Washington DC.

Schmidt-Hebbel, Klaus, and Luis Servén. 1997. "Savings across the World: Puzzles and Policies." World Bank Discussion Paper No. 354. World Bank, Washington, D.C.

Shah, Hemant. 1994. "Credit to Farmers and Small Businesses." Background Note. World Bank, Washington, D.C., November 28.

_____. 1995. "Argentina: Financing of Small and Medium Enterprises." Background Note. World Bank, Washington, D.C., October 5.

_____. 1996. "El Salvador: Rural Credits and Role of New Financial Products and Technologies." Background Note. World Bank, Washington, D.C., July 11.

_____. 1997. "Towards Better Regulation of Private Pension Funds." Mimeograph. LAC Regional Office, World Bank, Washington, D.C.

Shome, Parthasarathi. 1992. "Trends and Future Directions in Tax Policy Reform: A Latin American Perspective." *Bulletin for International Fiscal Documentation* 46:452–66.

Silvani, C., and J. Brondolo. 1994. "An Analysis of VAT Compliance." Mimeograph. International Monetary Fund Fiscal Affairs Department, Washington, D.C., November.

Squire, Lyn, and Sethaput Suthiwrt-Narueput. 1997. "The Impact of Labor Market Regulations." *The World Bank Economic Review* 11(1):119–44.

Stiglitz, Joseph E. 1986. *Economics of the Public Sector.* New York and London: W.W. Norton.

_____. 1994. *Whither Socialism?* Cambridge and London: The MIT Press.

Subbarao, K. et. al. 1997. *Safety Net Programs and Poverty Reduction: Lessons from Cross-Country Experience.* Washington, D.C.: World Bank.

Talvi, Ernesto. 1996. "Exchange Rate-Based Stabilization with Endogenous Fiscal Response." Inter-American Development Bank (IDB) Working Papers Series 324. Inter-American Development Bank, Washington D.C.

Talvi, Ernesto, and Carlos A. Vegh. 1996. "Can Optimal Fiscal Policy Be Procyclical?" Inter-American Development Bank and UCLA, Washington D.C. and Los Angeles.

Tanzi, Vito. 1996. "Fiscal Federalism and Decentralization: A Review of Some Efficiency and Macroeconomic Aspects." In *Annual World Bank Conference on Development Economics 1995*, edited by Michael Bruno and Boris Pleskovic. Washington, D.C.: World Bank.

Tanzi, Vito, and Howell H. Zee. 1996. "Fiscal Policy and Long-Run Growth." IMF Working Paper WP/96/119. International Monetary Fund, Washington, D.C.

Ter-Minassian, Teresa. 1996. "Borrowing by Subnational Governments: Issues and Selected International Experiences." IMF Paper on Policy Analysis and Assessment PPAA/96/4. International Monetary Fund, Washington D.C.

Theil, H. 1971. *Principles of Econometrics.* New York: Wiley.

Tiboni, Constancia. 1994. "The Reform of Argentina's Federal Tax

Administration Office." In *Civil Service Reform in Latin America and the Caribbean: Proceedings of a Conference,* edited by S.A. Chaudry, G.J. Reid, and W.H. Malik, World Bank Technical Paper No. 259. World Bank, Washington, D.C.

Tommasi, M., and A. Velasco. 1995. "Where Are We in the Political Economy of Reform?" Mimeograph. New York University, New York, May.

UNCTAD. 1994. *Directory of Import Regimes.* New York: United Nations.

UNESCO. 1994. *Medicion de calidad de la educacion: Resultados.* vol. 3. UNESCO Regional Office for Education in Latin America and the Caribbean, Santiago, Chile.

United States Department of Health and Human Services. 1995. *Social Security Programs Throughout the World.* United States Department of Health and Human Services, Washington, D.C.

Valdés, Alberto and Tom Wiens. 1996. "Rural Poverty in Latin America and the Caribbean." Paper prepared for the Second Annual World Bank Conference on Development in Latin America and the Caribbean, Bogota, Colombia, July.

Varangis, Panos, Takamasa Akiyama, and Donald Mitchell. 1995. *Managing Commodity Booms and Busts.* Washington, D.C.: World Bank.

Varangis, Panos, and Don Larson. 1996. "Dealing with Commodity Price Uncertainty." World Bank Policy Research Working Paper 1667. World Bank, Washington, D.C.

Waiser, Myriam. 1997. "Social Equity and Education." Background Note. World Bank, Washington, D.C., May 1.

West, Edwin G. 1997. "Education Vouchers in Principle and Practice: A Survey." *The World Bank Research Observer* 12(1):83–104.

Williamson, John. 1996. *The Crawling Band as an Exchange Rate Regime: Lessons from Chile, Colombia, and Israel.* Washington, D.C.: Institute for International Economics.

Wolff, Laurence, Ernesto Schiefelbein, and Jorge Valenzuela. 1994. *Improving the Quality of Primary Education in Latin America and the Caribbean: Towards the 21st Century.* World Bank Discussion Papers 257. Washington, D.C.: The World Bank.

World Bank. 1990. *World Development Report 1990: Poverty.* Washington, D.C.: World Bank.

_____. 1993a. *Housing: Enabling Markets to Work.* Washington, D.C.: World Bank.

_____. 1993b. *World Bank Lending for Small Enterprises, 1989–1993.* Washington, D.C.: World Bank.

_____. 1993c. *World Development Report,1993:Investing in Health.* New York: Oxford University Press for The World Bank.

_____. 1994. *Averting the Old Age Crisis.* Washington, D.C.: World Bank.

_____. 1995a. *Chile: The Adult Health Policy Challenge.* Washington, D.C.: World Bank.

_____. 1995b. *Guatemala: An Assessment of Poverty.* Washington, D.C.: World Bank.

_____. 1995c. *Labor and Economic Reforms in Latin America and the Caribbean.* Regional Perspectives on World Development, World Bank, Washington, D.C.

_____. 1995d. *Mexico: Rural Financial Markets.* Washington, D.C.: World Bank.

_____. 1995e. *Priorities and Strategies for Education.* Washington, D.C.: World Bank.

_____. 1996a. *From Plan to Market: World Development Report 1996.* New York: Oxford University Press for the World Bank.

_____. 1996b. *Global Economic Prospects and the Developing Countries, 1996.* Washington, D.C.: World Bank.

_____. 1996c. *Managing Capital Flows in East Asia.* Washington, D.C.: World Bank.

_____. 1996d. *Poverty Reduction and the World Bank: Progress and Challenges in the 1990s.* Washington, D.C.: World Bank.

_____ 1996e. "Targeting At-Risk Youth: Rationales, Approaches to Service Delivery, and Monitoring and Evaluation Issues." World Bank, Washington, D.C., February.

_____ 1997a. "Crime and Violence as Development Issues in Latin America and the Caribbean." Paper prepared for the Inter-American Development Bank Conference on Urban Crime and Violence, Rio de Janeiro, Brazil, March 2–4.

_____. 1997b. "Competition Policy and Mercosur." Mimeograph. LAC Technical Department, World Bank, Washington, D.C.

_____. 1997c. *Managing Government Exposure in Private Infrastructure Development.* Proceedings of a World Bank Conference, Cartagena, Colombia, May.

_____. 1997d. "Peru: Second Social Development and Compensation Fund, FONCODES II: Beneficiary Assessment." World Bank, Washington, D.C., March 19.

_____. 1997e. "Portfolio Improvement Program: Social Funds Review." World Bank, Washington, D.C., March 19.

_____. 1997f. *Private Capital Flows to Developing Countries: The Road to Financial Integration.* Washington, D.C.: World Bank.

_____. 1997g. "Sector Strategy Paper: Health, Nutrition and Population Sector." Mimeograph. World Bank, Washington, D.C., April 14.

_____. 1997h. *World Development Indicators, 1997.* Washington, D.C.:World Bank.

_____. 1997i. *World Development Report, 1997: The State in a Changing World.* New York: Oxford University Press for The World Bank.

Young, Alwyn. 1995. "The Tyranny of Numbers: Confronting the Statistical Realities of the East Asian Growth Experience." *Quarterly Journal of Economics* 110(August):641–80.

WORLD BANK LATIN AMERICAN AND CARIBBEAN STUDIES

VIEWPOINT SERIES

Latin America after Mexico: Quickening the Pace
By Shahid Javed Burki and Sebastian Edwards

Poverty, Inequality, and Human Capital Development in Latin America, 1950-2025
By Juan Luis Londoño
Available in English and Spanish

Dismantling the Populist State: the Unfinished Revolution in Latin America and the Caribbean
By Shahid Javed Burki and Sebastian Edwards

Decentralization in Latin America: Learning through Experience
By George E. Peterson

Urban Poverty and Violence in Jamaica
By Caroline Moser and Jeremy Holland
Available in English and Spanish

The Long March: A Reform Agenda for Latin America and the Caribbean in the Next Decade
By Shahid Javed Burki and Guillermo E. Perry

Black December: Banking Stability, the Mexican Crisis and its Effect on Argentina
By Valeriano García

Prospects and Challenges for the Caribbean
By Steven B. Webb

PROCEEDINGS SERIES

Currency Boards And External Shocks: How Much Pain, How Much Gain?
Edited by Guillermo Perry

Annual World Bank Conference on Development in Latin America and the Caribbean: 1995
Edited by Shahid Javed Burki, Sebastian Edwards, and Sri-Ram Aiyer

Annual World Bank Conference on Development in Latin America and the Caribbean: 1996
Edited by Shahid Javed Burki, Sri-Ram Aiyer, and Rudolf Hommes